D1066362

A THEORY OF
THE LABOR MOVEMENT

A THEORY OF
THE LABOR MOVEMENT

BY

SELIG PERLMAN, Ph.D.
PROFESSOR OF ECONOMICS, UNIVERSITY OF WISCONSIN

REPRINTS OF ECONOMIC CLASSICS

AUGUSTUS M. KELLEY · PUBLISHERS
NEW YORK 1970

First Edition 1928

(New York: The Macmillan Company, 1928)

Reprinted 1951, 1964, 1966, 1968 & 1970 by
AUGUSTUS M. KELLEY · PUBLISHERS
REPRINTS OF ECONOMIC CLASSICS
New York New York 10001

.   .   .   .

I S B N   0 678 00025 5
L C N   66 18323

.   .   .   .

PRINTED IN THE UNITED STATES OF AMERICA
by SENTRY PRESS, NEW YORK, N. Y. 10019

To
J. R. C.
and
N. D. C.

PREFACE

Twenty years ago the author of this book, like most of his college generation in Russia, professed the theory of the labor movement found in the Marxian classics. "Labor" was then to him—he realized afterwards—mainly an abstraction: an abstract mass in the grip of an abstract force. For, despite the copiousness of the statistical and sociological evidence adduced by Marxism for the view that the workman is bound, in the very nature of capitalism, to espouse the cause of revolution,—and despite Marxism's intense concern with concrete labor movements, from Chartism to date,—it remains true that, at bottom, the Marxian theory of the labor movement rests upon a species of faith,—namely the faith that history has appointed the labor movement to be the force which eventually will bring society to the third and final step in the Hegelian dialectical scheme of evolution.

Shortly afterwards (having in the meantime transferred himself to the American environment), by an unusual stroke of good luck, the author joined the research staff of Professor John R. Commons. Here he became acquainted with Professor Commons' method of deducing labor theory from the concrete and crude experience of the wage earners. This method is brilliantly demonstrated in his article on the *American Shoemakers*,[1] where a theory

[1] This article was reprinted as Chapter XIV in his *Labor and Administration* (Macmillan, 1913).

of industrial evolution as well as a theory of the
labor movement were evolved from the testimony
(in a series of reported conspiracy cases) given by
sweat shop bosses, "scabs," strikers, merchant capitalists, and manufacturers. In this approach the
Hegelian dialectic nowhere occurs, nor is cognizance
taken of labor's "historical mission." What mo-
nopolizes attention is labor combatting competitive
menaces—"scabs," "green hands," and the like;
labor bargaining for the control of the job.

On joining in Professor Commons' pioneering undertaking of a history of American industrial society, the author started with the socialistic movements among immigrant workmen during the sixties
and seventies. Here, in a field apparently of little
significance, the author stumbled upon a veritable
gold mine: he discovered that out of these overlooked movements among the German and other
foreign wage-earners there finally emerged the non-
socialistic program of the American Federation of
Labor. What an absurd and topsy-turvy order of
things! (For to the Marxian and to the socialist in
general it is "normal" for a labor movement to
"ascend" from "pure and simple" unionism to a
socialistic class consciousness; never to "descend"
from the second to the first.) Yet that was, clearly,
the product of the genuine and prolonged experience
of the Strasser-Gompers group of unionists who fell
away from their original faith reluctantly indeed.
This discovery gave the author another impulse in
the same direction. Obviously, working people in
the real felt an urge towards collective control of
their employment opportunities, but hardly towards similar control of industry. The events of

the day in the American labor movement—the failure of the socialists within the American Federation
of Labor and of the Industrial Workers of the World
without, to hold their own after auspicious débuts
shortly before, added strength to the author's new
convictions in formation.

When, at the outbreak of the European War, the
German labor movement espoused the national
cause, with the trade unions unexpectedly calling
the tune to the Social-Democratic piper, the author
set himself to studying the inter-relationships between the economic and the political movements in
that country. Here he stumbled upon the idea that
there is a natural divergence in labor ideology between the "mentality" of the trade unions and the
"mentality" of the intellectuals; and that, given
the opportunity to exist legally and to develop a
leadership from among its own ranks, the trade
union's mentality will eventually come to dominate.
In Germany the trade unions had emancipated themselves from the hegemony of the intellectual revolutionists in 1906—with the "Mannheim Agreement." That a trade unionism so emancipated will
be deaf to the call of revolutions and will think in
terms of its national industry from which spring
both wages and profits has been proved over again
by the events in Germany since 1918.

The Russian Revolution and the ease with which
the Bolshevists seized power sent the author review-
ing his Russian history to account for the weakness
of the "ruling" classes of Russia—a weakness
which was psychological and profoundly in contrast
with the strength of German capitalists in 1918-
1920 and with the fighting prowess of British capital-

ists in 1926. As a result, these three factors emerged as basic in any modern labor situation: first, the resistance power of capitalism, determined by its own historical development; second, the degree of dominance over the labor movements by the intellectual's "mentality," which regularly underestimates capitalism's resistance power and overestimates labor's will to radical change; and, third, the degree of maturity of a trade union "mentality." Then, after further analysis and generalization, the goal of "organic" labor crystallized out as "communism of opportunity," and the intellectuals divided into types distinguishable as "ethical," "efficiency" and "determinist-revolutionary." And finally, capitalism, instead of being a sheer material phenomenon, turned out to be the "effective will to power" of the capitalist class.

The author welcomes this opportunity to express his deepest gratitude to the late Mrs. John R. Commons for her unstinted encouragement and suggestion not only in connection with this book but indeed through all his years at Wisconsin. He also wishes to acknowledge gratefully the generous help of Professor E. A. Ross and of Mr. Louis C. Zucker.

S. P.

Madison, Wis.
April, 1928

CONTENTS

xi

INTRODUCTORY

CHAPTER I

TOWARD A THEORY OF THE
LABOR MOVEMENT

The present book does not claim to give a full history of the several national labor movements, which the author has chosen as the most significant —the British, the German, the Russian, and the American. Rather it gives a survey of the historical development of these movements in order to show the grounds upon which the author, in the course of more than fifteen years of study and research, has arrived at his theory of the labor movement. It is his belief that the present time affords a unique opportunity for stock taking in the realm of such theory. First, because during the throbbing dozen years just past, filled to the brim with war and revolution, both capitalism and the labor movement have undergone a testing heretofore undreamed of. At no other time in modern history has society shown itself so nearly "with the lid off" as since the Russian Revolution. Nor has the labor movement ever before been made to render so strict an account to the outside world, as well as to itself, of what its deep-lying purposes truly are, as during the crowded decade which witnessed the successful Bolshevist Revolution, the decisive defeat of Communism in Germany (largely with the aid of the organized labor

movement itself), the class war in Britain culminating in the general strike, the progressive metamorphosis of American capitalism into a "welfare
capitalism", with the arrest of the growth of American unionism, notwithstanding the economic prosperity—to say nothing of the eclipse of French unionism and of the destruction of any independent
labor movement in Fascist Italy. Second, the present appears an opportune time for a reëxamination
of the theory of the labor movement, since, even in
the eyes of the Communists, the revolutionary era
has been succeeded by a "temporary" stabilization
of capitalism.

Three dominant factors are emerging from the
seeming medley of contradictory turns and events in
recent labor history. The first factor is the demonstrated capacity, as in Germany, Austria, and Hun-
gary, or else incapacity, as in Russia, of the capitalist group to survive as a ruling group and to withstand revolutionary attack when the protective hand
of government has been withdrawn. In this sense
"capitalism" is not only, nor even primarily, a
material or governmental arrangement whereby one
class, the capitalist class, owns the means of production, exchange, and distribution, while the other
class, labor, is employed for wages. Capitalism is
rather a social organization presided over by a class
with an "effective will to power", implying the ability to defend its power against all comers—to defend
it, not necessarily by physical force, since such force,
however important at a crisis, might crumble after
all—but to defend it, as it has done in Germany,
through having convinced the other classes that they
alone, the capitalists, know how to operate the com-

plex economic apparatus of modern society upon which the material welfare of all depends.

The second factor which stands out clearly in the world-wide social situation is the rôle of the so-called "intellectual", the "intelligentsia", in the labor movement and in society at large. It was from the intellectual that the anti-capitalist influences in modern society emanated. It was he who impressed upon the labor movement tenets characteristic of his own mentality: the "nationalization" or "socialization" of industry, and political action, whether "constitutional" or "unconstitutional", on behalf of the "new social order". He, too, has been busily indoctrinating the middle classes with the same views, thus helping to undermine an important prop of capitalism and to some extent even the spirit of resistance of the capitalists themselves

The third and the most vital factor in the labor situation is the trade union movement. Trade unionism, which is essentially pragmatic, struggles constantly, not only against the employers for an enlarged opportunity measured in income, security, and liberty in the shop and industry, but struggles also, whether consciously or unconsciously, actively or merely passively, against the intellectual who would frame its programs and shape its policies. In this struggle by "organic" labor [1] against dominance by the intellectuals, we perceive a clash of an ideology which holds the concrete workingmen in the center of its vision with a rival ideology which envis-

[1] Trade unionists and intellectuals use alike the term "labor", which has an abstract connotation. But, to the trade unionists, "labor" means nothing more abstract or mystical than the millions of concrete human beings with their concrete wants and aspirations. And it is in this sense that the author uses it throughout this book.

ages labor merely as an "abstract mass in the grip of an abstract force."[1]

Labor's own "home grown" ideology is disclosed only through a study of the "working rules" of labor's own "institutions". The trade unions are the institutions of labor today, but much can be learned also from labor's institutions in the past, notably the gilds.

It is the author's contention that manual groups, whether peasants in Russia, modern wage earners, or medieval master workmen, have had their economic attitudes basically determined by a consciousness of scarcity of opportunity, which is characteristic of these groups, and stands out in contrast with the business men's "abundance consciousness", or consciousness of unlimited opportunity. Starting with this consciousness of scarcity, the "manualist" groups have been led to practising solidarity, to an insistence upon an "ownership" by the group as a whole of the totality of economic opportunity extant, to a "rationing" by the group of such opportunity among the individuals constituting it, to a control by the group over its members in relation to the conditions upon which they as individuals are permitted to occupy a portion of that opportunity—in brief, to a "communism of opportunity". This differs fundamentally from socialism or communism,

---

[1] I use frequently the term "ideology" in imitation of the usage of socialist intellectuals taken over from Napoleon's term applied by him in contempt to the idealists of his day. I find, however, that the term has quite the same meaning as that which scientists call "ideas" and "theory", philosophers call "idealism" or "ethics", and business men and working men call "philosophy." Unionists speak of "the philosophy of trade unionism." If they were "intellectuals", they would call it "theory", "ideology", "ideas", or "idealism", or "ethics", all of which I sometimes include in the term "mentality."

which would "communize" not only "opportunity",
but also production and distribution—just as it is
far removed from "capitalism". Capitalism started
from the premise of unlimited opportunity, and arrived, in its classical formulation, at "laissez faire"
for the individual all along the line—in regard to
the "quantity" of opportunity he may appropriate,
the price or wage he may charge, and in regard to
the ownership of the means of production. "Communism of opportunity" in the sense here employed
existed in the medieval gilds before the merchant
capitalists had subverted them to the purposes of a
protected business men's oligarchy; in Russian
peasant land communities with their periodic redi-
visions, among the several families, of the collectively owned land, the embodiment of the economic
opportunity of a peasant group; and exists today in
trade unions enforcing a "job control" through union "working rules".

But, in this country, due to the fact that here the
"manualist" had found at hand an abundance of
opportunity, in unoccupied land and in a pioneer
social condition, his economic thinking had therefore
issued, not from the scarcity premise but from the
premise of abundance. It thus resulted in a social
philosophy which was more akin to the business
men's than to the trade unionists' or gildsmen's.
Accordingly, the American labor movement, which
long remained unaware of any distinction between
itself and the "producing classes" in general,—
which included also farmers, small manufacturers,
and small business men,—continued for many decades to worship at the shrine of individualistic
"anti-monopoly". "Anti-monopoly" was a pro-

gram of reform, through politics and legislation, whereby the "producing classes" would apply a corrective to the American social order so that economic individualism might become "safe" for the producers rather than for land speculators, merchant capitalists, and bankers. Unionism, on the contrary, first became a stabilized movement in America only when the abundance consciousness of the pioneer days had been replaced in the mind of labor by a scarcity consciousness—the consciousness of job scarcity. Only then did the American wage earner become willing to envisage a future in which his union would go on indefinitely controlling his relation to his job rather than endeavoring to afford him, as during the anti-monopoly stage of the labor movement, an escape into free and unregulated self-employment, by winning for him a competitive equality with the "monopolist".

In America, the historical struggle waged by labor for an undivided expression of its own mentality in its own movement was directed against the ideology of "anti-monopoly". But in Europe the antithesis to the labor mentality has been the mentality of the intellectual.

Twenty-five years ago, Nicolai Lenin [1] clearly recognized the divergence which exists between the intellectual and the trade unionist, although not in

[1] "The history of all countries attests to the fact that, left to its own forces, the working class can only attain to trade union consciousness,—that is, the conviction that it is necessary to unite in unions, wage the struggle against the bosses, obtain from the government such or such labor reforms, etc. As to the socialist doctrines, they came from philosophic, historic and economic theories elaborated by certain educated representatives of the possessing classes, the Intellectuals. In their social situation, the founders of contemporary scientific socialism, Marx and Engels, were bourgeois intellectuals." Lenin in *What Is To Be Done?*

terms of an inevitable mutual antagonism, when he hurled his unusual polemical powers against those in the Social-Democratic Party, his own party at the time, who would confine their own and the party's agitational activities to playing upon labor's economic grievances. He then said that if it had not been for the "bourgeois intellectuals" Marx and Engels, labor would never have got beyond mere "trifling",—going after an increase in wage here and after a labor law there. Lenin, of course, saw labor and the trade union movement, not as an aggregation of concrete individuals sharing among themselves their collective job opportunity, as well as trying to enlarge it and improve it by joint effort and step by step, but rather as an abstract mass which history had predetermined to hurl itself against the capitalist social order and demolish it. Lenin therefore could never have seen in a non-revolutionary unionism anything more than a blind groping after a purpose only vaguely grasped, rather than a completely self-conscious movement with a full-blown ideology of its own. But to see "labor" solely as an abstract mass and the concrete individual reduced to a mere mathematical point, as against the trade unionists' striving for job security for the individual and concrete freedom on the job, has not been solely the prerogative of "determinist-revolutionaries" like Lenin and the Communists. The other types of intellectuals in and close to the labor movement, the "ethical" type, the heirs of Owen and the Christian Socialists, and the "social efficiency" type, best represented by the Fabians —to mention but English examples,—have equally with the orthodox Marxians reduced labor to a mere abstraction, although each has done so in his own way and has pictured "labor" as an abstract mass in the grip of an abstract force, existing, however, only in his own intellectual imagination, and not in the emotional imagination of the manual worker himself.

PART I
HISTORICAL

CHAPTER II

THE RUSSIAN REVOLUTION

In Russia, the Revolution came at a time when her capitalism was in its youth, and her laboring class totally without the training which labor acquires only when it has long been opposing to capitalism a trade unionism of its own making and under leaders out of its own class. It was, in fact, as though in England, in 1834, on the morrow of the Industrial Revolution, the masses of the factory population, organized for the first time in the Grand National Consolidated Trades Union, had by their threatened "National Holiday" or general strike, destroyed capitalism.

The successful Revolution of Russia, in 1917, displayed two original and greatly unexpected peculiarities that are full of the greatest significance to students of the world labor movement. The first is that her capitalism, which, having barely begun to industrialize the country and should, if Marx were correct, have been distinguished by a power of resistance, bespeaking virile youth, actually displayed the weakness which Marx had forecast for an already senile capitalism in its last stages of decline. Russian capitalism stood in sharp contrast with the older capitalism of countries like Germany which were far more advanced industrially, but where capitalism has successfully withstood the many revolutionary attacks since the end of the War. The other Russian peculiarity, closely interrelated with the first, is that the factory workers, although numerically still an insignificant part of the population and altogether new to the ways of organization, still have lent themselves eagerly as the unflinching instrument of the revolution. For this rôle, Marx had cast the working classes in capitalistically "mature" countries, with their greater numbers and presumably "mature" class consciousness. But in reality the latter, although trained for decades in organization, have generally played false to the Marxian prediction, and have willingly contributed towards the stabilization of capitalism in its times of peril. To be sure, the Revolution in Russia was precipitated by the lost War and by the War-created exhaustion. In Germany and Austria, however, where the defeat suffered was even greater, and where the old ruling groups, bereft by revolution of the protection of government and armies, were likewise left to look out for themselves and their possessions, the defenders of the established order yet knew how to discover adequate substitutes for the vanished military monarchy and how to attain a new preponderance by the use of all forces at hand, even including the portion of the working class organized in trade unions. In Russia, on the contrary, the scales registered altogether differently, when the disastrous war had removed from them the armed hand of the government, permitting an unhampered weighing against one another of the supporters and the opponents of the economic order based upon private property.

The "Ruling" Classes

It is an irony of fate that the same Revolution which purports to enact into life the Marxian social program should belie the truth of Marx's materialistic interpretation of history, and demonstrate that history is shaped by both economic and non-economic forces. Marx, as is well known, taught that history is a struggle between classes, in which the landed aristocracy, the bourgeoisie, and the proletariat are raised successively to rulership as, with the progress of society's technical equipment, first one and then another class can operate it with the maximum efficiency. Marx assumed that when the time had arrived for a given economic class to take the helm, that class would be found in full possession of all the psychological attributes of a ruling class, namely, an indomitable will to power, no less than the more vulgar desire for the emoluments that come with power. Apparently Marx took for granted that economic evolution is inevitably accompanied by a corresponding development of an effective will to power in the class destined to rule. But whatever may be the case in the countries of the West, in Russia the ruling classes, the gentry and the bourgeoisie, clearly failed in the psychological test at the critical moment. This failure is amply attested by the manner in which they submitted practically without a fight after the Bolshevist *coup d'état.*

The explanation for this failure of the "ruling" classes one must seek in Russia's peculiar historical development, primarily in the exclusive dominance which the factor of government played in her making. Where the historian of the West is obliged to deal with numerous, more or less independent factors—crown, feudal aristocracy, free municipalities, Established Church, non-conformity, merchant gilds, craft gilds, "interlopers"—the Russian historian who concentrates solely on government will not miss any of the mainsprings.

For one thing, "Muscovite" Russia,—the Russia centering in Moscow, which emerged in the Sixteenth Century from underneath the Tartar yoke—never truly developed a strong feudal class. The origins of Muscovite Russia lie back in the Twelfth Century, when foreign invasion drove the Russian people from the old settled and commercially advanced country on the lower Dnieper, with Kiev as its capital, to seek safety in the Northern woods. In the North, the Russian community, which formerly had known how to check its princes by a strong commercial patriciate and by the institution of the popular town assembly, became reconstructed upon an ultra-monarchist principle. For, now the princes became not only her political rulers, but they combined with political power an absolute ownership of the land (all-important now because commerce had completely given way to a self-sufficient agriculture), in addition to a managerial leadership in the difficult work of pioneer settlement.

Among the many independent principalities in the North, Moscow was at first one of the lesser ones. But her rulers knew how to make use of the rivalries of the other princes and of the cupidity of their Tartar suzerains to add one principality after another to their domains, until the process of "gathering up the Russian land" was completed. The numerous princes whom the Grand Princes of Moscow thus mediatized went to make up the upper crust of the Moscovite nobility, the Boyars. Lower down in the scale were the military and civil servitors of lesser rank. Such was the background of the Russian feudal class.

It was an unusually weak and unambitious feudal nobility. Even the "Boyar" was, in fact, no more than a steward of the Czar's estates and a leader of a posse defending his property. The most he dared to do was, surreptitiously, to obstruct the carrying out of the Czar's intentions. He dared not try to impose the will of his class upon the crown. Finally, with the peasantry passing under serfdom,—a process which was only complete by the middle of the Seventeenth Century,—the landed nobility became entirely too preoccupied with their estates, and with fastening their domination upon their still rebellious serfs, to give thought to political ambition. This non-political character of the nobility and, for that matter, of all the other classes—the clergy, and the few merchants, and townsmen—went even so far that it was considered merely a burden to be obliged to attend the representative "assemblies of the land", which the monarchs frequently convoked during the Sixteenth and Seventeenth Centuries. The last assembly with a semblance of legislative power met in 1642, and none met after 1698.

It was upon such an apathetic and subdued nobility, no more than a shadow of the Western landed aristocracy, that Peter the Great's program of modernization burst like a hurricane at the end of the Seventeenth Century. The nobles detested his innovations as the very handiwork of the Antichrist, but submitted without a murmur. Peter's auto-

cratic will succeeded in changing the tradition-wor-
shipping nobles and servitors of the state into "cul-
tured Europeans" and modernized bureaucrats.
Under his successors, especially Catherine the Great,
this "modernization" went on apace. It failed,
however, to instil an aspiration to occupy an independent position in the Russian body politic. For
that, there was lacking both class solidarity and a
class fighting spirit. It quite sufficed if the monarch
bestowed remunerative posts in the state service and
other favors, together with a free hand to exploit
the peasants. Catherine, who especially favored the
nobility, made an effort to give them some political
independence by voluntarily turning over to them
the local administration, and by decreeing, to that
end, that they organize themselves into provincial
associations. But so little did they care for political
power and active class prerogative that, aside from
their purely administrative work, the associations of
nobles were never more than social organizations in
the conventional sense of the word.

During the Napoleonic wars, a group of the
younger aristocrats became imbued with European
life and civilization, and organized a secret association to force a written constitution. They formed the
famous "Decembrists", whose military revolt in
December, 1825, was crushed by Nicholas I. Neither
then nor at any other time would the autocracy
admit any one to share in power nor deal as with a
political independent with any class. Thereupon followed a period of thirty years of the darkest political reaction, to be broken only by the defeat in the
Crimean War, and the accession of Alexander II.
Early in the new reign, the peasants were given

freedom with land, but burdened with a crushing indebtedness. The debt was taken over by the government to be collected in forty-nine annual installments, together with the other taxes, and paying the landlords in government bonds, which they quickly converted into cash and dissipated. In the half century between emancipation and the World War, the Russian nobility held the better half of the land, and enjoyed numerous privileges, such as monopoly of the military and the higher civil offices, numerous educational advantages at government expense, and cheap land credit from the government at rates far below the market. Nevertheless, the nobility steadily lost ground, and their lands kept on passing to the merchant class and partly also to the richer peasants. Many of the nobility went into the liberal professions and indeed made splendid contributions to Russian civilization. Likewise the political liberal movement drew heavily from the more enlightened landlords. Down to the revolution of 1905, the organs of provincial self-government, the "Zemstvos", so-called, were run by liberal landlords, who from time to time, were even emboldened to make demands for a national constitution and parliament. The revolution of 1905, however, with its agrarian disorders, threw the leadership of the nobility back to the reactionaries. And when the revolution had simmered down to the bogus parliament of the Duma of 1907, with the electoral law so amended as to give the landlords the majority, they truly fulfilled all that was expected of them. But, liberal or conservative, enlightened or backward, the gentry of Russia never was a "political" class in the same sense as the English or the Prussian. Neither on a historical background of abject servility to a Byzantine monarchy nor on a past of privileges without a share in power, could an effective will to political power, a capacity to subordinate individual or clique whims and ambitions to a well considered class interest and class program, have developed. These psychological traits a "ruling" class must not fail to have. The introduction of the culture of Western Europe, and acquaintance with the independent participation in government by European nobilities,— (independent even where, as in Prussia, it went with an external submissiveness to the crown,)—could not undo the work of ages long past. In this lack of unity lies, mainly, the miserable failure of the "White" movements of 1918-1921, despite unlimited support by foreign powers.

Muscovite Russia never had independent towns and self-governing gilds. Novgorod and Pskov, the Russian members of the Hanseatic League, lost their independence completely when it was their turn to submit to the "gatherer of the Russian land", operating from Moscow. The commerce of Russia was either carried on by foreigners, like the English Muscovy Company, or by a relatively few native merchants, who neither formed merchant gilds nor claimed borough rights. The old Russian towns were mere centers of military and civil administration, where to the "official" inhabitants and their house serfs was added a promiscuous population of petty tradesmen and a few artisans of either free or servile status. Russia missed altogether the stage of civilization which in the Western countries rested upon the craft gilds, since the bulk of the handicrafts of Russia were carried on by the peasantry on the landlords' estates or in their own village homes. So that Russian capitalism, when it finally did arise, came up not from the natural roots of a medieval commerce and trade, but principally as the creature of the government.

In the reign of Alexis, the father of Peter the Great, in the latter part of the Seventeenth Century, Russia began to advance toward the goal of a modern military state. Peter accelerated this movement enormously. But to be able to contend with Sweden, the greatest military power of the North, Peter saw that Russia needed industries, metallurgical, shipbuilding, cloth manufacturing, etc. To meet this need, he energetically espoused the mercantilist policies generally dominant in that day.

But Russian mercantilism was necessarily different from mercantilism elsewhere. In the West of Europe, mercantilism answered in an equal measure the needs of an expanding state and of a vigorous middle class, the latter being no less ardent in the pursuit of gain than the former in the pursuit of conquest.[1] In Russia, on the contrary, when Peter wanted manufactures, they had to be introduced mainly by government action. Hence Russian mercantilism was predominantly a state mercantilism. Even where Peter and his successors were able to enlist private initiative by money subsidies and grants of serf labor,—instead of building up a class of independent entrepreneurs, he merely created

[1] Contrast this with the Tudor mercantilism in England. The Tudor rulers, with all their absolutistic propensities, still, on matters of commercial policy, had their ministers keep in the closest touch with the traders, seeking their counsel and employing them as agents—this resulting in such a thorough interaction between crown and merchant class that it is difficult to say with whom there lay the greater initiative.

industrial bureaucrats with little or no initiative of
their own, who kept looking to the government.

The government continued as the sole prop of the
larger industries of Russia down to the second half
of the Nineteenth Century. The disastrous Crimean
War, 1854-1856, caused the government to embark
upon a most extensive railway building program. It
reached its greatest intensity between 1868 and 1874,
when one billion roubles were invested. Thereupon
the government railways, both when under construction and in operation, were added to the army and
navy as industry's chief and unfailing customer.
Soon, however, industry acquired a partly independent footing. While the government, to be sure, built
its railroads for strategic and partly fiscal reasons
(to bring to the peasant the necessary money for his
taxes by facilitating a grain export on a larger
scale), it was also creating incidentally a unified
internal market, which made mass production of
articles of common consumption profitable for the
first time.

Following the unification of the internal market,
in the last quarter of the century, Russian industry
truly began to develop by leaps and bounds. Textiles, the metallurgical industries, and, later, mining
and oil, vied with one another in multiplying output,
expanding their plants, and increasing their capital-
ization. While only too many of the big establishments were foreign-owned and foreign-managed, a
Russian industry and a Russian class of big business
men were arising nevertheless. A significant peculiarity of this feverish industrial and business expansion was that it resulted in a remarkably high
concentration of production in a restricted number

of large units. There was lacking a gradual evolution out of handicraft and out of a "domestic" or merchant-capitalist system, with the characteristic gradation in the sizes of the units from very small to very large which can be found where a normal development has taken place. The huge establishments of the new Russian industry resembled so many high peaks arising abruptly, as it were, from the plains, with no foothills.[1] Russian big business, unprotected on its flanks by a sizable class of medium and small business men, was particularly exposed to revolutionary attack.

Although by the end of the century, Russian industry, having expanded to great dimensions by a generous flow of foreign capital, had already outgrown its former complete dependence on the government as a customer, the relations between them nevertheless failed to undergo a radical change. For the addition of several less direct aids to the nation's industry, like a heavily protective and in some notable cases a truly prohibitive tariff, did not detract from the rôle played by profitable contracts handed out by a government which managed a huge railway system and purported to be the biggest armed power in the world. The government, on its part, fearful lest the new industrial power should in the end begin to dispute its own supremacy, was loath to let industry alone. To point out but one example: All modern states long ago passed general incorporation laws, extending to everyone the privilege of business incorporation, provided a few given form-

[1] In Russia the ratio of large establishments (employing 200 or more) to medium sized establishments (employing 50 to 200) was, in 1913, as 1 to 7.4. In Germany that ratio was, in 1907, as 1 to 50.7.

alities were complied with. In Russia, on the contrary, it was oftentimes a matter of years of lobbying in government departments before a new business corporation would be duly authorized. To Russian business men, the government policy of keeping business under its thumb was, of course, distasteful; still, they never neglected to make the best of the situation. For instance, when the sugar producers found themselves facing ruin from cutthroat competition, they appealed to the Minister of Finances, who immediately created a government-enforced "trust", and assured them huge dividends. The ultimate effect of all this can hardly be overestimated. A generous government could disburse bounties, enact prohibitive tariffs, give hugely profitable orders; it could hold the consumer down while the industrialists picked his pockets. It stands to reason, then, that since business success was assured by keeping on good terms with the government rather than by relying on one's own "tooth and claw", plus dynamic power and organizing ability, the business class of Russia, and especially those who enjoyed the greatest success, could develop only into a class of industrial courtiers. And when the bountiful government fell, the courtiers were not to be turned overnight into stubborn champions of the rights of their class amid the turmoil of a revolution. The Bolshevik leaders refused to credit the Russian "bourgeoisie" with any wish to emulate the example of the French bourgeoisie, which in its revolution, in the year 1789, did not flinch from destroying and clearing away the débris of the old régime. They declared that the fear of the impending working-men's revolution had already driven the Russian capitalists for good into the arms of reaction. In this belief they were completely in the right. However, they would still have been right had they added that, not only would the Russian capitalists fail to fight for the progress of the country, but they would equally fail to show fight in the defense of their own privileges. Russian capitalism had, since about 1880, the complete external appearance of capitalism elsewhere, and, by virtue of the magnitude of the scale of its productive units and its very feverish growth, even seemed to have outstripped foreign capitalism, at least in the *tempo* of its growth. So far, however, as having an effective will to live, so far as being really rooted in the social soil is concerned, such appearances were completely deceptive.

Only a little needs to be said about Russian religious life as a possible factor in the resistance to the Communist revolution. Down to Peter the Great, the Church had been, next to the monarchy, the most powerful institution in the land. The Church played a major part in aiding the princes of Moscow to "gather up the Russian land", and was primarily responsible for national self-preservation during the centuries of Tartar domination. So great in those days was its prestige and the prestige of its head, the Patriarch of Moscow, that even Ivan the Terrible, the most unrestrained tyrant history has known, felt he had to exercise caution when it came to the Church. In the Period of Troubles, 1598-1613, the Church was the rallying center for the two patriotic classes, the lower nobility and the merchants, who led in the ejection of the Polish invader and in restoring internal order. But Peter would not suffer in his realm an office almost equal in dignity to the throne. So he reduced the Church to a mere department of the state administration, placing it under a Holy Synod, with an omnipotent lay procurator at the head. It was not until the fall of the Romanovs in 1917 that the Church regained its freedom—only to come upon the hard times of the Revolutionary period. During the two centuries of serfdom to the state, the Established Church lost whatever power it ever possessed to evoke in the communicants a spirit of resistance to any sort of oppression.

Nor had Russia experienced a religious Reformation that might have trained and developed, in the struggle for religious freedom, a class of non-conformists with a disciplined, self-reliant capacity to withstand dictatorship from whatever direction. The resistance by Russia's millions of Old Believers, whose non-conformity consisted in rejecting some formal changes in rite and liturgy effected by Patriarch Nicon in the Seventeenth Century, took a different direction from the non-conformity of England and Scotland. While, on the whole, the effects on personal character may have tended to be nearly alike, making for sobriety, self-reliance, industry,— the very virtues conducive to economic success,— the Old Believers never resisted authority, but sought to emulate the early Christian martyrs.

It was from such "defenders" of the established order — this nobility, this "bourgeoisie", this Church,—that the resistance to the Communist revolution had to come.

The Rôle of the Peasantry

The weakness of the "ruling" classes in the fight on behalf of private property may be explained in part by their want of an ally in the peasant. No Thiers could rally a Russian peasant army for the suppression of a communist proletariat by an appeal to their property interest—simply because the Russian peasant was reared for centuries in an atmosphere of communistic land property, in the "mir". To make matters worse for the propertied classes, the peasant's strongest craving was for the land of the landlords. This was the only sort of currency which he would accept in payment for political support. In November 1917, when the Bolsheviks seized the government, one of their first acts was to satisfy the peasant's land hunger, by turning over to his use all the land. They had then, for a time at least, a free hand so far as eighty-five per cent of the Russian people were concerned.

The peasant's "mir", or agrarian land commune —the most basic and the most discussed Russian social institution—may be non-technically defined as a self-governing democratic association of all the peasant families belonging to a given village. It had the legal right to own land, and, subject to supervision by special authorities, to make land allotments, periodic or otherwise, to its members, and to conduct by the same democratic procedure whatever business pertaining to the land, such as purchase and lease of additional land, or whatever other matters of communal government, that might arise. The "mir" was established in a modern form after the emancipation of the peasants in 1861,

which included a land settlement with the former
owners, private landlords and the state itself. The
"mir", following a time-hallowed custom dating
from long before emancipation, parcelled out the
land to individual families in narrow strips of arable
and meadow, figured for each family on its size or
relative needs. The strips, which went to a family,
were rather numerous and scattered throughout the
entire holding of the "mir"; this in the interest of
equality, so that each might enjoy the use of land of
every degree of desirability, both as to quality of
soil and nearness to the village. Further, the family
allotments were subject to periodic re-divisions, and
to a complete one on the average once in ten or a
dozen years, and a partial one more often—to take
care of changes in family size and status. Furthermore, the size of the allotment, i.e. the number of
strips allowed, determined the amount of the tax,
which, until 1906, included also the annual installments on the debt for the price of the land agreed
upon by the settlement at the time of emancipation,
a debt which the state had then taken over from the
private landlords. And finally, until 1887, the
"mir" was collectively responsible for defaulted
taxes. This, simply and schematically, is a picture
of the workings of the curious institution of the
"mir". Thus the "mir" owned the land, but the individual peasant owned the other means of production, horses, cattle, implements, farm buildings, as
well as the means of consumption. The peasant family cultivated its strips and naturally enjoyed the
fruit of its toil, out of which it supported itself and
paid taxes. The control which the "mir" exercised
over the productive process was a by-product of the

practice of land communism, coupled with the three-field system [1] of agriculture; it made a uniform method of cultivation practically obligatory upon all peasants. There was a compulsory insurance through obligatory contribution of a share of the harvest towards a communal store of seed in case of famine, and a system of mutual neighborly help, in the nature of the "barn raising" of the American pioneer farmer. With this exception, production, as well as distribution, were strictly individualistic.[2]

The "mir", like the mediæval gilds, surrounded every side of their members' lives. It stamped their economic as well as their "political" and social thinking. The Russian peasant has always been a practical "anarchist", not just because of his proneness to spontaneous acts of destruction against the landlords, but in the sense of being so enveloped in the primitive social cell of the "mir" as to offer an

---

[1] Under which one-third of the arable lies fallow each year to give the soil an opportunity to recover its fertility.

[2] It seems vital to bring out in this connection the two conflicting theories as to the historical origin of the "mir". Professor Kluchevsky, Russia's greatest general historian, contends that the land control by the commune arose out of the necessity of guaranteeing the fiscal interest. That is, the government resolved as early as the Fifteenth and Sixteenth Centuries that the taxes of the peasant population, then as yet not brought under serfdom and therefore free to move about, could be gathered only under a collective liability by the entire village community for the total amount. Therefore the government was obliged by the logic of the new situation to give the communes a free hand in allotting the land in such a manner as would assure, so far as possible, each individual family's ability to pay. On the other hand, Professor Semevsky, an authority on Russian agrarian history, holds that agrarian communism was established at the initiative of the peasants themselves. The investigations of Russian scholars into land conditions in Siberia, where, owing to the recent settlement, "mirs" were originated under the very eyes, as it were, of the investigators, bear out Professor Semevsky's view. Whichever be the truer explanation after all, it is scarcely open to doubt that until the situation created by the recent Revolution, the peasantry's attachment to the "mir" was both genuine and unqualified.

excellent example of a thoroughly "non-political animal". For, to him, the "mir" itself, with its utter informality and with the utter absence of material and mental gold brocade connected with the few "offices" which it had, seemed not at all a "government", but an "an-archy". It is no mere accident, therefore, that the greatest anarchists of our time, "philosophical", as well as "propagandists by deed",—Bakunin, Prince Kropotkin, and Count Tolstoy—were Russian nobles with a thoroughly agrarian horizon. When they spoke of anarchism, they meant a social organization that was as much a non-government (an-archy) as the Russian peasants' "mir". "Government", on the contrary, stood in the peasant's mind for the central Imperial power, which took his sons for soldiers and forced him to sell a vital portion of his hard won means of subsistence for taxes, and gave nothing, or next to nothing, in return. In brief, the Russian peasant's "political" ideal was an anarchistic Russia, a loose federation of "mirs" or rather groups of "mirs", with a central "government" discharging but a few simple functions, largely of the "service" order, but above all, content to leave him and his "mir" alone. Such was also the political ideal of the early "populistic" socialists as well as of the nearest modern throw-back to the latter, the "Social-Revolutionaries of the Left". This party, which the Bolshevists had won for its ally in the revolution of October 1917, by agreeing to its land program, later turned its terrorist wrath on the Bolshevists, when it saw that the new Soviet régime, far from letting the peasant escape being "governed", meant instead a program of regimentation, of forcibly pumping communism into the village, of requisitions for the "Red Army", and of using Russia merely as a means to the end of world revolution. So far, however, as the peasant himself is concerned, like the non-political animal that he was and still remains, his resistance to the Communist dictatorship took the economic form of an unorganized but effective agriculturists' strike. And the Communist government, appreciating both the strength of the peasants' weapon and his unpolitical character, acted upon the correct diagnosis that the danger, however grave, called for no sharing with the peasant of the political power for which he had no clear desire, but rather for a general loosening of the bonds of government to permit a peasant economic autonomy in the localities—the New Economic Policy of 1921.

The "mir" owed its survival and strengthening after emancipation primarily to the government's fear of there arising a politically dangerous landless proletariat. But it owed it in part, also, to the very influential ideology of the nationalistic slavophile school of thought, which seized upon this solidaristic institution to claim for Russia a supremacy over Europe, and insistently urged that in its safeguarding lay the best assurance of Russia's avoiding the class struggles of the West. What the government, even up to the revolution of 1905, failed, however, to perceive, was that the same land system which presumably was to have assured the conservatism of even the poorest peasant, because it gave him an inalienable claim upon an equal share with his fellows in the collective economic opportunity, really defeated the government purpose. For the true sheet anchor of social conservatism is a class of

substantial peasants after the West European manner—"big peasants" with adequate land and capital,
progressive in their methods of cultivation, and
withal the acknowledged leaders in their communities. Different altogether was the Russian type of
"strong" peasant. The land he cultivated was not
his own, but a part of the communal land. It lay
not in one compact block but scattered in many
strips. He could not add to it by purchase from his
poorer neighbors,[1] since like himself they did not
own their land. Further, he was lockstepped with
the whole community as to method of cultivation,
namely, the three-field system. Hence he found only
one way to grow wealthier than his neighbors, that
is, turning "Kulak", or "fist", or usurer, who
loaned corn to his destitute fellow villagers in the
winter and the spring and made them pay three
prices in labor in the summer. The "Kulak" element accounted perhaps for about five to ten per
cent of the village. Below it was the great mass of
medium peasants who could make ends meet unless
hit by misfortune, especially with the aid of the
wages earned by some members of the family in the
factories in the cities, or else from handicrafts plied
at home. And lowest came the "poor" peasants,
the horseless, near-proletarian peasants, the twenty
per cent, and higher.

While there failed to come with economic stratifi-
cation a class of Russian *Bauern,* a rock of Gibraltar
to "throne, fatherland, and church", the progressive impoverishment of the great bulk of the peas-

[1] He could, of course, buy land of a neighboring landlord, which
then became his private property, but he could not make a unified
farm out of such purchased land and his allotment from the "mir."

antry for a period of forty-five years after emancipation was slowly undoing whatever influence for conservatism may have been contained in the time-hallowed organization of peasant life. The situation may be had at a glance from the figures following. From 1861 to 1900, the peasant population increased 90 per cent, the area of their cultivation (by purchase or by renting, as communes or as individuals) only 20 per cent, and the output per acre stood still or even slightly went back. In 1860, there were 4.8 desiatin [1] per adult male; in 1880, 3.35; and in 1900, 2.59 desiatin. It was only in the land shortage and in the crushing taxation, all the heavier since it included redemption payments for the land received with emancipation, that the peasants saw the sole explanation of their chronic poverty and semi-starvation. Not in the three-field system with its waste of land, nor in the "mir" with its destruction of any incentive either to check the birth rate or to individual improvement in agricultural methods. The remedy, accordingly, was to hand the land unconditionally to the tillers—wiping off the past debt, and making available to the twenty-two million peasant families the 110 million desiatin of the landlords' land, plus the usable portion of the state domain, in addition to the 140 million they already held.[2] In this remedy the whole village concurred without exception, from "Kulak" down to the poorest peasant. For even the "Kulak", although he made it his business to appear thoroughly reliable when the authorities were around, could trust to the excellent technique he had developed for controlling

[1] One desiatin equals 2.7 acres.
[2] These figures hold for the time of the abortive Revolution of 1905.

the "mir", that when the "mir" became enriched, his interests would not be overlooked. So much for the "conservative" order of the village life.[1]

To the government, however, the true character of the little village cosmos was only revealed in the election to the first Duma in the spring of 1906. Disregarding the "agrarian disorders" which kept recurring with more and more frequency since 1902, the cabinet of Count Witte, Russia's first "constitutional" government, so framed the electoral law as to throw a decisive influence to the peasantry. Great indeed was the dismay when a radical house was returned. To be sure, the Duma lasted but three months, but it definitely sealed the fate of the "mir", so far as the government was concerned. It had been tolerated and protected in the past because of the support to the existing mainstays it was presumed to give, notwithstanding the acknowledged handicaps it put upon production. It now lost every raison d'être. So, with the first Duma out of the way, the new strong government of Stolypin coolly decreed the destruction of the "mir" by "temporary" administrative decree.

Under the new order of things, any "mir" was empowered to resolve, by a simple majority, upon its own dissolution. Of still greater importance was the right granted to every individual family to petition for separation out of the "mir". Government bodies were set up to effect a division of the communal lands among all families in the case of complete dissolution of the "mir", and between the

[1] In the black soil region of Southern Russia, the "mir" was not a factor. There, however, the peasantry had been given so little land at emancipation that the hunger for the landlords' land, if anything, was stronger than in Central Russia.

individual families separating out and the remaining families, if the majority of the "mir" resolved to go on as before. The land thus assigned to individual families became their unrestricted private property. The law prescribed that every effort should be made to provide the separationists with farms in as few pieces as possible, and to encourage them strongly to build homes upon their new farms, away from the village. All in all, one million and a half of the total of 22,000,000 peasant families took advantage of this law from 1906 to the outbreak of the war. The "separationists" came from both extremes. "Strong" peasants sought to gain the freedom to employ more modern farming methods than the "mir" organization permitted. Needless to say, they were spurred on to that step by the favored treatment which they knew they could expect at the hands of the local land administrators in the matter of adjudicating the intricate conflicting rights. At the other end of the scale were the poorest peasants, many of them city wage earners, who no longer had the means nor the desire to work their land, and to whom their allotment in the village was a burden, combined as it was with a restricted personal freedom due to the "mir's" control over them. These had long been eager to cut loose, but were heretofore held back by law.

While it is difficult to conclude what sort of a peasantry might have emerged in the end, had not this process been brought to a stop by the War, it is nevertheless clear that after seven years of governmental encouragement, the great majority of the peasantry still continued true to the "mir", and generally viewed those who separated out as traitors to their class. And while the conditions of Russian agriculture had indeed improved in that period, and still more during the War—partly due to the new law, but mostly to the favorable prices on agricultural commodities on the world market— the land hunger of the peasantry, from the poorest to the "Kulak", continued unabated. And it was the clear perception of that dominant fact, together with their correct appraisal of the general longing for peace with Germany, which enabled the Bolshevists to seize power without serious opposition.

The Wage Earning Class

Russia's wage earning class first arose with her factory industries, that is, without antecedents in an urban artisan class. Consequently, Russian labor was obliged to do without the essential aid towards acquiring a self direction which could have been imparted to it only by an old established artisan group, trained in organization, as was the English, by centuries of experience with journeymen's societies.

The first factory workers were serfs; they were either state serfs permanently attached to a "possession" factory, that is, a factory located on the state domain and owned by or rented to an entrepreneur of the business class, foreign or Russian;[1] else they were the serf operatives of factories established by private landlords on their own estates. By 1840, the "possession" serfs were already free, and

---

[1] This unusual arrangement was dictated by the necessity of providing a labor force to entrepreneurs who, not being of the nobility, were legally barred from owning serfs. When such a factory changed hands, its attached working force went with it; it could also add to its labor force by purchase.

could hire out for wages, thus constituting Russia's first free wage earning class.

The emancipation of the peasants and the subsequent industrial development added greatly to the numbers of industrial workers. That was partly the consequence of the communal system of land ownership, which quickly created a land shortage and a surplus village population, since on the one hand it prevented a change from the wasteful three-field system, and on the other encouraged reckless propagation. It was also partly the consequence of the progressive destruction of the peasant handicrafts due to the superior competitive power of the factories operated with free labor. Yet much as the peasant influx to the cities resembled the cityward movement at the time of the English enclosures, it gave, under the Russian circumstances, a factory population with village ties still intact. As late as 1907, an investigation in Petrograd disclosed that out of 570 workers picked at random, only 260 were completely without village ties, 122 were still working their land, 111 had retained their land but worked it no longer, while 77, landless themselves, were regularly remitting a portion of their earnings to relatives in the village. This retention of village ties had both a good and a bad effect. On the one side, it offered an insurance of a kind against industrial unemployment; on the other side, however, this mass movement from country to city and back again with the changing seasons rendered the condition of labor poor and unstable, and had its most serious effect on housing conditions. A German observer said: "There can be nothing more melancholy than the Viborg workmen's quarter in Petrograd, with its streets where poverty and neglect stalk hand in hand. The houses are for the most part dirty wooden barracks enclosing evil smelling courtyards overfilled with every kind of refuse; while the various odors of foods in preparation coming through from the windows are enough to cause nausea in all but the least sensitive persons. The whole enormous Viborg quarter contains not one public park." Another German said: "In my opinion, since the Russian factory workers, due to wretched housing, are absolutely precluded from living a decent family life, their housing in employer-owned barracks, far from being an evil, is a true benevolence." In the great industrial centers, low wages and high rents compelled the Russian worker to be content, for himself and his family, with a mere "corner" in a room costing him two or three roubles [1] per month, so that not infrequently one room would hold four families.

An extensive investigation made in 1907, when wages still betrayed the effects of the revolutionary tide running at its highest, showed that the Petrograd metal workers, who were the highest paid workers in the country, had 50 per cent of their number earning 1.50 roubles per day, 38 per cent from 1.50 to 2.50, and 11 per cent above 2.50; with a general average of 1.67 roubles per day. Were the average Petrograd metal worker to purchase the same quantity and quality of foods consumed yearly by a typical workingman's family in Berlin, and were he to dwell in one of the better types of Berlin workingmen's houses, he would have had to spend for these two items alone the annual sum of 597

[1] A pre-War rouble equalled 51½ American cents.

roubles, or nearly one hundred roubles in excess of his total annual earnings. It explains why the Russian worker never bought any but second-hand clothing and why he housed himself in a "corner." For the decade from 1901 to 1910, distinguished by a great industrial expansion, as well as by strikes and revolution, it was reliably estimated that average Russian wages rose 18 per cent, while the cost of living had risen more than 37 per cent, and in Moscow fully 50 per cent. The lowest paid groups, as shown by a 1910 Moscow investigation, were the workers in textiles, who formed nearly one-fourth of Russia's three million factory workers, and of whom one-half were women. While 50 per cent or more of the metal workers received thirty roubles per month, only 1.9 per cent of the flax and jute workers, 8.8 per cent of the cotton workers, 10.3 per cent of the silk workers, and 15.2 per cent of the workers in wool received that wage. However, it rose to 35.3 per cent for the workers in the "mixed textiles" group. On the matter of hours of labor, the revolution of 1905-6 did cause a permanent reduction from twelve and eleven to ten and nine hours.

Russian labor legislation dates in a rudimentary way from the eighties and the nineties. Its enactment was motivated throughout by the aim to minimize to some extent the resistance to law and order from a working class driven to total despair. An employers' liability law was passed in 1903, but gave the injured workmen such illusory rights that during 1904-6, 18,994 out of the total of 23,915 accidents were "amicably" adjusted between employer and employee without any reference to state authority! Upon that, the law of 1912 was no slight advance, as it provided for a medical benefit and for a cash payment of two-thirds of the wage beginning with the fourteenth week after the injury, in addition to a pension to dependents in fatal cases. Finally, the employers were obligated to insure against accidents to their employees in employers' mutual funds, which were given the power to administer the benefits subject to court appeal. In the same year, compulsory sick insurance was introduced with sick funds by establishments. The employer contributed two-thirds to the employees' one-third, but was given a proportionate predominance on the board of directors and a much greater one in the appeal bodies.

The behavior of the labor movement in the revolution was due largely to bad conditions of employment and of the workingmen's life in general, forced upon labor by a capitalism yet in its early stages and not as yet won over, whether by law or by a conversion, free or forced, to a belief in the "economy of high wages". However, one will find a cause of at least equal moment, more particularly as to its effect on labor psychology, in the struggle of trade unionism barely to survive.

When trade unionism has concentrated labor's attention and thought on concrete industrial situations, rather than on the "class struggle" in general and on "exploitation" in general; when it has brought together the labor ranks under leaders out of their own class; when, with the growing numbers and stability of the organizations in their care, these leaders have begun to think independently of their former mentors from among the intellectual class; then with such a trade unionism, there comes to labor a philosophy and outlook all its own. This, without abjuring the aim of an ultimate labor revolution, will nevertheless, in practice, begin more and more to stress the economic instead of the political; and when important steps are to be taken, will more and more weigh their effects on the welfare, opportunity, and liberty of the average workingman rather than their significance as links in a chain of action leading toward an "ultimate destiny" of human society.

Once such a trade union apparatus has become a "going concern", it needs no longer the impetus of spectacular victory nor even of continuous successes in a moderate way in order to keep hold on minds. It is enough that it does not "lie down", that it does not overlook real opportunities, that it keeps up a steady pressure, and that prospects are not wholly hopeless. However, this assumes that the trade unionism in question has already possessed itself of the irreducible minimum of legal immunity indispensable for its very existence.

In Russia, the fate of the trade union movement prior to 1917 was decided not by what the employers did, but by what was done by the government. Its ups and down, accordingly, followed the business cycle much less than the ups and downs of the political revolution. The first wave of labor strikes came in Petrograd in the middle of the nineties, having been set in motion by the intellectuals of the Social-Democratic movement, of whom Lenin was one. Of necessity, the leadership in this and in the economic movements for another decade had to come from the revolutionary intellectuals, since they held a monopoly on the vital knowledge of how to proceed with mass movements under a forced "underground" existence. It was only after the railway strike of October 1905 had given the trade unions a half acknowledged and a half factual legality of existence, that we find a Russian labor movement come forth under leaders risen from the ranks. And, significantly, these leaders, "labor leaders" in the full sense of the word, then managed not only to get into their hands the economic organizations, which would not have been surprising, but also down to the final triumph of the government, they led the very political movement as well. So strong indeed then was this new leadership that had arisen directly from the workers, that it compelled the mutually hostile intellectuals of Bolshevik and Menshevik factions in the Social-Democratic Party to go at least through the motions of making peace, although their differences had already become absolutely irreconcilable.[1]

[1] Gregory Zinoviev in his *History of the Russian Communist Party* relates the following:
"The Bolshevik and the Menshevik leaders were compelled to seek unity following the revolutionary struggle of the end of 1905, under the pressure from the masses. This constitutes an exceedingly interesting episode in the history of our party. In fact the masses have more than once forced the Bolsheviks to seek reconciliation with the Mensheviks. And this is not strange. Still in 1917 one could hear it said: 'Why split? If the Bolsheviks will join with the Mensheviks and even the Social Revolutionaries, then we shall surely overthrow the bourgeoisie and Czarism.' In all events, in 1905 there commenced a strong movement in favor of unity. In a number of places united Committees of Bolsheviks and Mensheviks were formed, which created common committees on a party basis, and carried on the struggle together. The consequence was that the Central Committee had to enter into a like federative relation with the Menshevik Organization Committee. Later, under pressure from the masses was called the Unity Congress of the party, which was held in Stockholm. . . . The Mensheviks captured the victory at the Stockholm Congress. . . . There was nothing left for the Bolsheviks but formally to submit, since they were in the minority. And the workers were demanding unity."

The first well developed *genuine* unions, to be distinguished from the *bogus* police-organized and police-managed unions in Moscow in 1901 and elsewhere, were the printers' unions in Moscow and Petrograd. The former had in 1903 a membership of 5000, or one-third of the total craft, and won the ten-hour day and a twenty-five per cent wage increase. The Petrograd printers, who were, in June 1905, 25 per cent organized, conducted statistical investigations of labor conditions in their craft, had a strike fund and a conciliation committee, and were engaged in working out their first trade agreement. Both unions were, of course, illegal. In 1904, the oil workers of Baku, following a seventeen days' strike, obtained a collective agreement with the employing companies, with a reduction from 11½ to 8 and 9 hours, a wage increase, and sickness insurance at the employers' expense. This union was also illegal.

With the "legalization" promised in the Manifesto of October 17, 1905, a mass growth of unionism began. Thus in Petrograd the number of unions

Zinoviev's "masses" were the wage earners then for the first time organized and led by men risen from their own ranks. In other words, "organic" labor, albeit as yet in the beginning of its self-consciousness, raised its voice to issue to the revolutionary intellectuals the order to bury their differences, to them so important. But Zinoviev proceeds to show how the Bolsheviks carried out this mandate from the "masses": "But in actual fact the Unity Congress had in no way united the Bolsheviks and Mensheviks and we left Stockholm in reality two factions. Several of our comrades, whom we used to speak of as 'hostages', were taken into the Central Committee. At the Congress itself, the Bolsheviks created their own inner and from the party standpoint, illegal Central Committee. This period in the history of our party, when we were in the minority both in Central Committee and in the Petersburg Committee, and had to carry on our special activities secretly, was a difficult and painful one for us."

The Workers' Herald, February, 1926.

rose from 14 in June 1905, to 24 in the following January, and to 40 one month later. In February, also, the first city trades' council in the country was formed in Petrograd, with a printed organ of its own. Moscow had in November 1905, 23 unions with 25,000 members, and in the next ten months the number of unions rose to 50-60. In Charkov, Nijni-Novgorod, and dozens of other towns, the same occurred. The suppression of the armed rebellion in Moscow in December 1905, caused a temporary retrogression, but on June 9, 1906, when the first Duma was dissolved, there were in Petrograd 30 unions, with a membership of 40,000, of whom 10,000 were metal workers and 7000-8000 printers. Moscow had then 30,000 unionists. The political strike by the Petrograd printers, in protest against the dissolution of the Duma, caused the closing, at the end of July, of 37 unions with 40,000 members.

The best organized of all were the Petrograd metal workers. They had an illiteracy of 8 per cent, contrasted with 77 per cent for the whole country and 20 per cent for Petrograd as a whole. This union developed a structure on the representative principle, with a provision for a popular referendum, and had three paid full-time officers. It published a paper, employed four lawyers in its legal aid department, and one physician, and in the spring of 1906 began to pay out-of-work benefits. It was, however, the printers who established the first national trade union in April 1907.

As already brought out, the fate of the unions was decided by their position under the law. Prior to October 1905, trade unions and strikes were of course strictly forbidden by the criminal law. In accord with the promise in the October Manifesto of freedom of economic association, the government promulgated the law of March 4, 1906, "legalizing" trade unions. While it permitted preliminary organization without a permission from the government, the provincial governor, presiding over an official board, had to confirm the constitution and the right of the union to a permanent existence. Furthermore, the law expressly refused to legalize strikes or any other forms of trade disputes. Neither were unions permitted to federate locally or nationally, so that city trades' councils and national trade unions continued illegal.

The law went on to enumerate the causes for which a union was liable to official dissolution, and these were further broadened by subsequent official interpretation. The actual scope of the legality granted emerges clearly from a statement, in 1912, by the Petrograd Administrative Bureau of supervision in justification of its denial of official confirmation of the constitution of a petitioning union. It found, first, that the condemned constitution had as one of the union's purposes the engaging in peaceful arbitration of differences between employers and employees; second, that it provided legal aid for members; third, that it provided medical aid; fourth, that it established branch unions; and, fifth, that it provided for weekly instead of annual collection of dues. All of these activities the Administrative Bureau held to be illegal. To insure against a "resurrection", the decision ordered that the funds of the union it thus destroyed must not be turned over to any union that might take its place, but turned over to a general charity organization. The same official body enunciated at the same meeting, relative to another case, that unions did not possess the right to do the following: First, to work for the "spiritual and moral uplift" of members; second, to grant out-of-work benefits; third, to have other benefit funds; fourth, to provide legal aid; fifth, to conduct lectures, *musicales,* and other educational work; sixth, to hold correspondence with outside persons or institutions; and, seventh, to deposit its funds in other than the Imperial State Bank. By way of contrast, employers' associations could legally engage in lockouts, blacklisting, and could employ whatever other means they wished for combating strikes and unionism.

Although immediately after October 1905, the trade unions had become separate entities from the revolutionary political parties, the government feared that a new political movement, arising out of the trade unions, might perhaps nullify its own victory over the revolution. Consequently, it turned on the unions the full force of its coercive mechanism. It emboldened the employers to follow suit, and a wave of systematic lockouts, beginning in Poland and the West, spread thence to all industrial districts. The lockouts ended with a victory for the employers in all cases except the Moscow printing trades. The unions managed, however, to withstand annihilation from this combined attack for another year, due to the revival of industry in 1907. Yet the final outcome was inevitable. In 1907, there were in the whole of Russia 652 unions with 245,000 members; in the beginning of 1912, that number had shrunk to 15,000. In the provinces, where the administration knew no restraint whatsoever, unionism was completely annihilated. But even in Petrograd, 22 out of 52 unions went under from July 1907 to July 1908, while in eight of the largest ones surviving, the membership fell off 75 per cent. In 1910, Petrograd had but seventeen unions, with 7000 members. In Moscow, the débâcle was even worse, the movement falling off from 46 unions with 48,000 members in 1907, to 20 unions with 3500 members in 1910.

No wonder, then, that when, with the business boom of 1912, the labor movement revived, it was again thoroughly dominated by the intellectuals of the revolutionary parties. In the measure that governmental reaction triumphed, leadership tended to pass back to the intellectuals. In the political movement, the intellectual leadership had come back with the government's successes in 1906; in the economic movement, it had to await the full destruction of the trade unions.

In the light of the lessons from post-revolutionary Germany, the effects of such destruction can hardly be overestimated. Had Russian labor unions been let alone during the dozen years that elapsed between the two revolutions, it is not at all unlikely that they might have permanently remade the ideology handed down by the intellectuals, in the pragmatic mold of a trade unionism that seeks primarily to enlarge labor's opportunity and knows that it has "more than its chains to lose". Consequently, when the government drove the trade unions back underground, it only succeeded in foisting upon labor for good the leadership of the revolutionary parties with their conception of industrial problems carried over uncritically from the political sphere.

Thus, though the government spared capitalism the daily pains of an adjustment to the rising power of labor, it thereby sealed capitalism's fate.

The statistics of strikes show a rise from 222 strikes with 46,623 participants for 1910, to 2032 strikes with 725,491 strikers in 1912. It is significant that while there were almost no political strikes in 1910, 1300 out of the strikes of 1912 were political, with 545,813, or more than two-thirds of the total number of strikers participating. The political protest strikes in 1912 were enormously stimulated by a massacre of strikers in the Lena gold fields in Siberia, in which the number of killed and disabled reached 500. The same preponderance of political over economic strikes held during 1913, with 379,366 strikers out of a total of 678,564 from January to September. The strike wave reached its highest point in the first seven months of 1914, during which nearly 1,450,000 struck, of whom 322,287, or fully one-tenth of Russia's total factory wage earners, struck in the one month of July.

With War and mobilization, strikes came to an end. Until late in 1916, the War period was one of high prosperity and great industrial expansion. By the end of 1916, however, a change was clearly impending. There was increasing difficulty in provisioning the cities, due both to a diminution of agricultural production brought on by an excessive mobilization of man power, and to a growing inadequacy in transportation. In Petrograd, prices of articles of workingmen's daily consumption had risen since 1913 from 50 to 100 per cent, but the wages of only the most highly skilled had kept pace. For the majority, wages rose but from ten to twenty per cent. To render the picture more real, one must add a material increase in unemployment, resulting from the growing economic dislocation. All in all, no better stage setting for a labor revolution could be had. A three-million mass of physically exhausted workers, who for the past two years had been driven unmercifully hard to supply the enormous needs of a fighting army many times its number; a rapidly shrinking real wage, except for a relatively few; long queues in front of the food stores; an unrest growing from day to day, without a trade union organization to express it and give it a trade union meaning. Thus the Revolution's chief instrument was a laboring mass with minds like "virgin soil", open to whatever seeds the intellectuals of the revolutionary parties might choose to sow.

THE INTELLECTUALS AND THE REVOLUTIONARY PARTIES

The lack in the "ruling classes" of political talent with an effective will to power, the absence of a middle class, the position of the peasantry which was destined to range it against the existing order, and, finally, the outlawing and destruction of any trade unionism whatsoever—all these combined to give to the philosophies and programs of the intellectuals of the revolutionary parties an extraordinary weight and potency, once the army ceased to obey the old government. If the issues which actually have shaped the events since the Revolution can be brought, with an ease unthinkable elsewhere, under the theoretical formulæ with which the revolutionary parties have operated for long; if these general formulæ have seemed in effect to sum up the development of Russian social reality; it has been only because of the structure of the Russian community and the conditioning backgrounds of its several classes. These were such as to have given what amounted to a really free hand to a determined group of persons whose faith in the "scientific" validity of their program was unshakable, and who had the self excusing disregard of the "unavoidable" suffering caused by their labors which is common to all scientific vivisectionists. For, the Russia after the Revolution may boldly be said to have been made by the several thousand Bolshevists who joined the Party before 1917.

In the beginning, to be sure, power came to them because they were the only ones to have appraised correctly the intensity of the peasants' craving for the landlords' lands, the yearning of the unorganized and badly exploited factory workers for a reckoning with the boss, as well as the strength of the universal craving for ending the war with the Central Powers. Their unequalled skill, however, showed in knowing how to make use of the elemental driving power of these mass wishes, not only to destroy the old, which had in fact destroyed itself, but to erect a new social mechanism with themselves as engineers. Though they paid the price of "strategic retreats" here and there, as, for instance, their shift in 1921 to the New Economic Policy, when the "elemental" balking of the peasantry proved too much for them, the Bolsheviks have with this new state mechanism now succeeded for well nigh a decade in keeping a hostile world at bay, and, what is perhaps a stronger testimonial, in continuing to steer it in the same general direction as was given by their original philosophy. It is this supreme power of destroying as well as of building, given over into the hands of a few,—a phenomenon which Russia's whole unusual history had labored to produce,—that vests the development of Russian revolutionary thought and the social background of the intellectual revolutionists with a significance that can be scarcely overrated.

The intellectuals as a class were born of the determination of the government to "modernize" the nation. In no other country did the government feel it so incumbent upon itself to "make" an educated class, while dreading at the same time the inevitable political effects of its own creation. Bright lads of the lower orders of townsmen, parish priests, and even peasants, though they cannot be said, as a rule, to have received encouragement worth mentioning, managed to go through the lower grades. Once qualified, thus, for higher learning, they found the portals to an intellectual career open to them.

The educated class drew heavily from the impoverished lower nobility, which, in measure as it became educated, developed strong liberal tendencies. Education and the higher intellectual life being an importation from abroad, the prestige of foreign thought was always high in Russia. Not in vain did Marx ridicule as mere "intellectual gastronomists" the ultra radical scions of the Russian nobility who, having gone abroad and fallen under the influence of foreign radical social thought, became more "royalist than the king himself".

He must have meant the anarchist Bakunin, with whom he clashed, and others like him. But the edu-

cation of the West failed to make over into West-
erners, either liberal or Marxian, all Russian intellectuals. On the contrary, during the greater part
of the Nineteenth Century, the dominant school of
thought harped on Russia's "peculiarity", the conservative "Slavophiles" equally with the revolutionary "Narodniki", or Populists. Our concern here,
however, is only with the radical "intelligentsia",
both "Narodnik" and Marxian.

Aside from the "Decembrists," the group of educated aristocratic army officers who, in 1825, attempted to change the government by a military revolt, the Russian intelligentsia as a self-conscious
class dates from the forties. The "men of the forties", so called, gave to Russia a type of "repentant
nobleman", repentant of the crimes committed by his
fathers against the peasantry. This generation of
intellectuals left an indelible imprint even upon its
detractors, the "men of the sixties", who repudiated
and ridiculed it, charging it with having forgotten, in
the eloquence of its words, that words without action
are worse than useless. For, they it was who "discovered" the "mir", and laid the foundation of a
Russian homegrown socialism. The intellectuals of
the sixties were not of the nobility primarily. They
were bold and individualistic plebeians, proudly pro-
claiming themselves free from contamination by the
aristocratic tradition. They were the "Nihilists"
and later the "Narodniki".

The "Narodniki", or "Populists" of the seventies, were socialists with a typically Russian agrarian horizon, more correctly agrarian anarchists.
Their main idea was that in the West, with its capitalism gripping both city and country, and with

political democracy the heritage of past revolutions, the road to socialism already lay through a revolutionary political movement of wage earners. On the contrary, they held that, in absolutist Russia, socialism, avoiding completely the painful capitalistic period, could be evolved directly out of the "mir". For there, in the place of a vigorous factory system, many millions of peasant handicraftsmen were still ministering to the wants of the people, and there, moreover, the wisdom of the masses had preserved in Russia's 109,000 "mirs", a solidaristic basis of social organization.

It was, according to the "Narodniki", the duty of the intellectuals to enlighten the peasant masses as to the full significance, both actual and potential, of their institution, the "mir", and to organize them through the country. They believed that the peasants, thus enlightened and organized, ignoring the existing government and avoiding the false lure of the political democracy so dear to the liberals, would, through a national assembly, proclaim that henceforth the land was the peasants', and that a new Russia has arisen, a Russia of loosely federated and completely self-governing peasant communes. This was precisely a program of an anarchism indigenous to a rural society organized like the Russian. And if the "Narodnik" agitators who, as the saying ran in the seventies, "went into the people", failed to awaken the peasantry, but, instead, awakened the government to the danger of their agitation, it was not because the "Narodniki" did not fit their philosophy to the fundamental horizon of the village. The failure lay only in the mental sluggishness of a peasantry, serfs but yesterday, deeply distrustful

of any self proclaimed friends, and still dreaming
that the next act of the Tsar-Liberator would give
them the land without their lifting a finger.

The non-political educational campaign, having
brought arrest, imprisonment, and exile, political
terror was taken up in 1878 as a means of reprisal
and prevention of cruelty to revolutionists. The few
years that followed were truly the heroic period in
the history of the Russian intelligentsia, when a
mere handful of intellectuals fought a sanguinary
duel with the government of the mightiest empire.
That duel culminated in the violent death of Alexander II on March 1, 1881.

In the end, the government proved the victor. By
1883, the terrorist organization collapsed. Thereupon for seventeen years, the "Narodnik" movement continued on the plane of mere theoretical discussion. The essentially "Narodnik" belief that
socialism would come out of the "mir" and by the
efforts of the peasantry, remained. But the anarchism of the seventies had already given way to a
demand for political democracy. That led by degrees to a *de facto* rapprochement with the liberals,
although it tended to be obscured for long by the
stress laid upon terrorist actions. Likewise, the
initial extreme intolerance for capitalism, the complement of the belief in the socialist potentialities of
the "mir", more and more tended to change into a
virtual acquiescence in capitalism for the city, even
if it was still to be kept out of the village at all
hazards. This practical evolution towards a political liberalism covered not only the theoretical period,
but continued uninterrupted also during the years
after "theory" had given way to action, with the

organization, in 1900, of the Social-Revolutionary
Party. It went on, although probably still unper-
ceived by the Party itself, through the revolutionary
years 1903-1907, then during the ensuing reaction
and temporary disintegration, and finally through
the Party's brief but phenomenal efflorescence between the February and October revolutions of 1917.
It was in substance a gradual exchanging of the
original rural horizon for a more urban one, and
furthermore, an urbanization with a conservative
slant. This urbanization of viewpoint told in the
conversion to political democracy, just as it told in
the tacit admission of the great part the industrial
capitalists were to play in the future Russia, and
even in the acquiescence, in 1917, in a continuation
of the war with Germany. To be sure, the Party
remained true to its traditional demand for land
"socialization", that is, the transfer of all the land
to the "mirs" upon the basis of "equalized land-
use". But even that was subordinated in 1917 to
the political problem. Yet, for a time, the peasantry
failed to notice the change in their advocates and
political leaders, which, together with the flocking
to its standards of the sort of persons who are usually attracted to a government party, accounts for
the Party's prosperity in the spring and summer of
1917. It was only when, later in the year, the left
wing split off that we find the typical peasant attitude again represented politically. For the program
of the Social-Revolutionaries of the Left was nothing but a clear throw-back to the rural anarchism of
the seventies: First, by virtue of its "political"
ideal, envisaging Russia not as a centralized state
which, by its very nature inevitably would become the

oppressor of the local communes, but as a "free" peasant Russia; and second, by virtue of the land arrangement after the October revolution, which the victorious Bolsheviks permitted these, their allies in the overthrow, to bring about. Furthermore, when in 1918, the Bolshevik government, forced in part by the military situation and in part prompted by its program of communism, embarked upon a program —the very antithesis of peasant anarchism—of force in the villages, then the alliance gave way to war, although the Left Social Revolutionaries preferred to effect the break on the issue of foreign policy. They were promptly suppressed by the better organized Bolsheviks, but there can be no doubt that at the time their social program truly reflected the actual mind of the bulk of the peasantry.

The defeat, in October 1917, of Kerensky's Social-Revolutionary Party by the Bolshevists in league with the former's own left wing was decisive, and no less decisive was the Bolshevik triumph in 1918 over the Social-Revolutionaries of the Left, which left them masters of the political situation. This renders it completely clear that the intellectual factor which had actively remade Russia did not come from a Russian rural setting, but instead was of foreign origin and with an urban appeal—Marxism. This is not at all meant, of course, to rule out as a factor the historically conditioned situation in rural Russia, for the Bolshevists were soon to learn by experience that the elemental force of Russia's every day rural actuality could not be coerced for long without evoking catastrophic consequences. It is meant merely to indicate that it was solely from the Marxian trained intellectuals, with their phenomenal boldness derived from a conviction that their teacher had provided them with a master key to all hidden mysteries of social development, past, present, and future, that there came the factor of activism, which today, after ten years, continues in the same relationship to Russian society as is the master mariner's to hulk, masts, sails, and wind.

There are in Marxism two distinct strands, one a historical-sociological and the other an activist-revolutionary. These were closely interwoven in Marx himself. But, in the course of the socialist movement, these strands have often been sundered.

The historical-sociological strand came first into play and was employed harmoniously by all Russian Marxians. George Plechanov, the father of Russian Marxism, had turned away from the "Narodnik" philosophy, and later founded, in 1883, the first Marxian study group among the Russian revolutionary exiles and university students in Switzerland. In that and in related groups, future Bolsheviks and future Mensheviks, and even future liberals and reactionaries "evoluting" as temporary Marxians, jointly employed Marx's materialistic interpretation of history as a heavy weapon against the "Narodnik" dream of Russia's reaching socialism without having to pass through capitalism. To crush the "Narodniki", all Marxians alike stressed, in their polemic, the basic conception of the Marxian theory, that society's development has for its dynamic factor not the free human will, not even the will of the "Narodnik" "heroes" leading the "mass", but the gradual growth of its productive forces, which, with the inexorable immutability of natural law, determines the sequence of one social order after another—the patriarchal order, feudalism, capitalism, and socialism. Hence there could be for Russia no shortcut to socialism. On the contrary, socialism would come there, as elsewhere, only after a capitalistic development of sufficient duration and intensity had prepared for it by industrializing Russia, by revolutionizing her stagnant agriculture through the capitalist dynamic drive for gain, by disrupting the amorphous village into a landless proletariat on the one side and peasant entrepreneurs on the other, and finally, and chiefly, by causing enough millions of her peasants to be "thoroughly boiled in the factory boilers" so as to create an urban wage proletariat. This urban proletariat, aided by the proletarians in the villages, would have the numbers and the strength for a successful socialist revolution.

For nearly fifteen years after Plechanov's beginning, the Marxians, without distinction as to ultimate destination in the political line-up, kept pounding at the "Narodnik" view that the peasantry *per se* was socialistic and would become the main support of the revolution. At this stage, they all predicted in one voice that the next Russian revolution would be a "bourgeois", or capitalist, revolution, which, as the French revolution had done, would abolish absolutism and give the land to the peasants. And although they admitted that the organized Social-Democratic workers were destined to play a weighty and independent rôle in that revolution, pushing the capitalists to ever greater and greater thoroughness in making a clean sweep of the débris of the old order, the labor revolution would have to wait until capitalism and the "bourgeoisie" would have completely discharged their historical function.

This unity, however, in the Marxian ranks, lasted only so long as the "Narodnik" philosophy continued a formidable enemy, and so long as there had not yet begun any mass stirrings of labor, bringing the revolution down from the clouds into reality. By the end of the nineties, Marxism definitely triumphed in the intellectual combat.[1] The frequent strike movements by the factory workers, especially the textile operatives, of whom 30,000 struck in Petrograd in 1895, more and more clothed the revolutionary idea with the vestments of reality. Henceforth the main combat shifted to within the Marxian group itself, causing a permanent line of division, which, whatever the concrete issue at any given time, at bottom betrayed a separation between those Marxians who have chiefly inherited from their master his historico-sociological (evolutionary) side,—the Mensheviki,—and the others upon whom the spirit of Marx the activist-revolutionist has descended,—the Bolsheviki. Looking at the matter from no pedantic theoretical standpoint, which would lead to an application of the methods of the "Higher Criticism" to the writings of Marx in an effort to discover which of the factions had interpreted the teacher rightly, but from the point of view of a common sense psychology, enlightened by the opportunity for retrospection, the whole matter

[1] This, however, did not hinder the Social-Revolutionary party, which was organized in 1900 by younger generation "Narodniki," from developing during 1901-1907 a tremendous following among the intellectuals, mainly students, who were drawn to it by its daring acts of revolutionary terrorism against the government. By contrast, the Social-Democrats who, being believers in mass action only, rejected individual terror, appeared timid and puny spirited revolutionists.

will appear as follows: The Mensheviki created the inevitable impression throughout the revolution of 1905-6, as well as in 1917, that they comforted their souls with the injunction against a purely labor revolution in a still backward country, legitimately deducible from Marx, the evolutionary sociologist. The Bolsheviki, on the other hand, have shown throughout a joy in bending the Marxian historical thought to placate a "will to revolution" inexorably seeking an outlet in action—altogether in the spirit of Marx the revolutionist. It would seem, further, that this separation came only in part from diverging objective appraisals of the revolutionary possibilities contained in given situations. Chiefly it was determined by differences in temperament and mental make-up in general. Some were capable of a real "will to revolution" without counting the costs too closely; others shrank at critical moments from the possible consequences to society of revolutionary change.

The issue boiled itself down to the "hegemony", or supremacy, of the proletariat in the forthcoming "bourgeois" revolution. The first round, from 1898 to 1900, was fought between the "economists" and the political actionists, the latter led by Plechanov and Lenin, at that time standing shoulder to shoulder. The "economists" maintained that, since Russia was on the threshold of merely a "bourgeois" revolution, it was labor's part to concentrate chiefly on economic action, on struggles for the amelioration of its conditions in industry, leaving, for the present, political action to the bourgeois parties. The "economist" tendency was suppressed, but the same issue of the rôle of the proletariat in the "bourgeois'' revolution, soon reappeared in the struggle between the Mensheviki (minority) and the Bolsheviki (majority), causing, in 1903, a party split which has never been healed.

According to the Mensheviki, led by Plechanov and Martov, while revolutionary labor, owing to Russia's belated political evolution, was destined to play a weighty and independent part in the "bourgeois" revolution, it could not, however, in the nature of things, assert a real "hegemony". On the contrary, mindful that the order emerging from that revolution could be nothing else than an advanced form of capitalist political democracy, labor would have to confine itself to forcing the "bourgeoisie" as far to the left as possible, without, however, attempting to usurp the latter's leading place. In practice, the Menshevist position implied, first, a coalition with the industrial capitalists for a life and death struggle against autocracy and feudalism; second, a radical solution of the agrarian question by expropriation of the landlords in favor of the peasants; and, third, a solid entrenchment by labor to serve as a steadily growing basis of operations for the ultimate labor revolution,—in the state, through labor legislation, and in industry, through an unrestricted freedom of combination and trade unionism. The Mensheviki, therefore, accepted the Russian industrial capitalists as a genuinely revolutionary class within the limits of capitalistic democracy, fully convinced that when the proper time came, it would not hesitate to fulfill the historical task of the middle class, while the politically backward but land hungry peasantry would aid in the decisive victory of the democratic cause by the overwhelming weight of its numbers.   Beyond the political revolution, the Mensheviki visualized themselves as a Russian edition of the German Social-Democracy, except that they would be in the more favorable environment of an advanced political democracy.

The Bolsheviki,[1] led by Lenin and his group of intimate followers, admitted, of course, as Marxians, that the labor revolution could not as yet be on the immediate program.   However, they totally rejected as a necessary consequence that labor should forego an immediate revolutionary "hegemony".   On the contrary, they regarded the "hegemony" of labor as a sheer necessity, in view of the surrender which they considered inevitable of the Russian industrial capitalists to monarchical reaction.   The Russian capitalists, the Bolsheviki asserted, were bound to seek an agreement with the absolutist monarchy in the very initial stage of the revolution, for the reason that the advanced state of revolutionary maturity of labor would throw it into a panic of fear for its continued existence and cause it to declare itself satisfied with even slight concessions from the government.   Consequently, the destruction of the autocracy and of the remnants of the landlord régime would have to be brought about not by the "bourgeoisie" but by labor and the peasantry declaring a joint dictatorship.   Such a revolution, after all, would remain, in substance, a "bourgeois" revolution, even with the substitution of the peasantry for the industrial bourgeoisie.   For, the peasantry in this stage would be an undifferentiated class led by its "petty bourgeois" "Kulak" element and

[1] Later several of the outstanding Mensheviki, like Trotzky, became allied in views with them.

would be driven to make a thorough job of the revolution by its lust to lay hands on the privately owned land. This would preserve the essentially "bourgeois" character of this revolution, notwithstanding the "hegemony" of labor.

The Bolshevik "will to revolution" told also in their scheme for the organization of their party. The Menshevists, who, in that as in other respects, thought themselves the more correct Marxians, advocated decentralization of power and democracy within the party, which they justified on the ground that revolutions are always spontaneous and elemental phenomena, depending on a revolutionary mass psychology boiling up from the depth of the labor movement. In other words, the pace of revolutions cannot be forced, no matter how intense the "will to revolution" might be at the party's top. By contrast, Lenin envisaged the revolution as evoked by the purposeful and relentless action of a select body of "professional revolutionists", picked and trained by the leaders at the top and serving as faithful transmitters to the local organizations of the revolutionary direction and determination issuing from the top. With the existing police régime in Russia, they maintained, party democracy could be conducive only to weakness and inertia.

A vital constituent in the train of thought leading up to the Bolshevist tactics has been an optimistic analysis of the revolutionary situation in the West of Europe, matured, as they believed, by a ruthless imperialism, itself the result of a general capitalist breakdown from overproduction. The Bolshevists' insistence that, despite Russia's extreme economic backwardness, the revolutionary pace must be forced far in advance even of that of West European labor, may be made to harmonize with the fundamental Marxian historical conception only by assuming a strong conviction that the capitalistic world as a whole has already entered the period of social revolution. From this conviction, it could then be made to follow that Russian revolutionary labor, far from having to trail behind labor in other countries, might well precipitate the world revolution. That is, it could do so if it knew how to take the right advantage of the opportunity for seizing power presented by the very backwardness of a country with eighty-five per cent of its people still in a semi-servile state.

To continue with the Bolshevist forecast of the course of the revolution: With the seizure of dictatorial power by labor and the peasantry, tantamount to the suppression of the political power of the industrial "bourgeoisie" and the expropriation of the landlords, revolutionary labor, which heretofore went hand in hand with the peasantry as a whole, undifferentiated into classes, would now carry the class struggle into the village by driving a wedge between the "Kulak" element and the poor, practically proletarian peasants. When this process would have been completed, the urban proletariat, now in league with the proletariat and near-proletariat of the village, would then put across the real labor revolution by suppressing the "bourgeoisie" in the village. After that would come the reign of socialism or communism, the end of capitalism.

The Bolshevist tactics, now in retrospect so supremely important to the world's history, were formulated in the heat of the revolutionary period,

1903-1906, covering the beginning, the culmination, and the suppression of the first Revolution. It is indeed an irony of fate, that the Menshevists, who, because of their greater moderation, considered themselves the greater realists, should have proved the farthest removed from a true appreciation of the real distribution of power among Russia's social classes. Yet the Bolshevists, although their "will to revolution" did not carry them, as might have been expected, beyond the chance of sighting the real situation in Russia, proved no less disastrously wrong in their estimate of the world situation. This, however, as the whole world knows, has not prevented them from erecting an apparently unshakable political dictatorship over one-sixth of the globe.

CHAPTER III

THE GERMAN REVOLUTION

Just as the upheaval in Russia has disclosed a social constitution shaped in a peculiar historical mold, so the Germany after 1918 has demonstrated how a "normally" developed Western community might achieve a self stabilization when thrown out of equilibrium by war and revolution. Like absolutist Russia, the German Empire had stood in the minds of all as an amalgamation of the principle of a feudal monarchy with modern capitalism, and in each the monarchical, pre-capitalist partner has appeared in a rôle of unquestioned dominance over the other. But whereas in Russia the factor of the state was everything, in modern Germany the political factor of the monarchy was largely a screen behind which a self-reliant class of industrialists was building up its own might. This might was not in wealth alone, which in times of acute revolution may add but little to resistance power. It was in the form of a highly complex and delicately adjusted economic mechanism, on which even avowed revolutionists would shrink from laying inexperienced hands. And hand in hand with this growth in power, went a cultivation of a masterful spirit making surrender unthinkable. This efficient and power-loving capitalism did not grudge to the French middle classes the laurels for the defeat of Feudalism. For itself it was content to leave the state apparatus in the hands of the monarchy so long as the latter understood how to further the interests of German industry and of its owners, by tariff policy, by placing diplomacy in the service of commerce, by permitting cartels and monopolies, and by encouraging export trade through freight rate and other privileges. Especially they trusted the monarchy to safeguard them by anti-socialist laws and strike and picketing restrictions from revolt from below. To gain this security they even submitted willingly to the Bismarckian social insurance program, unwelcome though its financial burden upon industry might be. However, once the military collapse in the field spelled the monarchy's doom, there appeared in its place, flanked by reliable allies, such as the landed nobility, the middle class, and a farm owning peasantry, the industrialist class as a new self-confident champion for the established economic order. Herein, then, is one difference between the Russian and German revolutions.

But if the sole characteristic of the German revolution had been the power of resistance and the strategic ability shown by the capitalists, its lesson to the social investigator would have been neither very great nor unique—for it is their weakness in Russia that has about it all the lure of the exceptional. What makes Germany stand out in interest is the unparalleled clearness with which the inherent, but little suspected, tendencies of labor in an advanced phase of capitalism have come to light in the vicissitudes of her labor movement. These tendencies revealed themselves at a time when labor ceased to be exposed to the unchecked efforts of a primitive and youthful capitalism to exploit, but had already acquired a shelter in a functioning trade unionism. And, topping it all in interest, is the spectacle of the never ceasing conflict, over a space of more than fifty years, between the upper or middle class intellectual in the labor movement and the trade union leader and organizer risen from the ranks. This is disclosed to us as we trace through years the rise of the trade unions and their leaders from a place of disdained inferiority in the labor movement to "equal rights" officially with the intellectuals, then even to a practical supremacy over them. In this consummation one sees at the same time how organized labor is finally coming to unfold itself, unshaped by the intellectuals, in accord with its own spontaneously formed aspirations. These are a summation of the hopes and expectations of concrete human beings, namely those who are paying union dues, are carrying on strikes, and are voting for candidates for political office.

The Sources of the Strength of German Capitalism

Germany's, especially Prussia's, modernized class of territorial nobility, the class which contributed Bismarck and Hindenburg, has been capitalism's main support in its struggle for life. The "junkers" were sworn monarchists, but their relation to the monarchy was totally different from the one between the nobility and the crown in Russia. With the junkers, a profession of absolute loyalty did not obscure the consciousness of their own independent contribution to the might of the ruler, totally distinguishable from the concrete military mechanism of power, of which, to be sure, they as officers were a pivotal part. On more than one occasion, when they suspected that the crown had grown somewhat forgetful of their own economic interests, they let it be known in no unmistakable terms that they might be forced to revise their relationship to the ruling dynasty. Their great weight in the social scale, with or without an established government holding sway, came from a unique psychical blending of the indomitable "will to power" of the mediæval feudal lord with a capacity for a sustained self-discipline in the pursuit of the modern aim of efficiency and economy, which was the contribution to mankind of rational, calculating, and persistently profit-seeking capitalism.

The German landed nobles, in addition to their grip on the army, the higher central bureaucracy, and local administration, have known how to make a profitable commercial business of operating their estates. Thus to the natural loyalty felt for them by a peasantry that was mentally still dominated by the rural tradition, there was added an unquestioned economic leadership, and, especially in the case of the numerous and weighty class of peasant owners, a common vital interest in the agricultural protective tariff, which the junkers, being close to the governing power, have always been skillful in manipulating. Consequently, when the revolution came, it was behind them that the peasantry ranged itself, seeing, like them, in the urban revolutionists a destructive force dangerous to all the cherished mainstays of their conservative rural civilization —religion and good morals, obedience by inferiors to their social superiors, and, most important of all, their economic prosperity.

Doubtless the strongest single factor which caused the extreme divergence of paths between the Russian and German revolutions lay in the conditions of their respective peasantries. Fate had been kinder to the German peasant. He was emancipated more than half a century earlier than the Russian, and he was not forced, as the Russian, to continue lockstepped with his fellows in a communal régime. He could become an individual proprietor and had an incentive to making improvements and to a greater efficiency even as a mere tenant. Unlike the Russian peasant, he did not have everything to gain and nothing that was personally his to lose from a clean sweep of the existing property titles. He therefore threw his weight into the social scale on the conservative, pro-property side; and along with him went the small peasant, part independent and part wage earner, and even the wholly wage-earning landed proletariat.

Quite removed from the peasant, but on the same side of the alignment, was the educated and well trained official class—the state administrative hierarchy, the clergy, the professors and the teachers. Prussia and Germany had developed, as no other country, by a long historical process, an officialdom with an unequalled tradition for dutiful service. Like the landed class, with which they are often connected by family and social ties, this officialdom owes its social strength to a blending of the older with the modern—of the traditions of a bureaucracy which served Frederick the Great with a thoroughly modern intellectual equipment and scientific training. It is among them, also, that nationalism, since Bismarck's achievement the creed of all classes, has become most firmly rooted. This class regards itself as the sheet anchor of the German nation in contrast with the mercurial free lance liberal intellectuals; and events have indeed proved that, hard-pressed economically though it has become with the catastrophe to the mark, it has invariably added a material weight on the conservative side far beyond its numbers. On the same side will have to be reckoned, of course, the Churches, both the Lutheran and the Catholic. Though the great and influential political party answerable to the latter, the party of the Center, has been, since the revolution, a decisive factor for liberalism and for the Republic, it is, however, universally accepted that should social revolution become the issue, the definitive opposition of the Church, proclaimed in papal declarations and through the many decades of assiduous anti-socialist propaganda, would leave no doubt as to which side it would join.

So far nothing has been said of the industrial and commercial middle class. Though over the same period the process of the concentration of capital has brought an ever greater and greater part of the nation's economy directly or indirectly under the rule of "big business"; though the largest industrial establishments have immeasurably outdistanced in output, in product, and in the number employed, the medium sized and small establishments; yet no tendency of the middle class to disappear, predicted by Marx, can as yet be observed, as shown by the following table:

NUMBER OF ESTABLISHMENTS AND OF PERSONS EMPLOYED

Year	Small Establishments (1-5 Employees)		Medium-Sized Establishments (6-50 Employees)		Big Establishments (51 Employees or more)	
	Establishment	Employees	Establishment	Employees	Establishment	Employees
1882	2,882,768	4,335,822	112,715	1,391,720	9,974	1,613,247
1895	2,934,723	4,770,669	191,301	2,354,333	18,953	3,044,267
1907	3,146,134	5,383,233	270,122	3,688,838	32,122	5,363,851

Evidently the two and a third million new employees in the big establishments, added from 1895 to 1907, came not from the urban middle class, but from the country districts.

On the political side, the German middle class has been more backward in its development than the Social-Democratic wage earners. After its unsuccessful attempt to democratize the government by the revolution of 1848, it was willing to accept, with an occasional constitutional "flare-up", as in the early sixties, a superficially modified absolutist régime. When Bismarck took out of its feeble hands the task of national unification, and the troops returned victorious from three wars, the lapse from the ideas of 1848 was complete. Compared with the political supineness of the middle class, the wage earning class was far in advance. But the political quietism of the "bourgeoisie" did not in the least denote complete inertia. On the contrary, having abandoned political ambitions, the middle class threw itself with all the greater fervor into industrial and economic activity, with the result that England had to abandon its proud claim of being the "workshop of the world". In no other country has economic "rationalization" been carried so far and to such success by a class of able and daring business men. On the technological side, this "rationalization" meant the closest union of science with industry, bringing the discoveries of science into the workshop and applying the methods of management learned in industry to organizing for scientific research and discovery. On the purely economic and price determining side, competition had been made to yield to the capitalistic collectivism of the "Cartel". As decade followed decade, the complexity and the efficiency of German industry grew apace. The banks and financial institutions became one delicately adjusted economic organism with industry and commerce—an organism forever growing in size as well as in complexity, and with its eye more and more turned to the foreign market. Also, the country itself was becoming more and more industrial, more and more urbanized, more and more dependent for its rising standards of living and welfare on an industry functioning without interruption, and selling abroad. To operate such an industry called for the best brains of the nation, and for an economic training and a length of economic apprenticeship, of which the laboring class and its leaders, with their heads in the political clouds, were, until the revolution, completely unaware. However, to qualify for rulership under the new conditions, one had to pass an economic and not a political examination.

Bismarck's "monarchical and paternal state"— to use his own expression—had made a bid for the fealty of labor through a program for social legislation, solemnly promulgated in the Emperor's Declaration of 1881. "If the state will show a little more Christian solicitude for the workingman", he said in a speech to the Reichstag at the time of the most rigorous enforcement, in 1884, of the anti-socialist law, "then I believe that the gentlemen of the Wyden program (Social-Democrats) will sound their bird call in vain, and that the thronging to them will cease as soon as the workingmen see that the government and the legislative bodies are earnestly concerned in their welfare." But the attempt then and there to kill the political revolutionary labor movement failed. The German working people were already sufficiently removed from the days of Frederick the Great and serfdom to have any feeling of humble gratitude for benevolence from their superiors. But neither had they already gone through the recasting mold of a stabilized and functioning trade unionism. They were a "class-conscious fighting proletariat" under an intellectual leadership.

The Period of the Supremacy of the Intellectuals in the Labor Movement

On the heels of the political revolution of 1848 came a short-lived though country-wide movement by journeymen in the different trades to organize trade unions. This was virtually suppressed by the counter revolution of 1849, and finally outlawed by a decree of the Council of Allied States in 1854, calling for the dissolution of all socialistic and communistic labor organizations. Therefore, when a German labor movement began with Ferdinand

Lassalle's "Open Letter to the General Committee concerning the convocation of a General German Labor Congress at Leipzig" in May 1863, it was a new beginning. He wrote: "The laboring class must constitute itself as an undivided political party, and make the general, equal, and direct suffrage the main issue. Only through representation in the legislative bodies of Germany will the laboring class be able to satisfy its legitimate interests in politics. Labor must begin forthwith a peaceful and lawful agitation for the suffrage with all the means available within the existing law." Taking up the various issues which the Liberals were then holding up before the working class, such as savings banks, invalidity insurance, health insurance, etc., he exclaimed: "Is it your aim to make the individual worker's misery more bearable? Or is it your aim to raise the standard of the whole working class above its present level? That, indeed, should be your aim!" To that end, however, no co-operative societies as advocated by Schulze-Delitzsch will serve—owing to the "iron law of wages". "That iron law, which, under existing conditions under the rule of demand and supply, determines wages, is as follows: the average wage tends to be reduced to the price of the customary necessaries of life employed for the maintenance of existence and for continuing the race. This is the point around which actual wages oscillate with a pendulum-like motion, without being able to swing away for long too far in either direction." And, summing up in a phrase his entire labor program, Lassalle said, in his principal theoretical work directed against Bastiat and Schultze: "The only way out for the laboring people can therefore lie through that domain in which they still rank as human beings, that is through *the State*." For, with its conquest of political power, labor can then turn it into an instrument for abolishing capitalism and the "iron law of wages"—by setting up co-operative producers' associations with state credit.

Lassalle's labor program is thus the purest expression of the mentality of the revolutionary intellectual yet found. Trade unionism with its everyday concrete and often "pettily" involved problems, which only those with shop experience can duly appreciate and help solve, was automatically ruled out as hopelessly incapable of effecting change in a situation absolutely dominated by the "iron law of wages". But labor politics,—in which the intellectual is far more at home than most trade unionists can ever hope to be—with its general issues, which gain from abstract and philosophical statement, and with the broad scope it offers for parliamentary and agitational skill and oratory, was exalted above everything. The hard and severe struggle, long concealed, which German trade unionism was obliged to engage in, first, formally to maintain its political neutrality alongside the powerful Social-Democratic Party, and then for an equal voice with that Party, in making momentous tactical decisions affecting both alike, is therefore traceable to this conception of the labor movement which germinated in the mind of Lassalle, the famous lawyer and the brilliant intellectual. With the growth of the movement, the Lassallean influence became a hindrance to be overcome: this notwithstanding that it was due to his genius as an agitator that the broad masses of the

German workingmen first absorbed the idea of the solidarity of labor, which has served trade unionism in good stead equally with the political Party.

By contrast, Marx was almost a "narrow" trade unionist. In his reply to Proudhon in his *Poverty of Philosophy,* published in 1847, he assigned to the trade unions the same significance for the organization and triumph of labor which the mediæval communes had for the bourgeois middle classes. And he unequivocally condemned every effort to make them subservient to any political party, as sounding their death-knell. "The trade unions are the schools of socialism. . . . All political parties . . . without exception . . . arouse in the workers but a passing enthusiasm; the trade unions, however, grip the laboring masses for good. . . . They only are capable of realizing a true labor party and of offering a bulwark of resistance to capitalism". Thus Marx, in an oft-quoted conversation with Hamann, the treasurer of the General German Metal Workers' Union.

Yet it was the Lassallean and not the Marxian conception which ruled the German Social-Democracy after it had emerged triumphant from the ordeal of the twelve-year period of exceptional legislation. Even August Bebel, who, with Wilhelm Liebknecht, had first brought Marxism to German labor, who had won a signal victory for it in a labor convention as early as 1867, and who, thereupon, became instrumental in organizing many trade unions as parts of Marx's International Workingmen's Association, had the following to say, at the Party convention in 1893, concerning the prospects of trade unions in Germany:

"In Germany, the state system of workingmen's

insurance took away from the trade unions that branch of activity, and has in effect cut a vital nerve, as it were. For, benefit systems had meant enormously in the furthering of unionism in Britain and among the German printers. Labor legislation has likewise preëmpted many other lines of activity which properly belong to trade unions: and from all indications it will continue to do so, even increasingly, in the future. . . . With each extension of the state's competence, the sphere of trade unionism is bound to become more and more restricted. . . . We might organize into trade unions all we want, but when capital will bring its domination in industry generally to a par with that in the industries controlled by Krupp and Stumm . . . *then surely it will be all up with the trade unions;* then *political action only will be able to turn the trick.* As a matter of natural and normal development, the trade unions will find all their vital threads cut one by one." At the same convention, Liebknecht joined Bebel in warning against expecting too much of trade unionism, and he said, a year earlier: "Before the trade unions will have a chance, the banners of socialism will already have been waving over the citadels of capitalism."

German trade unionism was born under a distinctly political constellation. Three political parties, two Socialist and one Liberal, reached out simultaneously in 1868 to act the midwife. The Liberal, Dr. Max Hirsch, influential in the workingmen's educational association,[1] went to England to

---

[1] The predominant form of labor organization prior to the repeal of the prohibition against combinations in Saxony in 1861, in Prussia in 1867, and in the other German states in 1868.

import the British model of an "amalgamated" union, which he found fitting so well with the liberal philosophy of *laissez-faire* and self help. But already at the national convention of the same educational associations of the year before, August Bebel, a brilliant and intellectual young mechanic, had been elected chairman in his place. Bebel was no longer a radical Liberal, but had succumbed, under Liebknecht's influence, to the charm of Marx and the International, and with his well known capacity for effective agitation and leadership, he was a force to conjure with. Knowing this, the Lassalleans took alarm and called a general labor congress in Berlin for the purpose of launching a trade union movement controlled by themselves. Hearing of this in England, Hirsch hastened back, and appeared, uninvited, before that Congress. However, he was refused a hearing and was forced to leave.[1]

Upon Lassalle's death in 1864, Von Schweitzer and Fritsche—the latter a workingman—had taken over the management of the political General German Workingmen's Union, organized by him the year before, which in 1868 numbered over 125,000 members. Von Schweitzer and Fritsche now came to this General Labor Congress with a detailed program for organizing labor in 32 trade groups, but under a rigid centralization, with themselves at the head. Their program was, of course, adopted, and at the next trade union Congress in 1869, it was reported that thirteen national trade unions had been

---

[1] He thereupon organized the Hirsch-Duncker trade unions, which have survived, although little significant numerically, to date. Duncker was a liberal printing employer who was Hirsch's coadjutor.

formed, which a year later had a total membership of over 20,000. Von Schweitzer showed, however, a typical Lassallean contempt for trade unions when, out of a clear sky and notwithstanding that the trade unions were apparently making headway, he dissolved them and reorganized them on a mixed basis by eliminating trade distinction and placed them under a still stricter control by the political organization. This pulling up by the roots, of course, did not do the organizations any good; so that by 1871 three-fourths of the membership had left, and after more zigzagging, aided by police persecutions, the whole movement went to its official death by dissolution in 1874; although the real death had taken place considerably earlier.

The trade unions launched by the Bebel group were given a more considerate treatment. At the convention of the educational associations in September 1868, an affiliation with Marx's International Workingmen's Association was officially announced and the latter's program accepted *in toto,* including the emphasis on trade unionism. It is obvious that, as with Marx himself when he wrote the Inaugural Address of the International in 1864, the English type floated as a model before that convention. For it resolved that "whereas experience teaches that sickness, invalidity and old age can best be cared for by the trade unions, the convention directs the members and especially the executive committee to put their best efforts into the formation of nationally organized trade unions." Shortly thereafter Bebel published a constitution modelled on the English ideas both as to structure and benefit systems. Several trade unions, a few regional but mostly local, were organized within a few months.

The period 1868-1878, the latter being the year of the passage of the anti-socialist law, which outlawed both socialist and trade union organizations, was one of experimentation and of trial and error. As organizations active on behalf of their membership, the trade unions counted for little, for they were regularly beaten even during the high tide of prosperity following the victory over France. This was, therefore, primarily a period of mental germination. By degrees the trade unionists were feeling their way toward workable principles. Political neutrality was one such principle. The advantages of complete independence as organizations—the members as individuals were for the most part Social-Democrats—of any political party were beginning to be brought home by the stability of membership and other successes of the national unions of the tobacco workers and the printers, organized in 1865 and 1866 respectively. These successes encouraged an active trade unionist, York by name, and a member of the Bebel Social-Democratic Party, to formulate a plan for definitely unifying all scattered unions into national trade unions: to free them of their debilitating dependence upon both political parties by coming out for a complete political neutrality; to establish a uniform system of benefits in all unions; to systematize their methods of struggle against the employers: in brief, to realize to the full the British model of unionism. Bebel gave him full encouragement, and in June 1872, a convention of unions affiliated with the International Workingman's Association, representing over 11,000 members, endorsed York's program. Obstacles were encountered, since the continued harassing by the government made political neutrality seem like running away from the enemy. With York's death early in 1875, the whole movement ceased.

Unity of the socialistic unions came at last automatically with the unity of both political groups, the Lassallean and the Bebel-Liebknecht Social-Democrats, in 1875. And the same trade union conference which effected that unity also declared for political neutrality and for national organization by trades. But the Lassallean spirit told even in this conference of trade unionists: its appeal to the workingmen to join the unions of their trade read that "although organization into trade unions is totally inadequate to improve materially and permanently the conditions of labor, it is urgent, as a means of affecting temporary improvement, of furthering education, and of developing class consciousness." This is as much as the socialistic trade unionists in 1875 were willing to claim for themselves.

Little or nothing was accomplished, due to lack of energy, police difficulties, preoccupation with politics, and an outright lack of good will in Social-Democratic quarters. And whatever organization there was, was swept away by the government in 1878, following the passage of the anti-socialist law. From the end of October to the middle of December, of the twenty-five existing national unions fifteen were thus dissolved, including even the originally neutral unions of printers and tobacco workers. And the majority of those which had escaped this fate up to then preferred to dissolve voluntarily, only five unions surviving. The trade union press and even the workingmen's mutual benefit societies succumbed to the same fate.

During the period of the anti-socialist law, the police of the several states were empowered "to prohibit associations of any kind, which by promoting Social-Democratic, socialist, or communist tendencies, aim at the destruction of the existing order of state and society; also all associations in which such tendencies were apparent enough to endanger the public order, and, in particular, the good relations between the various classes of the population." 1878-1890 was therefore a heroic period in the history of the Social-Democracy. Having in 1890, triumphantly defeated the best police system on the Continent, it emerged filled with a just self-confidence. However, for trade unionism, it was a period of unmitigated misfortune, since whatever glory there was in resisting persecution redounded solely to the advantage of the political party. Moreover, with the general labor interest turned to the political arena, whatever feeble lessons of value had been learned by the trade unions of the seventies were now completely forgotten, and were replaced by opposite teachings, which later had to be unlearned before any progress could be made.

The widest effect on the trade unions was produced by the wholesale application of the law of 1850, relating to political associations, rather than by the more rarely applied anti-socialist law as such, or even by the notorious Puttkammer strike decree of 1886 [1] which gave this law a sharpened interpreta-

---

[1] This decree virtually outlawed picketing and even striking altogether where a wage strike appeared as being "incited by Social Democratic agitators".

tion. For here the effect was not only relative to the right of the unions to exist, but went much deeper, driving into the labor movement a new fundamental conception of proper labor tactics and of trade union organization, namely the new so-called "localist" conception, which ran directly counter to the "lessons" of the seventies. Under that law, local political associations were strictly forbidden to federate. Therefore it sufficed for a national trade union to touch in only the slightest degree upon a subject which could be interpreted as being political, to bring itself within the category of political associations, and therefore subject to dissolution. Now that the Social-Democracy had been driven underground, it would, for the time being, have been suicidal, so far as the allegiance of the broad masses of labor were concerned, for the trade union movement, on its part, to be satisfied with a political neutrality. Hence the idea arose and gained great popularity that, since national trade unions could exist only on condition that they should relinquish the sole function for which they were instituted, namely, the political and radical education of their members, the only fit form of organization was the local one, mainly political and agitational in nature. By a loose and practically invisible method of a wider co-operation through so-called "Vertrauensmänner", they could avoid complication with the law and escape police detection. Economic struggles, on the other hand, were to be looked after by "wage committees" chosen in public meetings by trade, also locally. Such was the new idea, and, in view of the growing embitterment of the working people against the government, it is clearly to be seen that, even though at the end of the period, the national trade unions had ten times as many members as the "localists", yet the great spiritual prestige of the latter, as revolutionary unionists without fear and without reproach, was bound to put the national unionists on the defensive. They were handicapped by their insistence on "every day" union work and on political neutrality; this especially, since the "localists" were given aid and comfort by many important leaders of the Social-Democratic Party from among the intellectuals, who gravely doubted whether the leaders of the national trade unions were genuinely revolutionary. Consequently this twelve-year period did much effectually to weaken the trade unionists' prestige, and to exalt the intellectuals', and burdened trade unionism with having eventually to dig out from under the political landslide engulfing it—a task which was only completed after fifteen years.

To return to the events following the passage of the anti-socialist law. The first two or three years were years of deathly silence. The labor movement lay disorganized and stricken by the terror of government persecution and of police espionage. But slowly and gradually it began to recover. The first steps were the foundation of a number of new trade journals, containing at first nothing but strictly inoffensive trade matter, then venturing to bring accounts of wage movements and strikes in the various parts of the country, and soon, with the then general discussion and criticism of the government's social legislation measures, steering into deeper and more strictly forbidden channels. Economic prosperity came to supply the usual impetus to wage move-

ments. Trade unions were again springing up, even
if, for reasons of prudence, they chose the disguise
of purely mutual benefit associations and had their
strikes conducted nominally by special strike committees selected at mass meetings. After 1883, many
national unions were being freely established, the
printers heading the procession, then the hatters,
stone masons, and others. By 1890, fifty-eight
national unions had entered the lists, with a total
membership of 277,000, in addition to a large number of local unions unaffiliated with national unions,
both for reasons of "localist" scruples and otherwise. The regained and much enhanced power of the
strike was attested by the strike of 12,000 Berlin
bricklayers in 1886, and by the strike of 100,000
Ruhr miners in 1889. What helped in this revival of
open organization was the social-conservative movement inaugurated by the court preacher, Stöcker,
with Royal approval, aiming to win the working
people away from Social-Democracy by bringing
home to them the "social" character of the German
monarchy. To this end, a certain lessening of the
police prohibition against public meetings of workingmen was indispensable, and with that came a
relenting all around. Also, the leaders of the national unions had learned how to steer between the
Charybdis of police reprisals and the Scylla of
scathing "localist" denunciation of themselves as
renegades to the proletarian cause.

In 1890, after the failure of the anti-socialist law,
the many heretofore isolated unions came together
in a species of a national federation. This was
precipitated by the formation of a strong employers'
association for Hamburg and vicinity, for the an-

nounced purpose of a common lockout policy against
organized labor and to render impossible the celebration of the labor May holiday.[1] Hence, on August 7, 1890, the president of the Metal Workers'
National Union invited all the presidents of the
"free" unions (this excluded the anti-socialist liberal Hirsch-Duncker unions with a small membership) to a conference in Berlin to counsel together
as to the best means of meeting the employers'
attacks. The conference, which met on November
6, resolved in favor of a general federation with the
national union as a basic unit, and elected a "General Commission" to serve as a connecting link between the affiliated unions, and to render aid both
in organizing and in solving their financial difficulties. The first General Trade Union Congress,
which met a year and a half later, in March 1892, at
Halberstadt, with 198 delegates representing about
350,000 members, pointed to the changing situation
which permitted an open existence to a vigorous
Social-Democratic Party, and rendered any union
meddling with politics totally unnecessary. It thus
once and for all time disposed of the issue of national
organization *versus* "localism", which was identical
with the issue of politically partisan or neutral
unions. The "localist" delegates, speaking for 10,-
000 members, withdrew from the congress and from
the federation. Thereafter only the close relationship of the "localists" to some of the leading Social-
Democrats lent them any significance, and at times
placed them in a position to cause trouble between

[1] The international Socialist and Labor Congress, which met in
Paris in 1889, declared the celebration of the First of May as a
labor holiday obligatory upon all national labor movements.

the two movements. However, though always numerically small (with 7,000 in 1892 and 17,600 in 1907),[1] they yet continued to be a troublesome fringe until after 1907 they became merged with the syndicalist movement.[2]

The new federation was given few stated powers, with a constitution strongly resembling the American Federation of Labor. The function of directing and financing strikes, which the General Commission had assumed after the Berlin conference, was taken away from it by the Congress at Halberstadt, leaving the whole matter to the constituent unions. Craft unionism still predominated, although the issue of craft *versus* industrial unionism furnished the liveliest discussions. The first ''industrial'' unions were of the metalworkers (1890), the leather workers (1892), and the woodworkers (1893), which took the lead on the industrial side. City trades' councils, *Gewerkschafts-Kartelle,* were provided for, and, as in the American Federation of Labor, they were stripped of any right of interference in the relations between the trade unions and the employers; they therefore served primarily as a ''connective tissue'' in matters of organization, propaganda, education. In addition, they were given the highly important function, under the German circumstances, of preparing for the elections of the representatives of labor on the various official boards, of supervisory charge of social insurance and other matters; and, later, of providing for legal aid to union members through special ''labor secretariats.''

[1] In that year, half of their number amalgamated with the national unions.

[2] Syndicalism never gained a foothold in Germany.

As said above, the trade unions were in the first half of the nineties completely overshadowed by the Social-Democratic Party. That party had attained dazzling heights of success. Compared with the doubling of the Social-Democratic vote from 1886 to 1890, which reached the number of 1,427,300 in the latter year, with 35 members returned to the Reichstag, the trade union membership, diminishing from 277,000 in 1891 to 223,000 in 1893, and rising only to 259,000 in 1895, looked anything but impressive. So high did the self-confidence of the party run that at the convention of 1891, Bebel did not hesitate to state his "conviction that ultimate success lay so close that few of those present here will fail to live to see it". And Vollmar, the leader from Bavaria, prophesied in 1893 that in another five years the Social-Democracy would rule the country. Accordingly, then, the trade unions were viewed with condescension and even disdain.

The trade union difficulties came not only, nor even principally, from the employers, from the narrow interpretations by the government and by the courts of their legal rights, nor from the depressed business conditions in the first half of the nineties, but from their own lack of certainty as to a proper procedure. In order that they might strike out on the road which had made British unionism stable and strong, an internal struggle had to be fought against revolutionary prejudices, owing their origin to the intellectual radicals who heretofore had ruled supreme. These prejudices had now become lodged in the minds of minority leaders, generally local, but whose strength and prestige were strongly nurtured by past tradition. The battle between the trade-union mentality on the one side and the revolutionary intellectual mentality on the other, was fought out in the trade union movement around two main points, namely union out-of-work benefits and trade agreements.

In view of the extensive system of social insurance which the law provided, but which failed to include unemployment insurance, the latter remained the only form of mutual insurance that the unions could employ as a means for self stabilization and for counteracting fluctuations of membership.

In 1892, ten national unions paid such benefits, but in the next six years their number was increased only by two. The objections were many. First, that since unemployment was caused by capitalism, its costs should not be borne by the workers. A fear was felt that out-of-work benefits, healing as they would, if only in a puny way, the worst effects of capitalism, would cause a loss of revolutionary spirit, and, since they would raise union dues, they would push the trade unions into a hopeless morass of treasury worship. On the other side of the argument, it was pointed out that the printers, the "Englishmen" in German trade unionism, had suffered no loss in membership despite the last costly strike of 1892; also that the power of the strike could only increase if the employer would no longer be in a position to obtain strikebreakers by merely beckoning to the unemployed; and that members who would have helped by their contributions to build up an out-of-work fund would hesitate to leave the union and lose it all. In the end, the arguments on the affirmative prevailed, and the second General Trade Union Congress gave a fulsome endorsement to the principle, stating, reassuringly, that it would in no way obscure the "militant class character" of the organizations practising it. Six years later, at the congress which met at Stuttgart in 1902, the discussion had already advanced to the point of demanding state and communal contributions toward union unemployment funds (the so-called "Ghent system"), and even a complete state system of out-of-work insurance. A similar "imprimatur" was given to public employment offices with partial trade union supervision. The number of unions with out-of-work benefits rose from twelve in 1898 to 27 in 1904, to 41 in 1910, to 44 in 1916, and was in use by all unions after 1917.

The collective trade agreement with employers (Tarif-Vertrag) underwent a similar evolution before it was accepted. The printers pioneered in 1896 with the first national agreement. Agreements came next in building, woodworking, and in other mechanical trades. On the other hand, in the basic industries, coal and iron, unionism had no standing, showing throughout the intimate connection between union strength and "recognition". However, a veritable storm broke loose when the printers concluded their agreement. What the radicals saw in it was not a concession by the heretofore all-powerful employers that from now they were committed to sharing their power with labor, but an unholy abandonment of the sacred class-struggle principle. And what contributed strongly to this violent opposition was the idea which had become deeply rooted during the years of the anti-socialist law, that labor's ultimate emancipation lay only over the political route. Another crucial consequence of the predominant "political mindedness" of German labor, which expected industrial control to follow automatically upon seizure of political control, was that, although the trade agreement denoted the employer's relinquishment of his cherished "boss in my own house" idea, no one, even the trade union leaders themselves, thought to the very last of advancing labor's control in the shops by means of "shop rules" or "union working rules", which helped so materially British and American unionism to become entrenched in industry. The dispute over the trade agreement was finally settled when the general congress of 1899 disciplined the Leipzig city trades' council for having expelled the local printers' union on account of the agreement with the employers.

About the middle of the nineties came a turn of the tide for the trade unions, through the clear-sighted persistence with which leaders like Karl Legien, the German Gompers (who was in office for thirty years down to his death in 1921) and his group of associates, counteracted discouragement among the leaders of the constituent unions. They taught them the proper technique of conducting strikes, and how to build up stable and well-knit organizations. With skillful earnestness, the General Commission made itself both the guiding head and the connective tissue, and with the advent of business prosperity, positive results were at last shown. The total membership rose from 329,000 in 1896 to 493,000 in 1898, and to 680,000 in 1900. Four years later, it reached over a million; in 1905, it was 1,344,000, and in 1907 it rose to 1,865,000. The steady and sharp rise since 1895 proved conclusively that unionism in Germany had more than "taken".

The trade unions had also acquired an effectiveness
in defending their rights when threatened from the
side of the government. This was shown by their
well poised and impressive way of stating their case
to the country, in the so-called "Stumm era"
(named from von Stumm, the Saar coal magnate,
who led the onslaught from 1895 to 1899)—when
they were threatened by a succession of legislative
attempts to curtail the right to strike. All the bills
were defeated, due to a favorable political conjunc-
ture in the legislative chamber as well as to labor's
well executed campaign of self-defense. Whereupon
the disappointed employers, now entirely thrown
upon their own resources, turned to organizing
"yellow" unions and to reinforced anti-union measures in the shops. But so high had the prestige of
the unions already become with the working people,
that these very devices merely served to advertise
the trade unions far and wide, and brought about a
mass flocking to their banners, as witnessed by the
swelling membership in those years. The organized
workers, individually and as a group, found that the
union organization offered them shelter and protection as wage earners, insurance against unemployment, and frequently also sick, accident, and invalidity benefits, in addition to those they received under the law. The unions also by changes in the law
sought to enlarge the sick benefits as well as to
assure the rights of the workingmen under the existing law through the union legal aid institutions
and its watchful supervision of the election of labor
representatives on the several official and administrative insurance and industrial bodies. Thus they
realized that their trade union had already so thor-

oughly enveloped their lives on all sides that its
claim upon their loyalty had, by an imperceptible
growth, come to rival, if not to excel, the claim of the
Social-Democratic Party, even though they were tied
to the latter by all the threads of the past. However,
the party leaders failed as yet to realize that the
trade unions, which they had become used to dis-
missing with the remark that they were useful as a
"recruiting ground" for party membership, had
grown to a size and to a confidence in themselves
which would sooner or later bring on a rebellion
against an exclusive intellectual-political directorate
of the labor movement.

"Equal Rights" and Trade Union "Supremacy"

In 1892, the convention of the Social-Democratic
Party rejected a resolution making membership in
national trade unions obligatory upon all party
members. This was due to sympathy felt for the
"localists", who made up for their small numbers
by a reputation for a purer revolutionism than that
of the national unions. However, to salve the latter's feeling, Bebel spoke of the moral obligation
upon Social-Democratic workers to support trade
unionism. In reality, the mere fact of the organization of a central trade union agency was extremely
distasteful to many leading spirits in the Party, who,
harking back to Lassalle, contended that the success
of the labor movement is greatly dependent upon a
"unity of interest" in the minds of the working
people, a unity which the trade union leaders were
now turning into a dangerous duality. Therefore,
when in 1894, Karl Legien began to sound out the

various trade union leaders as to the advisability of a second trade union congress, he met with poor response. The central Social-Democratic organ, the *Vorwärts* in an article "What is going on?" even denounced the General Commission as pursuing "sinister schemes", and this resulted in two large trade unions demonstratively withdrawing from the General Commission. When the second Congress at last met, all these suspicions were given unrestrained vent. Legien, thereupon, justified the action of the General Commission: "The 'sinister schemes' had consisted in the suggestion to call a trade union conference on matters of social and labor legislation: the law of combinations, protection of labor, and factory inspection. There had been no intention of secrecy about it, and he could not but feel that these questions, though political, did truly belong to the field of trade union activities." A part of the Party press, however, were openly denying to the trade unions the right to deal with anything but the most immediate wage problems and insurance institutions, claiming for the Party whatever went beyond this. Many delegates, in defending Legien, minced no words. The printers, forever the most consistent and staunchest supporters of trade union independence, threw back the challenge with the retort that "the trade unions need no guardian; we are a sovereign people." After this, efforts were made on both sides to avoid new conflicts, and at the Trade Unions Congresses of 1899 and 1902, the complete unity in the labor movement was reaffirmed. But with the shifting in the relative distribution of power between the Party and the unions, due to the latter's new accession of strength, a showdown was inevitable, even had it not been precipitated by the issue of the political mass strike.

Although the voting power and parliamentary representation of the Social-Democracy had been growing apace since the eighties, it affected the state no more than before, for it had driven the other parties to a more ready co-operation against it. With this lack of advance, there came about 1904, a feeling of disappointment with parliamentarism in general, and a strong disposition fostered by "left-wingers", like Rosa Luxemburg, Karl Liebknecht, Klara Zetkin, and Karl Radek,—subsequently all Bolshevists,—to try extra-parliamentary means, such as the general strike and the political mass strike in the place of what they now termed "mere inactive watching". The trade union leaders, now at the head of prosperous going concerns, with many tangible achievements for labor to their credit, and with a brilliant future ahead of them, knew that the issue was bound to come up at the forthcoming Party convention, with more than a likelihood of carrying; therefore they could not remain inactive lookers-on at the serious efforts of these revolutionary intellectuals, which would, to a certainty, furnish the government with a welcome pretext for throwing the labor movement, the trade unions included, back into the state of the period of the anti-socialist law. They well remembered how, twenty-five years earlier, the trade unions had suffered even more than the Party, since for them legal existence is a veritable *sine qua non*. They also knew that to the employers, with whom the government was more and more sympathetic, the trade unions loomed much more dangerous than the Party. Neither did they want to repeat the experience with the obligatory May First holiday, an ever standing source of friction between them and the Party. For they had to bear the costs, since it devolved upon them to care for the working men discharged in consequence of the May holiday, without the opportunity to vote upon it. They therefore decided to determine their attitude towards the new issue without waiting for the Party to act first. Considering that the issue in question was a political one, this was nothing short of "lèse majésté". At the Trade Union Congress in Cologne, which met some months before the Party convention of that year, a resolution was passed, which was later declared mandatory upon all trade union members, as follows:

"The Congress emphatically rejects all attempts definitely to determine the tactics of labor by means of propaganda for the political mass strike; all organized workers are hereby put under the obligation to combat it with all their power. The Congress further refuses even to discuss the general strike as advocated by anarchists and by *individuals without any understanding of the economic struggle;*[1] the workers are strictly warned against permitting such ideas to divert them from their every day work of strengthening their organizations."

To this a reply came from the radical *Leipziger Volks-Zeitung* that "the trade union movement had ceased to be a proletarian movement; it is the movement of a labor aristocracy; nothing else".

The Social-Democratic Party which met later in Jena, when faced by this resolution, adopted one of

[1] Meaning the intellectuals in the Party leadership.

its own, which, while failing to give the fullest satisfaction to the extreme radicals, contained an express
menace to the unions, from their point of view.   It
read as follows: [1]

"The convention declares that in the case of an
attack upon the universal, equal, direct, and secret
suffrage or upon the right of combination, it becomes
the bounden duty of the entire laboring class to
defend itself with every available means.   The convention declares a most comprehensive use of the
strike *en masse* as one of the most effective weapons
for the repulsion of such a criminal encroachment on
the rights of labor, as well as for conquering additional basic rights."

The dispute continued.   But while the furious
fight over the situation was raging in the labor press,
especially on the Social-Democratic side, the political leaders were getting ready to "climb down".
First there was an unofficial conference between the
Party leaders and the General Commission in November 1905, at which Bebel, the old politician,
showed much zeal for reconciliation.   As the General Commission itself reported later on: "His recent utterances were hardly consistent with his attitude at Jena.   He declared that, of course, the Party
would do everything to prevent a general strike;
that should it become unavoidable after all, the
Party alone would carry it on, and would provide
the necessary funds; that the trade unions were

[1] At the International Labor and Socialist Congress of 1904 at
Amsterdam, it was held that "although the absolute general strike,
in which all work whatever ceases, is an impossibility, yet a general
strike in some industries of vital importance shall be considered as a
proper weapon of last resort for bringing about important social
changes, or whereby encroachments on the rights of the workers might
be warded off".

entirely free to take whichever attitude they wished
in this matter."

Some days later, a secret conference of the trade
union leaders took place, the minutes of which were
later published, through a breach of confidence, by
the *Vorwärts*. On this occasion, all the accumulated
ill-feeling against the pretensions of the Party broke
loose. The conference was "aroused with indigna-
tion over a large part of the Social-Democratic Party
which attacked the trade unions in the rudest and
most violent way". Boemelberg, the chairman of
the last Congress, regretted his oft-quoted declaration at the congress in 1902 that "Party and trade
unions are one"; had he known how it would be
misquoted, he would never have made it. Legien
finally made a ringing declaration of independence:
"that the trade unions felt no longer under any
obligations to accept in silence the unrestrained attacks by the Party press, but, from now on, they
would express their own opinion without restraint,
even at the risk of bringing on unpleasant discussions; that the trade union press would freely use
its right to criticize the actions of the Party in all
cases where trade union principles were at stake;
that for the trade unions the resolution adopted at
the Congress at Cologne remained valid, not the one
passed at the Party convention".

This unwavering attitude did not fail to create a
profound impression. It made the Party realize
that the trade unions had definitely outgrown its
guardianship; and it was sensible enough to yield.
Another conference between the Party leaders and
the General Commission took place, at which the
Party agreed to give up the claims of supremacy,

and, instead of trying to dictate, to co-operate with the General Commission on all common questions of importance. This agreement was ratified by the next Party convention at Mannheim in 1906, and became known as the "Mannheim Agreement", declaring that "in order to bring about united efforts in all actions which touch the interests of the trade unions and of the Party alike, these shall always be preceded by a full understanding between the central directive organs of both organizations". The General Commission, commenting at the next Congress at Hamburg in 1908 upon the new situation, said: "It is to be hoped that the frequent ructions between the Party and the trade unions during 1905 and 1906 will have a lasting good effect in that the complete co-operation, which now exists, will never again be endangered *by theorists and writers* who attach a greater value to mere revolutionary slogans than to practical work inside the labor movement". Thus the trade union movement won equal rights at last, and the "superior" intellectual radical had to capitulate before the embattled trade unionist.

After Mannheim, harmony reigned. The trade union organizations continued their successes and gained further prestige. The membership rose from 1,689,000 in 1906 to 2,017,000 in 1910, and to 2,573,-000 in 1913; that of the metal workers alone from 233,000 in 1906 to 557,000 in 1913. The total annual receipts of all unions increased from M. 46,000,000 [1] in 1906 to M. 82,000,000 in 1913, and their total funds for the same period from M. 25,000,000 to M. 88,000,-000. The annual amounts disbursed in benefits of all sorts by all national unions were M. 9,330,000

[1] A German Mark approximately equals 25 cents.

in 1906, and M. 31,750,000 in 1913. In 1913, of that amount M. 16,606,000 went for strike aid, M. 13,-536,000 for sick benefits, M. 11,532,000 for out-of-work benefits, M. 273,500 for extra aid in sickness and death, M. 1,506,000 for traveling benefits, M. 938,000 for victimized workers, M. 559,000 for invalidity benefits, and M. 414,000 for legal aid. The city trades' councils had separate funds to provide for their multifarious activities. In 1913, eight hundred such councils (where there had been 553 in 1906), with an affiliated membership of 2,311,000, had a total income of M. 2,311,000, or of M. 2,143,000, including monies collected as voluntary strike donations, and expended M. 2,145,000, of which M. 487,-000 for "labor secretariats" and legal aid, M. 234,-000 for labor temples, assembly halls and workingmen's hotels, M. 174,000 for elections of labor representatives to government advisory bodies, M. 168,000 for libraries, and M. 130,000 for agitation. The labor secretariats, which since 1902 were grouped nationally in a "Central Labor Secretariat", in conjunction with the General Commission, gave aid in 1913 to 683,000 persons, of whom 651,250 were trade unionists. So far as the highly important criterion of trade agreement is concerned, there had been in 1907 5324 agreements for 111,000 establishments, covering 974,000 wage earners; and in 1912, 12,437 agreements for 208,000 establishments, covering two million wage workers. Mention should also be made of the highly vital and comprehensive statistical work carried on under the General Commission and by individual national unions, and of the ever growing net of trade union publications headed by the *Korrespondenzblatt* of the General

Commission. To offset this showing of remarkable growth in membership, income, and numbers covered by trade agreements, there was the renewal since 1908 of the campaign for a law restricting the right to strike, and especially after 1911, a more rigorous interpretation by judicial and administrative authorities of the existing laws against the trade unions—which continued incessantly to the very outbreak of the War. This kept the unions perpetually on the defensive from the direction of the government.

Although officially the "Mannheim Agreement" was for the unions no more than a charter of "equal rights", actually their gains soon went far beyond mere equality with the Party. For while the unions were making one advance after another, not all was well with the Party.

Earlier in the decade, the Party had in convention, by the weight of an overwhelming majority, put down the "Revisionist" rebellion against Marxian orthodoxy led by Edward Bernstein. The latter, formerly the closest associate of Engels, had imbibed, during his years of exile which he spent in England, many of the views of the Fabian socialists, and, in 1899, came out with a theoretical broadside against "orthodox" Marxism and the established tactics of the Social-Democracy. Bernstein's strongest contentions were against forecasting for capitalism a speedy and violent death. Rather he emphasized its capacity for self-stabilization. On the practical side, "Revisionism" called for a new emphasis on "immediate demands", so vital to the interests of the concrete workingman and his family, a program which, while it bore a distinct intellectualist stamp by continuing to lay its chief stress on political action, still came quite near to the trade union point of view. However, at the time, the trade unions were too busy with the work of growing up, and were as yet still too humble in their own minds before the roaring lions of the Social-Democratic Party, to risk taking a hand. So the revolutionary orthodoxy celebrated a triumph. Revisionism was to all appearances laid to rest for good, and the Party continued in its old tracks, confident that it was going with the inevitable psychological mass current. Although sadly conscious that its influence in parliament lagged far behind its growing popular support, the Party remained confident that at subsequent general elections the curve of its success would maintain its old climb.

So matters stood on the eve of the election of 1907. It was a campaign fought on the issue of colonial expansion promoted by the government. The socialists centered on the view that colonialism and imperialism were capitalism's devices for escaping its final doom, besides causing bloody war, and must be fought to the end. On the governmental side, a strong popular appeal, led by the Kaiser, was made on the issue of patriotism. The results showed a slight increase of the total socialist vote over the preceding election, but a loss of nearly one-half of the seats in the Reichstag. This was a blow which neither the German socialists nor socialists abroad had anticipated. All socialists had come to expect continued successes by the German Social-Democracy with the inevitability of an astronomical phenomenon. Therefore all the greater was the disturbing effect upon those who had come to believe that while revolutionary orthodoxy, like virtue, was

its own reward, yet it also brought another and not
to be depised compensation in multiplied seats in
the Reichstag and in renewed lustre to the star of the
Social-Democratic Party. Just as the "Mannheim
Agreement" meant an external check upon the revolutionary enthusiasm of the intellectuals of the
Party coming from the practical trade union side,
so now, the election results of 1907 brought a similar
check from the Party's own direct experience. Between them, these two influences go a long way to
account for the party's changed "course". Despite
the unwavering devotion to the old symbols and
slogans, such a change came first to light in 1913.
Driven into a corner by shrewd government tactics,
the Party repudiated its old principle of refusing
under any circumstances to vote a penny to a capitalistic government. For the violation of this principle, the socialists of the South German States had
been severely reprimanded by the Party a few years
before. And now the Party itself voted for the government bill for a moderate capital levy to provide
for an enlarged army. The spirit of the "dead"
revisionism had come to mock its quondam execu-
tioner.

As revisionism thus came in practice to rule the
policy of the Social-Democratic Party, the last barriers were crumbling between the trade unions and
a virtual ascendancy over the whole labor movement.
Officially still in possession of only "equal rights"
with the political party, in reality the trade unions
already acquired a supremacy, although that
changed condition still needed the War and the
Revolution to become evident to all. The victory
now came, because the trade union program had

about it a definiteness and incisiveness which the Party's program no longer possessed. But in substance, this victory of trade unionism over politics was a victory, inside the labor movement, for the method which keeps testing social theory in the crucible of concrete experience—the best adaptation to social problems of the scientist's experimental method—over a method which can be experimental only partly and superficially. The "experimenting" by the political party is only a spurious and incomplete experimenting, so far as the labor movement is concerned,—for two reasons: First, in modern society the main current of experience flows through industry, the trade unionist's arena, not through politics, where the intellectual is at home and active. Second, the intellectual is hampered even in the limited experimenting which he conducts, by his basic preconception of labor as an "abstract mass in the grip of an abstract force". So that whatever salutary experience he may thus have acquired, tends before long to be erased from his mind by the more potent and more lasting influence coming from his basic thinking about the labor movement.

War, Revolution, and the Present Situation

On the eve of the War, the trade unions were once more going through a severe crisis with regard to their status under the law. With other adverse things, it was momentarily expected that the government would apply to all unions the interpretation of the Imperial law concerning associations, and would hold that trade unions were political bodies and thus subject to all the restrictions applied to such bodies.

Shortly before, such interpretation, applied to six unions, had already been upheld by the court. Thus, when the War was declared, an out and out dissolution of the unions was looked for. In effect, just the opposite took place. The government changed its "course" abruptly, and, in the interest of national unity, the persecution of the unions ceased, and they themselves were given a heretofore undreamed of recognition, both at the hands of the government and of the employers. This, of course, was virtually determined by the "Policy of the Fourth of August" —the policy of patriotic support of the government in the War. This was adopted by the Social-Democratic Party, and the trade unions, both through their General Commission and through the executive bodies of all individual unions [1] throughout the War gave this policy their enthusiastic and unflagging support. That the newly found patriotism was not just a phenomenon at the top, but penetrated deeply into the membership, is borne out by the materially greater losses in membership sustained by the "free" unions, compared with the liberal (Hirsch-Duncker) unions and with the much more important Christian unions.[2] Mobilization affected all three classes of unions alike, but the past radical policy of the "free" unions made their patriotism suspect to many of their members, despite the fact that

[1] The Congresses were dispensed with for the duration of the War.

[2] The Christian unions arose in the middle of the nineties, embracing both Catholics and Protestants, with their stronghold in the mining region of the West. Vehemently rejecting socialism as contrary to their religious faith, they were none the less genuine unions, and at times their militant tactics even brought them into co-operation with the "free" unions. In 1913, the percentages of organized labor for the several union groups were as follows: "Free" unions, 78; Christian unions, 9.5; "Yellow" (employer controlled) unions, 8.4; and Hirsch-Duncker unions, 3.3.

these unions were responsible within the party for the "policy of the Fourth of August". The "free" unions were reduced to 37 per cent of their membership, the Christian to 52 per cent, and the liberal to 58 per cent. So that the War-time gains were not in membership, as was the case in the United States and England, but in influence and status. These gains were as follows:

First, the legal status was greatly improved. Formerly, the employees on the railways, which were then owned and operated by the State, had been altogether forbidden to organize. In June 1916, after much negotiating with the government, they at last formed a union, but with this all-important concession: that, while refraining in the constitution from avowedly prohibiting the strike, no provision was made for a strike fund. In the same month, the Reichstag passed a law removing from over the heads of the unions the menace of being declared political associations, and in May 1918 the famous paragraph 153 of the industrial code, which rendered picketing subject to a jail sentence of three months, was repealed. But since strikes in War time were rare, the greatest benefit was derived from the industrial "recognition" which the law of "the auxiliary services" helped procure for the unions in the "heavy industries" hitherto closed to them. This law, providing for joint boards and for workers' shop representation, was passed at the end of 1916, and applied to all munition industries. The General Commission of the trades unions, reporting immediately after the Revolution, said that, with all its ruinous effects upon industry as a whole, that law "had materially strengthened the trade union organizations and enabled them to begin an upward swing. Therefore the system of labor representation provided by it, was taken over into the revolutionary legislation''.

However, recognition of unions by employers had been proceeding apace from the very outbreak of the War. It came about naturally, through the joint work of employer and union representatives on the multifarious welfare and wartime provision boards, set up by the government to deal with such matters as unemployment, industrial recruiting, rehabilitation, and so forth. The two sides were learning to know each other better under the favorable circumstances of the common War emergency. Thus gradually the joint relationship was shading out from the bare wage-contract of old into a new and manifold ''industrial-community'' relationship, upon which the union leaders were laying great store. Finally, when in the late summer of 1918, the doom of the monarchy—the main prop of the old industrial order—was sealed, the hitherto autocratic ''heavy industries'' fell into line, hoping to find in the trade unions the indispensable brake upon the rush to Bolshevism, which they already clearly envisaged. The new relationship was, on November 15, 1918, made industry-wide through the famous ''Agreement between the Employers' Associations and the Trade Unions regarding *Arbeitsgemeinschaften*'', which gave the union leaders all they asked for: full official recognition, disbandment of the ''yellow'' unions employer controlled and strike breaking, the abolition of all discrimination against union members, the eight-hour day, jointly managed employment bureaus, shop committees to watch over the

proper execution of collective agreements, and joint
conciliation boards by industry and for the country
as a whole.

As already mentioned, during the War the trade
unions gave consistent support to the majority faction of the Social-Democratic Party, which stood by
the "policy of the Fourth of August". However,
in June 1915, a call was published in the radical
Leipziger Volkszeitung, signed by many socialists,
among them twenty union leaders, condemning that
policy and foreshadowing the ultimate splitting off,
a year later, of a minority to form the Independent
Socialist Party. Thereupon the General Commission, and subsequently a conference of the executives
of all unions, held that "the views urged by the
factionists in the Party ran directly counter to the
essence of the trade union program and harmed the
effectiveness of the labor organization; their adoption would mean the loss of everything that the trade
unions have striven for and have achieved". This
view was endorsed by individual conferences of the
several unions. After that split in the Party actually
had occurred, a general union conference, in July
1917, rejected by unanimous vote the resolution of
the commercial employees' union calling on the
General Commission "to co-operate in all political
matters with *both* Social-Democratic Parties". An
article in the official union *Korrespondenzblatt,* in
1916, said: "This policy of the Fourth of August
is of the most vital interest to the trade unions; it
saves our land from invasions; it protects us from
the dismemberment of German territory and from
the destruction of our flourishing industries; it protects us from losing the War and from being bur-

dened for decades by indemnities. This policy safeguards our industries as well as our foreign markets.'' By contrast, the ''Independents'', who were
led by the outstanding intellectuals in the historical
Social-Democratic movement and included Bernstein, the ''revisionist'', as well as Kautzky, the
''orthodox'', were happy at last that they had found
their old ideals again,—an international solidarity
of the proletariat against the international exploiters. What they wanted was an immediate end to
bloodshed, an end to the violation of human rights
and liberties, to the suppression of speech and opinion. Filled with wrath against their own government, they apparently cared less about the effects of
their policies on the lives of the working people and
on German industry under the hard and irrevocable
conditions which war had laid upon them, than for
the spiritual comfort of a regained allegiance to their
old principles.

Had the Revolution come with the political labor
movement united in a single party; had the Social-
Democratic Party entered the Revolution with its old
self-confidence of the nineties or at the time when it
had put down the ''revisionist'' rebellion just a decade before the outbreak of the War, it would doubtless have led to a decisive backward swing of the
pendulum from the prestige of the trade union
leaders to that of the Party intellectuals. Only
temporarily, however, until the forces of industry
could have had time to assert their supremacy over
the ''political''. However, as the situation actually
developed, the Independents withdrew after a few
weeks from the provisional Revolutionary government, organized by the socialists after the flight of

William II, and that was soon to be followed by a non-socialist "bourgeois" majority in the election to the Constitutional Convention. In the meantime, those intellectuals who were still further to the "left" than the Independents,—the Bolshevist Spartacans under Karl Liebknecht and Rosa Luxemburg,—were making the Russian "Soviet" or "council" idea a force to be conjured with. But the slogan of "all power to the councils" was forestalled and blocked by a "majoritist" (Social-Democratic) control in the Berlin and national "Councils of Workers' and Soldiers' Deputies", which abdicated in favor of the democratically chosen Constitutional Convention. Thus the only outlet which the Party intellectuals, now joined by not a few former "bourgeois" economists, could find for their revolutionary impulse was in working for the "socialization" of industry (the term "nationalization" being taboo as smacking too much of the old bureaucratic control of the railroads "nationalized" by Bismarck).[1] On the other hand, for the trade union leaders, "socialization" held but the mildest kind of appeal. They worried much less about the form of *ownership* of industry, public or private, which to the intellectual is always the main issue, than about extending labor's *control* over industry, for which they had acquired a taste during the war and especially after the "Agreement of November 15".

In March 1920, the monarchists' rebellion, known

---

[1] They indeed held the fort in the Socialization Commission of 1919, but with the resignation of the socialist government the whole matter was shelved.

as the Kapp "Putsch", occurred. The government fled from Berlin, and it devolved upon the unions to save the Republic by means of a general strike. The returned government accepted the demands of its rescuers. These included both the appointment forthwith of a socialization commission, with trade union participation, to proceed energetically in the case of those industries already ripe for socialization, and the immediate taking over by the State of the coal and potash industries. However, little or no real pressure was applied in that direction. Responsible leaders did not want socialization; they merely felt that they had to take cognizance of its potency as a popular slogan. For, at bottom, they gravely feared that it could only further aggravate the shattered condition of industry. Only the "opposition" leaders in the unions insisted that labor wanted it. The Socialization Commission sat and came to an unfavorable conclusion. And by the end of 1921, the subject had dropped out even from discussion. By that time the unions and the labor movement as a whole had their hands full trying to keep their real wages from sinking out of sight, in addition to trying to keep up with the lightning-like developments on the capitalistic side, in the way of mergers, vertical trustification, and the like. On the matter of the basic reorganization of industry, they were therefore content with what they could get along the line of "industrial democracy". This latter, far from being a mere unformed wish or a dignified designation for mere opportunism, has grown into a well rounded out program, rivalling in theoretical close-knittedness the best of the compositions from the pens of the intellectual Party members.[1]

The conception which the trade unions held of industrial democracy expanded as events unfolded. At first the trade union leaders questioned or even feared the movement for shop councils. They based their hope for industrial democracy on nation-wide written agreements with the associated employers, by industry and for the country as a whole. Thus they saw the "November agreement" as the crowning success of their efforts for many years past and as the culmination of a movement which had begun in 1896 with the agreement in the printing industry. On the other hand, the idea of the shop councils was at the grave disadvantage of having first been proposed by the Bolshevist Spartacans, who would make such councils rivals to the trade unions themselves and the basis of a political dictatorship, rather than the beginning of a progressive shop democracy. When, however, this idea refused to down, but instead gained constantly in popularity, the trade union leaders were obliged to take notice of it. Furthermore, the menace of Bolshevism contained in the original proposal of shop councils had, in the meantime, considerably abated, owing to the voluntary surrender of power by the German "Soviets" to the Constitutional Convention. Therefore the trade union leaders ended by accepting the shop council plan. This acceptance, grudging at first, later became a wholehearted one, and the shop council became officially recognized as one of the three main

[1] It is for this reason that in the arrangement of this book, the best and most elaborate sample of it was placed, for purpose of clear contrast, side by side with the discussion on the intellectual. (See Chapter IX.)

avenues leading to industrial democracy. The two others were "economic parliaments" to legislate for a self-governing industry, and the industrial agreements already mentioned. The trade unions, however, took good care to bring the shop councils into an organic connection with their own structure, to subject them to union regulations, and to confine them to working within the scope of the collective agreements made by the unions themselves.

But even with trade union supremacy over the political Party now admitted, new and menacing difficulties engendered by the Revolution itself had to be met. The extraordinary growth in membership itself brought with it unexampled problems both in adjusting the administrative apparatus and in preserving the policies taught by past experience. The total membership of the "Federation of German Trade Unions", renamed from the "Trade Unions affiliated with the General Commission", rose to 5,479,000 in 1919, and to 7,890,000 in 1920.[1] These new difficulties, together with a clear demonstration of the trade union point of view, are set forth in an article by Hermann Mueller, president of the National Lithographers' Union, in "Die Neue Zeit", just before the Trade Union Congress in November in 1919:

"The trade unions did everything during the War to save Germany from the dangers menacing her. This was not from motives of super-patriotism. They, like the Social-Democratic Party, acted with a clear realization that this War would decide Ger-

[1] In close co-operation with the Federation of Trade Unions stood the organized clerical employees, in a federation of their own of eleven national unions, with a total membership in 1921 of 686,000.

many's 'to be or not to be'. How right they were in this, the peace treaty shows. Furthermore, this was not a question concerning the capitalists alone. The fate of the whole working class depended on the country's industries. That the German workingman had nothing to lose but his chains may have been true at the time when Marx and Engels wrote the *Communist Manifesto*. But it no longer applied to the workingmen of 1914. Step by step they had advanced, and had conquered conditions that were no worse, if not actually better, than in most other countries. All this was at stake if the War was lost. The ruin of the German industries meant also the breakdown of the German labor movement. The radical groups are not only losing sight of the general public welfare, but even of the interests of the working class. To them, their Party has become an ultimate end in itself. They are thoroughly unscrupulous in the choice of the means to strengthen their party. Hence their abominable propaganda, misrepresentations, and accusations. It is small matter to them what becomes of the German people, what of the working class, morally and economically. . . . How has all this come about? How can the workingmen who created their trade unions with so much hard and bitter effort, thus risk the fruits of their work? The answer is simple enough: the ultramodern militant leader builds not upon the old and tried members. For him the rapid growth of the unions was a godsend. Before the War, the unions affiliated with the General Commission were two and a half million strong. Now they have more than twice that number, notwithstanding the hundreds of thousands killed in the war and the many prisoners not yet returned. The term 'November Socialist' is much abused, but it well describes the situations in the trade unions, which are suddenly crowded with people who should have discovered their courage before the Revolution. These 'November unionists', now that they are paying their dues, are anxious to reap by the bushel and at once. Things are not moving fast enough for them. The fanatics of today are none other than those who formerly were either indifferent or even among the "yellows". They are the tools of the political radicals." [1] Mueller is only partially right in drawing the contrast between the experienced and the inexperienced unionists. He ignored the rival radical unions whose nucleus, formerly members of the old "localists", had had experience of a kind, and who by 1919 had won new recruits to the number of about 100,000. Besides these rival unions, there were within the Federation itself millions of new members who had come to plague Mueller and all the old leaders.

The "Policy of the Fourth of August" and the "Agreement of November 15" were the points especially singled out for attack by the radicals. The elections of officers, long delayed by the War, began to bring about rapid changes in the personnel of union leadership. The opposition won in the branch unions of the large cities, Berlin, Leipzig, Duesseldorf, and so forth, and also in a number of instances, the national offices. However, these changes were not without disappointments to their sponsors. Frequently, one chosen to a responsible union office would be recalled for failing to act as radically as he had talked as a candidate.

[1] *Die Neue Zeit*, June 1919, p. 291.

At the Congress held in Nuremberg in 1919, the conservatives outnumbered the opposition in the ratio of two and a half to one, though the radical minority in the membership at large was in all probability a more considerable fraction of the whole. At this Congress, the two factions, split on political lines, caucused separately as hostile bodies. The two factions again measured strength in the first country-wide election to the shop councils, which the law of January 18, 1920, authorized,—this time not in convention but in a popular vote amounting to a referendum. Karl Legien issued an appeal to uphold the trade unions against those who would make the shop councils a rival to them, and won decisively. At the Congress held in Leipzig in 1922, the hostility had already become much allayed. The official report read: ''The labor movement is on the road to recovery. There are now more of those who criticize objectively, with a true desire to remedy certain concrete evils, in contrast to the others who indulge in a wholesale condemnation, irrespective of merit. . . . As at Nuremberg, there were again special caucuses of the 'factions', just as there were 'faction speakers' at the general meetings. But this time an overwhelming majority protested against this sort of dragging of political party dissensions into trade union congresses. Also at Leipzig, the opposition was much smaller. It no longer indulged in personalities. It consisted mostly of new members.''[1]

Thus the revolutionary phase, when the outcome was still uncertain, had clearly come to a close. The older leadership firmly held its own.

[1] *Die Neue Zeit*, Vol. 40, 1922, p. 342.

Thereafter all revolutionary attacks dashed themselves against impregnable trade union positions.

By the middle of 1922 the problem of currency inflation, resulting in a rapid sinking of the real wage, assumed serious proportions. But it was nothing compared with the consequences of the occupation of the Ruhr by the French in January 1923. Currency inflation then reached "astronomical" dimensions. Unemployment, first caused by the "passive" resistance of the Ruhr industries, and later increased by the change to a new "strong" currency, the Rentenmark, ran into millions. The accumulated funds of the unions were reduced to worthlessness. The trade unions now faced an attack by the employers at all points,—on their real wage, on the revolutionary conquest of the eight-hour day, on the collective agreement, and even on their very existence. Since the organized employers were so commandingly in the saddle and evidently bent upon a thoroughgoing offensive, there was no longer any purpose in maintaining the "Central Joint Industrial Board." ("Zentralarbeitsgemeinschaft"). This had been created under the "Agreement of November 15", with the broadly conceived purpose of "facilitating joint dealing with all the economic and socio-political questions concerning German industry as well as with all legislative and administrative matters pertaining thereto". It was dissolved by the central trade union executive in 1924, and the several trade unions followed suit in their respective industries.

An enormous loss of membership betrayed the almost hopeless situation of the trade unions. On March 31, 1923, their membership stood at 7,427,000.

Six months later, it was still over seven millions, but on December 31 it had come down to 5,741,000, and sank in another year, in December 1924, to 3,975,000—a loss from the eight million high water mark in September 1922 of nearly fifty per cent. The severest losses tended to be registered by the unions in the "heavy industries". The trade union statistical bureau made two investigations, one in May and another in November 1924, regarding the eight-hour day. In May, in the seven largest industries, 54.7 per cent of the workers worked more than forty-eight hours per week, of whom 13 per cent worked more than 54 hours. In November, the former figure had fallen to 45.4 per cent and the latter to 10.7 per cent. The printers who showed 49.5 per cent in May showed 26.5 per cent for November. For the textile workers, the percentage had fallen from 82.4 to 66.0; in the metal industry from 63.5 to 53.1. By the number of establishments 33.5 per cent worked longer than 48 hours in May, and 24.3 per cent in November. The re-conquest of the eight-hour day was slowest in the larger establishments.

Throughout these troubled years, the Communists kept up a relentless campaign, from within and from without, to subject the trade union movement to their control. Their outstanding leaders, Karl Liebknecht, Rosa Luxemburg, and Franz Mehring, of the pleiad of remarkable revolutionary intellectuals in the old Social-Democratic Party, were dead, the first two having been killed by Nationalist soldiers early in the Revolution. Therefore the Communists were now led by leaders of lesser calibre and still lesser renown, who, as with Communists elsewhere, stood in tremendous awe of the exceptional group of intellectuals who were directing the Communist Party of Russia and the Third (Communist) International. However, such command at long range by persons who were outsiders and unversed in the German situation, even if they did display a brilliance in their handling of their own Russian problems, naturally had its serious drawbacks. The crisis which came with the occupation of the Ruhr by the French early in 1923, entailing the crash of the Mark and phenomenal unemployment, furnished the Communists with a most favorable opportunity. Nevertheless, their successes were confined to the political field only, where they polled a vote of 4,000,000 in the election of May 1924, although in the second election of that year, seven months later, they lost their gains. In the trade union movement, the most the Communists could accomplish was to capture a number of the city trades' councils. Out of these councils they endeavored by an "Opposition" conference at the end of 1923, preparatory to an "Opposition" congress, to create a nucleus for a rival national trade union movement. Later they shifted to "boring from within" the existing organizations. Their tactics, in both instances, failed to obtain appreciable results. The Central Committee of the Federation retaliated in 1924 by dissolving the trades' councils under Communist control; and the executives of the several unions, in joint conference in January 1925, unanimously resolved to apply the tactics of expulsion to all members opposing the official trade union lists in elections either to public industrial bodies or to works' councils.

Amidst all these difficulties, the trade unions found that their political interests were but inadequately represented in the legislative bodies by the intellectuals of the Social-Democratic Party. The report of the Trade Union Federation for 1924, in the section on the "political representation of the trade union interests", remarked that while the political neutrality of the "free" unions had never hindered the closest possible connection with the Social-Democratic Party, and the situation remained totally unaltered even when the Congress at Nuremberg in 1919 saw fit to abrogate the "Mannheim Agreement",[1] "there have taken place certain developments in the Social-Democratic Party which are causing great uneasiness in trade union circles. Trade unionists view with alarm the increase in influence and in numbers within the Social-Democratic Parliamentary Group of the so-called intellectuals. The cause of their uneasiness is that this type of a person evidently is strongly imbued with purely theoretical and radical notions, and, in the opinion of practical trade unionists, takes slight cognizance of the actual interests of the working people and of their organization. This has led to incongruous results. Thus, while the trade unions are generally charged with responsibility, particularly by the Communists, for every tactical move made by the Social-Democratic Party and its Parliamentary Group, they find that they are lacking the direct means of making the labor representatives pursue

[1] Because there were at that time two socialist parties, the Social-Democratic and the Independent. In 1922, the latter dissolved, and became reunited with the parent party, bringing back within the fold the old socialist leaders and as many of the membership as did not go over to the Communists.

proper policies in the national parliament and in the diets of the several States. This situation can only be remedied and the undesirable activities of the Party 'Opposition' can only be checked when trade unionists will become represented in the legislative bodies both directly and to accord fully with their numbers and weight.'' The report goes on to say that in line with this new policy, the Vice-President of the Federation was named, after negotiations with the Party, at the head of the list of candidates on the Social-Democratic list at Hamburg. And it concludes: ''The question is as yet far from solved. A thorough change in the situation cannot be attained merely by negotiating with the controlling organs of the party. The lists of candidates are made up by the district Party organizations, and pressure from the Central Committee is certain to encounter resentment and resistance.''

However, the ''control'' of the intellectuals, whom, notwithstanding their occasional refractoriness, the German labor movement will continue to use to the full, is no longer a very important issue. The real task is the elevation of the deplorable labor standards in a country weighted down by ever mounting reparation payments and in the teeth of an extremely aggressive and splendidly organized employing class, which finds in the country's plight a ready-to-hand argument for keeping those standards down. Nevertheless, whatever hardships or even crises the future may be holding in store for the German labor movement,—its experience, both in the past and in recent years, has amply prepared it to cope with them. From its revolutionary past, the German labor movement inherited a feeling of solidarity which is both broad and potent. It used to be Karl Legien's constant advice to the leaders in the several unions to concentrate on improving the conditions of the less skilled groups, since then the standards of the skilled will go up automatically. But the German labor movement has also learned that this, its spiritual capital, namely the readiness on the part of the individual member and on the part of the individual union to sacrifice for others and for the common cause, must not be dissipated in the pursuit of unrealistic and unattainable objectives, no matter how strongly such objectives might appeal to the romantic imagination. German unionism understands German industry thoroughly,—its managerial problems as well as its problems of marketing under the severest international competition history has yet known. Too, German trade unionism is fully aware that improvement in German labor standards depends upon a continuous solving of these problems. The German labor movement has therefore shelved, perhaps for good, its former radical anti-capitalism and is endeavoring, instead, through economic and political pressure, to get for labor the maximum from capitalism. And all the while, it is seeking to gain a position in German industry as an indispensable institution.[1]

[1] Many of the quotations and the greater part of the statistical material contained in this chapter are taken from K. Zwing's *Geschichte der deutschen Gewerkschaften* (Jena, 1922).

CHAPTER IV

THE BRITISH LABOR MOVEMENT

The convinced socialist, to whom socialism lies inevitably at the end of a no less inevitable line of social evolution, sees in the history of British labor the strongest of proof for his contention. For England seems to offer incontrovertible proof that modern labor can no more be diverted from attaining its mental maturity in a socialistic class-consciousness than can a boy from finding his in the grown man. Here indeed is the oldest continuous labor movement in the world, in the country with the first factory system and with the earliest capitalism. It is, moreover, a labor movement which, though for half a century so wedded to social conservatism as actually to have become capitalism's complement, eventually turned its back completely on middle class liberalism, and at the end of the Nineteenth Century came forth behind collectivist banners and under socialistic leaders. Now, a quarter century later, it has become the strongest hope of Western socialism. Nevertheless, though the validity of the socialist theory of the labor movement has thus apparently been established by the overwhelming weight of this British evidence, a complete study of all the circumstances and factors connected with the about face in the movement at the end of the last

and at the beginning of the present century contro-
verts this contention.

THE "OLD UNIONISM",
OR THE "NEW MODEL" OF THE FIFTIES

In the second half of the Nineteenth Century, organized labor in Britain,—so typical and so distinctive that to it was generally applied the appellation
"trade unionism", without the adjective "British",
—was a movement of skilled artisans. These artisans had inherited to a no small degree the tradition
of associated self-help and of a collective control
of their economic opportunity from the old journeymen's societies, some of which began as early as
the Seventeenth Century, a consequence of the disruption of class harmony in the craft gilds. During
the second quarter of the Nineteenth Century, the
"revolutionary" period in British labor history,
these organized artisans, partly through their own
experience, but also from observing the rawness of
the mass movements of the factory workers of the
industrial North, were taught forcibly the utter
hopelessness of a disorderly rush against the citadel
of capitalism. They saw how the syndicalistic Grand
National Consolidated Trades Union, the "One Big
Union" of 1834, which was at least 500,000 strong,
broke up at the first impact with the government
and the organized employers, due to the inner weakness of a movement which was more like a mob than
like an organization. They also saw the futility of
the Chartist political mass demonstrations, verging
on insurrection, which filled the latter thirties and
early forties. These artisans, thanks to a long

training in their own organizations, had already
quite outgrown any tendency to accept at par value
the millennialist currencies of either Robert Owen
or of Feargus O'Connor. They now became convinced that it was futile to use force against a régime which proved as deeply intrenched as British
capitalism, which was the fruition of a development
of over half a millennium, and was buttressed by a
still older political system. From that came a realization of the necessity of adjusting their utterances,
practices, and demands to the dominant note in
English life, and even to pick their weapons from
the intellectual arsenal of the dominant class if they
were to rise in the social scale at all. It meant practically abandoning the great class of the unskilled to
their fate, and concentrating on acquiring for their
trade organizations a greater internal stability and
a recognized status in industry and before the law.
This was, in other words, the program of the "New
Model" in unionism, born in the fifties.

In brief, the goal of this British conservative
unionism was a legal, political, economic, and social
equalization of classes—a thoroughly pragmatic
ideal of raising labor as a group and the laborer as
an individual. Characteristically enough, it pinned
its expectations far more on an improved *status* of
the trade unions, an immunity from the criminal
law and a "recognition" by the employers, than on
militancy and fighting preparedness, although it did
not neglect the latter. It demanded the abolition of
all political and legal disabilities weighing upon the
workingmen; of the denial of the political franchise;
of the employer's superior rights under the law of
master and servant, and of his freedom from liability

for injuries under the fellow servant doctrine; of the summary jurisdiction of the magistrates with their invariable prejudice against workingmen in matters of wage contracts; and of the generally undemocratic administrative and judicial state machinery. But they demanded, most emphatically of all, the cessation of the treatment of peaceful picketing as a criminal offense, and the exposure of trade union funds to embezzlement by dishonest officers. Next came a series of demands for facilitating the rise of the individual workingman out of his class: educational opportunity at public expense, safeguarding the patent rights of workingmen inventors, and peasant proprietorship. All of these, it was believed, would vitally contribute to an ultimate economic equalization of classes. But mainly that would result from stable trade unions. Such unions would know how to prevent fluctuations and loss of membership by a comprehensive system of benefits,—sick, and accident, superannuation, and death,—payable out of funds raised from high weekly contributions, that, coupled with the payment of strike and out-of-work pay for considerable periods at a time, would make possible placing a reserve price on labor's services.

The wage theory of this unionism was based on supply and demand. Wages will rise when the union controls and limits the supply of labor, hence the stress on apprenticeship, emigration funds, and abolition of overtime. At bottom, the trade policy was restricted to securing for every workman those terms which the best employers were willing voluntarily to grant. The protection of labor by law was condemned in principle—so deep had the gospel of *laissez-faire* and of self-help penetrated into the skilled artisan class. But in particular cases, it was sanctioned and pursued, like coal mines' acts and factory hours legislation. The real desideratum, however, was industrial conciliation boards and collective bargaining with the employers.

The Amalgamated Society of Engineers, formed in 1852 out of several related trade societies by the genius of Allan and Newton, gave this type of unionism its model constitution. It was two in one —a mutual benefit society and a trade union. As a benefit society, it had the local branch for its active unit, which received the weekly dues of one shilling, holding the money in trust for the national office, and disbursed the accrued benefits under rigid national rules. As a trade protective organization, the district organization was the active unit, functioning under the closest supervision of the national officers, who enjoyed in that capacity far greater discretion than in the matter of benefits. Leadership was now no longer by casual enthusiasts, but by "experts", carefully trained, or rather self-trained, for managing big organizations with huge funds and multiform activities, insurance, protective, legislative, and political—labor's going concerns in the full sense of the word. The other "Amalgamated" unions, like the carpenters and the boilermakers, copied this model.

By the middle of the sixties, we find the leaders of the "amalgamated" unions working as a "Junta" through the London Trades Council. They were keeping up a relentless pressure on Parliament, forever busily molding a favorable public opinion and besieging political leaders. Their actual politi-

cal power was slight, since none of their membership were enfranchised before 1867, and only a
limited number of the wage earning class after that
date. But their achievements, especially the new
legal status for unionism, so exceptionally favorable
that judges and the legal profession have not yet
ceased to deplore it, were astonishing. This
"Junta" period, in which the labor leaders of
Britain so inspired the public with confidence in
the essential soundness and moderation of their
movement, weathered all sorts of storms, and turned
the very attacks by enemies into promising opportunities, is perhaps the most notable chapter in
world labor history.

Yet, once the ambitious program of legalization
was accomplished, the whole clockwork in the mechanism seemed to run down. In the decade from
1875 to 1885, the British Trades Union Congress,
the annual "parliament of labor" which the leaders
of the "Junta" had first convoked in 1871 to mo-
bilize a maximum labor pressure on a recalcitrant
Liberal government, had but little left of the grandiose program of the sixties and seventies. These
congresses refused to enlarge their meager program,
despite even the retrogression in numbers, in
"recognition", and in influence, to which the industrial depression contributed most seriously. Nor
were they moved at first by the new ferment of
socialism and the ominous unrest among their own
membership.

WHY "NEW UNIONISM" WON

Fully to comprehend this somewhat puzzling mental inertia which seized the "Old Unionism", it is

imperative to realize more completely the background. The unions, as was seen, had begun as a subject class bent on rising to a higher level in society, but setting out on the long campaign with a complete knowledge of the obstacles and the opposition in their way, and with full awareness of their utter inability to win by purely coercive means. The successes proved great indeed, but the leaders have never forgotten that the victories were won by shrewd tactics rather than by force, and then solely by the aid of influential middle class friends. Therefore the movement has never ceased to be on its good behavior, and the concessions by Parliament and by the employers have carried an implied obligation resting upon union leaders to justify the confidence thus reposed. George Howell, one of the "front benchers" in the eighties, upon whom the mantle of these leaders had fallen, expressed that view clearly in conjunction with the attack he made upon the revolutionary "New Unionists" of the nineties. "When the unions of the United Kingdom", said he, "were demanding the repeal of the Criminal Law Amendment Act, they pleaded that they did not desire to coerce or to compel, but to persuade and induce." [1] Twelve years earlier, he had said: "Unionists have no more right to compel men to belong to a trade union than employers have to restrain workmen from joining or remaining in the union." [2] The Webbs stressed two explanations for the union leaders' practical abandonment of the strike, the weapon, *par excellence,* of coercion,—their engrossment in the work of administering their

[1] *Unionism, Old and New*, 139.
[2] *Conflict of Capital and Labor*, vii.

huge benefit funds, due to their incapacity to delegate work to subordinates, and their sheer conversion to the philosophy of the middle class. Rather does it lie in their consciousness of an obligation to keep faith with those who had accepted them on faith. But, while thoroughly explicable, this industrial pacifism could but lead to the downfall and displacement of the conservative leaders, since it arrested the labor movement mid-career before it had attained an adequate control of the job opportunities, even for the "labor aristocracy", to say nothing of the unskilled.

By contrast, one of the causes, if not *the* cause, of the unshakable grip of the American conservative union leaders, which continues to date, is that conservative union leaders in this country have, on the whole, always been more aggressive against the employers, and have striven more relentlessly for a full job control than have their radical rivals, so that whether or no they always succeeded in "bringing home the bacon", the membership could rarely complain that their leaders were "giving up without a fight". American conservative unionism, notwithstanding its limited "objective", falling far short of workers' control and the like, is a hard hitting unionism. Consequently, it has retained its grip on the members.

It is therefore full of significance for an appreciation of true labor psychology, that in order to carry the day, the socialistic "New Unionists", John Burns, Ben Tillett, and Tom Mann, attacked the old leaders not on the ground that they refused to embrace socialism but because they neglected opportunities for labor's further rise within the exist-

ing social framework. In fact, the leadership of
the labor movement has passed to these victors in
the famous dockers' strike of 1889, not because they
were socialists, but because they had made good
their claims as aggressive unionists. "How long,
how long", had appealed Tom Mann to the trade
unionists in 1886, "will you be content with the
present half-hearted policy of your unions? I readily grant that good work has been done in the past
by the Unions, but in Heaven's name, what good
purpose are they serving now? All of them have
large numbers out of employment even when their
particular trade is busy. None of the important societies have any policy other than that of endeavoring to keep wages from falling. The true unionist
policy of *aggression* seems entirely lost sight of: in
fact, the average unionist today is a man with a
fossilized intellect, either hopelessly apathetic or
supporting a policy that plays directly into the
hands of the capitalist exploiters." And John
Burns wrote, in 1887: "Constituted as it is, unionism carries within itself the source of its own dissolution. . . . Their reckless assumption of the duties
and responsibilities that only the State or the whole
community can discharge, in the nature of sick or
superannuation benefits, at the instance of the
middle class, is crushing out the larger unions by
taxing their members to an unbearable extent. This
so cripples them that the fear of being unable to
discharge their friendly society liabilities often
makes them submit to encroachments by the masters
without protest. The result of this is that all of
them have ceased to be Unions for maintaining the
rights of labor, and have degenerated into mere

middle or upper class rate-reducing institutions." [1]

Another weapon placed in the hands of the "New Unionists" was the old leaders' practical denial in practice of a labor solidarity wider than the immediate and rather narrowly conceived craft group. The rush to extend a helping hand to a group lower down in the scale may not be overpowering where, as in America, a fluidity of social classes has prevented labor from becoming psychologically compressed into one class. In England, on the contrary, the high spirited mechanic, by becoming the champion of the unskilled and unorganized, can best find vent for his rebellion against an implacable caste system which shuts him up in his own class. Under English conditions, therefore, only leaders who have gotten completely out of touch with the membership could come to overlook the emotional satisfaction that the practice of solidarity and of mutual sacrifice gives to those who feel oppressed by a common oppressor. At the same time it need not follow that solidarity in action is impossible without an ultimate revolutionary purpose. For its psychological effect is completely achieved when one is standing shoulder to shoulder with one's fellows in a contest for the next hundred yards in the enemy's territory, or for keeping territory already won, and need not be concerned with the infinite space beyond.

Still another fatal error of the old leaders was their rejection of the opportunity for labor's advancement by protective legislation, to which they came apparently, it is true, through sheer dogma-

[1] Quoted by Webb, *History of Trade Unionism,* 383-385.

tism imbibed from their middle class friends. Said
Howell: "They (the "New Unionists") look to the
State for aid. But history shows, especially industrial history, that self-reliance, self-help, by industrial effort, and mutual help, by associative effort,
are the only practical means whereby the conditions
of the people can be permanently improved." [1]
These leaders came to believe that the governmental
theory which suited a capitalism in the zenith of its
strength and in the full possession of world economic mastery also suited a laboring class, first
endeavoring to win a foothold. Thus they came to
overlook, purposely and persistently, a sure and
useful instrumentality, and were unable to offer
any excuse or extenuation of the error after their
own decisive success in dealing with the much more
difficult matter of legalizing picketing. To make
matters worse, a goodly portion of the labor movement, the cotton operatives and the miners, had been
successfully pursuing the legislative route for at
least two decades. No wonder, then, that the Trades
Union Congress, which met in 1890 in Liverpool,
was willing to give the labor movement into the
hands of the victors in the dockers' strike, who had
given labor a sense of the prowess of youth which
it had not known in years, and who were ready,
without prejudice, to push open any door beyond
which labor's advancement might lie. The important thing was not voting in favor of the "collective
ownership of the means of production, distribution,
and exchange", but entrusting direction to aggressive leaders.

While the impulse toward mass organization

[1] Howell, *Conflict of Capital and Labor*, X.

which the victory of the "new unionists" had given
to the labor movement soon spent itself, a mental re-
juvenation of the whole movement was doubtless
brought about. For British trade unionists again
found themselves facing new fields to conquer. At
last, they felt, the economic organizations had been
moved off the dead point. Thereupon, with the sense
of solidarity, so characteristic of the British workers, no longer inhibited by any narrow craft selfishness and timidity in action, they headed for the
unskilled and unorganized, and for a new aggressiveness towards the employers. Likewise, the
legislative opportunity, heretofore neglected, now
began to beckon most attractively, so that most of
the new energy began to flow in that direction.
Eventually, as we know now, the British trade union
movement was made to suffer for having its rescue
out of mental stagnation effected by socialists. For,
the new leaders, despite their splendid début as
trade unionists, mistaking their success as a mani-
fest revolution in ideas in the labor movement,
quickly turned to politics and legislation as their
main hope and enthusiasm, and in turn were guilty
of a serious oversight. It is only too apparent now
that these new socialistic leaders failed to perceive
that, while it functioned more or less satisfactorily
as labor's "foreign office", maintaining a steady
pressure on the British government, the Trades
Union Congress, headed by its Parliamentary (or
lobbying) Committee, yet fell entirely short of the
work of a labor's "home office", which should coör-
dinate and knit together the several organizations,
eliminating and preventing dual or rival unions, ef-
fectively encouraging federation, and so forth. Con-

sequently it was left for the post-War period, fully thirty years later, and in the heat of a period of acute industrial conflict flowing from a world wide economic maladjustment, to *improvise* a general *economic* federation of British labor.

The new trend in the British labor movement since the nineties is explained for the most part in terms of industrial depression, union stagnation, or a new class-consciousness coming from socialism. That the depression played a major rôle cannot be denied. But too much, it seems, has been made of the attractive force of socialism working by itself. True enough, the new orientation employed a socialist compass and spoke a socialist language. But what is overlooked is that socialism could exert upon the masses a strong pull in the new direction only because it came to them organically connected with religion. It was that, after all, which supplied a never diminishing drive, after the original impulse from the victories of the "new unionists" had in due season become spent. Continental socialists find it next to impossible to perceive the extent to which socialism's success among British labor is due to the religious vehicle it is employing. This oversight is the fruit of the assumption which now passes for axiomatic that labor's affinity for socialism is so powerful that it needs no sponsor nor special advocate. The British trade union movement had become, independently of the intellectuals and under its own leaders, a successful going concern, with a well-defined practice touching the daily and most vital interests of a membership of many hundreds of thousands. Therefore a conversion to socialism so wide and so late in the day would have been un-

thinkable, had it not been that the ideal of the new
social order came introduced as the sole practical
expression of Christian precepts, by leaders themselves for the most part deeply religious, and to a
working class whose devotion to the chapel perhaps
equalled and had certainly antedated the devotion
to the union. This is borne out by the fact that the
spread of socialism was not the work of the materialistic Marxian Social-Democratic Federation,
although it had graduated and influenced the first
"New Unionists", John Burns and Tom Mann, but
of Keir Hardie's Independent Labour Party. Max
Beer, a Continental socialist whose long residence
in England had taught him, however, to appreciate
the religious factor in the life of the British working
class movement, said the following of Keir Hardie:
"Socialism and labour politics were not subjects
for him to be reasoned and dogmatised upon. He
had little tuition, but a great deal of intuition. A
deeply religious, even mystical nature, although
born of free thinking, rationalist parents, he had
something in him of the primitive Christian, and he
rebelled against the injustice flowing from the division of society into rich and poor and the disintegration of mankind into hostile nations and warring
states. Socialism and the brotherhood of man—
these were his religious tenets, and to these he attached himself with all the spirituality that his rich
Celtic nature was capable of." And, speaking of
Hardie's first lieutenant, Bruce Glasier, Beer said:
"He enjoyed a much better training than his political leader. . . . Both of them belong, however, to
the same spiritual caste, which is religious and
mystical. For Glasier's socialism, too, was not ma-

terialistic or political; it had for him the meaning of an ethical religion, a practical service of humanity rather than any capture of political power and change of state administration. In his earliest book . . . he sums up his faith: 'Historically, socialism is more closely related to religious than political propagandism. It is from the prophets, rather than from the statesmen, economists, and political reformers, that the socialist movement derives its examples and ideals. Socialism means not only the socialization of wealth, not only the socialization of the means of production and distribution, but of our lives, our hearts—ourselves. . . . Socialism, when finally resolved, consists not in getting at all, but in giving; not in being served, but in serving. . . . Its ultimate moral, as its original biological justification, lies in the principle, human and divine, that 'as we give, so we live', and only in so far as we are willing to lose life do we gain life.''[1]

Another shrewd observer characterizes the aims of Keir Hardie's adherents in the following words: ''With the addition of a faith in socialism, the Independent Labour man generally shared all the virtues and limitations of the best type of his fellows. Very possibly he was an active socialist, quite possibly, also, he took a drop too much, occasionally, but he was even more likely to be a Methodist local preacher or perhaps a bigoted 'Rechabite'. . . . When he was 'religious', he filled the chapels of his district with a quaint mixture of socialist aspiration and evangelical doctrine; if he had finally severed himself from orthodoxy, he joined a 'Labour Church', where they sang hymns and offered prayers

[1] Beer, M., *History of British Socialism*, Vol. II, 310-312.

in the most approved fashion of British non-conformity. It was a socialism racy of the soil." [1]

The same writer shows how the influence of the Independent Labour Party men grew in the trade unions: "The majority of its earlier, as well as of its present members, shared the feelings and general life experience of the people among whom they had to work. . . . Their fellow unionists, instead of finding the Independent Labour men indulging in rhetoric about the rights of the workers, whenever any question of immediate trade policy was to be considered, generally found them the most useful members of the branch. Merely by reason of their fitness for the various posts, the branches found themselves continually choosing Socialists for offices, paid and unpaid, of the Trade Union world. . . . One consequence of this is curious enough. When not one in few of the Trade Unionists would have described himself as a Socialist, the Trades Union Congress, composed of delegates, elected almost entirely by Tories, Liberals, and men of no politics, startled the nation by passing a resolution in favor of the national ownership of the means of production, distribution, and exchange." [2]

And twenty-five years later, another keen-eyed observer wrote the following of "those wild men on the Clyde":

"Every year in Glasgow, the Socialist faithful gather together to preach and to pray in memory of Saint Keir Hardie. I went to this year's prayer meeting. The church was St. Andrew's, the largest public hall in Glasgow. Father and mother and the

[1] Brougham, Villiers, *The Socialist Movement in England*, 132-3.
[2] *Ibid.*, 132.

kids were there . . . up to five thousand. . . .
Chairman Rankine swung into straight gospel
preaching right soon—the gospel of Socialism. . . .
He used personal religious experience to vivify the
thing. One night, when sleeping in the open, he said
that he found himself on a sudden in the presence
and novelty of dawn. It was like something that
Socialism was doing to the world today. His words
put me in mind of the revelation of Saint John:
'The new light and the new day', he ended, on a
ringing note of ecstasy, 'are not far away'. Then
Maxton preached. He told them promptly the misery
was their own fault. They had been backsliders,
lazy and shiftless, lacking energy, lacking faith in
the religion that could serve them—Socialism. He
beat and flayed them for their Socialist sins, for
their supineness in action, their trade union laxity,
their social heresy, their little faith. And they
cheered him for these scourgings louder than for his
curse of the capitalist. They were Presbyterians,
and had the conviction of sin in their hearts. . . .
There was even more religion in George Lounsbury's
half-episcopal and half-evangelical sermon than
there was in James Maxton's. . . . 'Our movement
is the greatest religious movement the world has
ever known. Tell people the truth, I say: that capitalism is on its last legs, and ask men to join with us
in this, the only fight that matters, for the redemption of mankind'. . . . Then the choir rose and sang,
'O Beautiful My Country'." [1]

[1] Charles Rumford Walker, *Atlantic Monthly*, May 1926.

The "New Unionism" at Work and Its Balance Sheet

Having turned the labor movement toward legislation and politics, the "New Unionism" reopened the door to the intellectuals. The intellectuals of the preceding generation had been extremely useful to the "Old Unionists" as legal and political experts and as their sympathetic interpreters to the public when they were seeking for a new legal status for the unions. When that had at last been attained, and the political program became reduced to merely a few measures bearing the stamp of Gladstonian liberalism, and could be amply looked after by a few labor liberal M.P.'s, the occupation of these intellectuals in the labor movement seemed to be gone, and labor drew completely within itself. But when the "New Unionists" had succeeded in drawing labor's newly awakened aggressive energy into the channel of parliamentary social legislation and of municipal socialism (as the more easily attainable installment of socialism), the need again arose for the aid of the experts in public administration, economics, and political science. And finally the Taff Vale decision of 1901, rendering union funds liable to being levied upon for damages to employers, has forcibly recreated the situation of the sixties and seventies, when the labor leaders, thanks to the acumen of Frederic Harrison'[1] had been prevented in the nick of time from committing the fatal error of accepting legal incorporation, which would have forever kept them in the courts.

But in reality the intellectuals needed no invita-

[1] See Chapter VIII.

tion to associate themselves with labor. Moreover, they who now came swarming to labor's aid, were of a breed vastly different from Harrison and his fellow Positivists. While the latter, too, had a program which the labor movement was to have helped realize, it was only an idealistic "good citizenship" program, viz. to use its new strength and prestige coming from legal recognition "for the general welfare as well as for trade interest". The intellectuals of the new generation, on the other hand, trained as they were in the tenets of the Fabian Society and the new economics, were thoroughgoing collectivists, and esteemed it their life purpose as well as a categorical social duty to make the labor movement into a draft horse for their socialism. Compared with the old intellectuals, who were few in number and somewhat less persistent in "educating" their labor friends, since their main interest was, after all, in philosophy rather than in economics, the influence of the new intellectuals soon bade fair to become enormous. For, it must be said in all justice that hardly any other labor movement has been so well served by competent and painstaking researchers in the problems of labor, for whom no delving into the history, however ancient, of public administration, trade unionism, and consumers' co-operatives, was too tedious once it held the explanation of results valuable to labor. Furthermore, along with the "heavy" researchers, who were trusted friends-in-need to perplexed labor leaders, as well as labor's valuable and ingenious spokesmen on many a Royal Commission, a considerable body of "workers' education" teachers and organizers have been enthusiastically providing an intellectual

foundation to thousands of young workingmen, the
future leaders.

Yet, with all these extraordinary aids to the
spread of socialism, the typical trade union mentality has at bottom been affected much less than is
generally supposed. Following is a masterly description of the inner life in the British union movement at the time of the General Strike of 1926, from
the pen of a radical intellectual:

"In this land of the House of Lords, the trade
union movement is formalist, antiquated, firmly
rooted, and very strong. Its ritual and traditions
are very potent, and to extinguish an individual
union is a task almost beyond the powers of any
capitalist. In one union (the Boilermakers), it is
still obligatory for all members to address their fellows in the old fashioned way of 'worthy brothers'.
Or again, take the printing trade. The trade union
organization here is an incredibly complex matting
of powerful craft unions. Do not confuse the Printing Machine Managers' Trade Society with the
Machine Menders, or even with the Machine Rulers'
Society: distinguish these from the National Society
of Operative Printers and Assistants, and this in
turn from both the Typographical Association and
the London Society of Compositors. These, of
course, must not be confounded with the Lithographic Printers, still less with Lithographic Ar-
tists, or even with the Electrotypers' and Stereo-
typers' Society. The Association of Correctors of
the Press and the Printing and Paperworkers' Society no doubt presents no problem to the reader.
When he has mastered the exact function of these
bodies, and their membership, he may proceed to

consider the distinction between the National Union of Journalists and the Institute of Journalists, and the gulf dividing both from the Amalgamated Pressmen. These unions are not decaying relics. They are much alive and somewhat jealous. They are deeply rooted in the hearts and habits of the workers in the trade, and when all could be brought together, the power they wielded was immense."[1]

As in this strike, sympathy with the plight of labor in other trades will bring out the full membership of these numerous unions on a sympathetic General Strike. The unions as a whole will finance the Labour Party with its socialistic program and socialistic leadership, and more than half the membership will vote for its socialistic candidates. An occasional radical at the top may allow himself the leeway to "flirt" with Soviet Russia. But the heart of British unionism is still in these jealously revered organizations that stand guard over the collective economic opportunity of each group,—the jobs and the working conditions that go with the jobs.

We must now, however, return to the situation in its entirety created by the developments of the last quarter of a century between capitalism and the labor movement in Britain.

The turn of the century saw British industry, until then in the favored international position derived from its pioneering priority, being overtaken by the industries of Germany and the United States. The younger basic industries of the latter countries were now beginning to show the advantage of being unencumbered by antiquated equipment and by old

---

[1] Postgate, Raymond W., "The History of the General Strike", *Locomotive Engineers' Journal*, July 1926.

and set ideas in shop management and in commercial organization. In the United States, these basic and important industries, iron and steel, machinery construction and textiles, became organised on the principle of an utmost mechanization, with the use of semi-automatic or even automatic machinery, and with a minimum employment of skilled labor. The metal trades carried this principle to an acme of achievement through the application of another and more characteristically American cost-reducing method—the method of interchangeable parts, which had begun with Eli Whitney a century earlier and had evolved "quantity production" and a greater mass production than elsewhere. Three factors made possible the American methods: an enormous and ever growing internal market furnished by a population demanding the same standard goods from one end of the vast country to the other; an inherent lack of conservatism in a society which has erected individual advancement almost into a moral duty; and a factory working class drawn from the peasantries of Europe, to whom "union rules", "shop working rules", which in Britain were labor's conquests of a century long struggle, carried no meaning whatsoever. Britain, on the other hand, had established her industrial reputation by virtue of the solidity (which too often went with needless heaviness) of her products manufactured by a skilled working population and designed to meet the wants of her heterogeneous customers in the five Continents. This left her industrial managers with a strong predilection in favor of old and tried methods, which soon were raised almost to the dignity of national habits. Also, in her industrial relations Britain was now paying the penalty of the ruthlessness of her capitalism during and after the Industrial Revolution, which had sown in her laboring people an ineradicable distrust of their employers. In consequence of this distrust, working rules of the English unions, which they had hammered out in the struggle for decent living standards and a modicum of security and shop freedom, were clung to, regardless of their effect on output or even on ability to compete in the international market. Then, too, complicating the situation most seriously, had come a gradual depletion and partial exhaustion of the coal mines, which from the beginning have been the main prop of British industrial supremacy. And as a final aggravation came the economic consequences of the World War, causing a material shrinkage in international trade. The triumph of the nationalisms of the smaller nations had led to the erection of prohibitive, or nearly prohibitive, tariff barriers, in an effort to foster industries in heretofore agricultural communities. From the English standpoint, reparation settlements under the Treaty of Versailles, especially those involving the coal indemnity, were economically unwise. Truly, British industry and capitalism have been going through a fight for life. No longer could compensation of the laboring class and general labor standards repeat the steady climb as in the period between the fifties and the nineties. Progressive economists, like Schulze-Gävernitz would no longer go to England for the best living examples of the "economy of high wages" for the employers and governments of other nations. The "sheltered" industries, that is, industries selling to British consumers only, like the building trades, or like the railways, those in a position of natural monopolies, continued, under pressure by the unions, to hold favorable wage differentials as compared with Continental Europe. But other industries, like mining and shipbuilding, exposed to international competition, especially to the fierce post-War competition which a marked retrogression of continental labor standards and currency inflation had accentuated, gave to their labor either greatly reduced wages or less employment.

Yet it would be a clear mistake to conclude, from these conditions, that the doom of British capitalism is impending. The established order in Britain, based on property and private initiative, has come down to our own day with an overwhelming power of resistance to attack, as soon as fundamental issues affecting its further existence are at stake. British Capitalism has allowed the survival in practically all of its past glory, of vital remnants of the precapitalist aristocratic régime. The ruling classes in Britain, with an almost "scientific" rationality, have always known how to "bleed the revolution white", not by "Bloody Sundays" or by Bastille dungeons, but through implanting in her lower classes, by timely concessions, a deeply rooted constitutionalism.

The English aristocracy and gentry, totally unlike the Russian, whose weakness the Revolution had so thoroughly exposed, has been endowed with a political genius which it knows how to use both for the expansion of the Empire and for the preservation of the internal *status quo*. Much as the glamor of its economic fortunes has been tarnished by the consequences of the War, by the agricultural depression, and by crushing taxation,—there still remains, hidden away in the British upper class, a capacity for concerted and decisive group co-operation, an ability to assume an unquestioned leadership in an emergency—be it a foreign war or a General Strike, —and a quiet but indomitable determination to resist when no possible compromise is available. This vigorous survival of a pre-industrial feudal régime is one of the major pillars of the established order of things.

Modern industrial capitalism, while it has doubtless largely justified Marx's expectation of a progressive concentration of capital in manufacturing industries, culminating in the latest "vertical" and "world trusts", has not only failed to destroy the middle class, but has, on the contrary, gone on adding to it. It has done this because the constantly growing mass production in manufacturing brings about—perhaps necessitates—an ever growing number employed in goods distribution and in financial institutions of one sort or another. In manufacturing proper, progress now denotes both a replacement of labor by machinery and a multiplication of executives, sub-executives, employment managers, and the like,—in other words a new and rapidly growing industrial official class, which is becoming one of the main elements in a conservative middle class. If industrial capitalism has therefore been, with one hand, engaged in raising its own potential "gravediggers" in the shape of a wage earning class, as Marx said, it has, with the other, sufficiently counteracted that by multiplying potential defenders for itself.

The new ferment which came in with the "New Unionism" and with Keir Hardie's Independent Labour Party in the nineties, had to await the revolutionary Taff Vale court decision of 1901 before the whole labor movement showed a readiness to carry out by deeds the pivotal part of the new program,—independent political action by labor's own political party. This appeared first in the form of a "Labour Representation Committee" named by the trade unions, which J. Ramsay MacDonald, himself a religious and ethical socialist intellectual, with a background of the old rural yeomanry, carefully guided. After its dazzling initial success in the campaign of 1906, it renamed itself the British Labour Party. But under whatever name, from those early years of preparation for the début of the new party to the present, the British Labour Party has alternated with the trade unions as the bearer of the best hopes of labor. The labor movement as a whole has had periods of enthusiasm for politics, succeeding, and being succeeded in turn, by periods of aggressive economic action even bordering upon revolutionary syndicalism. This zigzagging motion of the labor movement has perhaps been unavoidable. England has an omnipotent parliament and a tradition that conservatives in power will not undo progressive legislation of the past. This has rendered advancement through political instrumentality no less secure, to say the least, than conquests by economic power and through bargaining. But, on the other hand, even a most attentive response by Parliament to the demands of labor is impotent to undo the effects of the changed position of the country's industry in the world economy. Thus, the "political" period, 1906-1910, which failed to realize the original expectations and ended in disappointment, was followed by a period, 1910-1914, marked by a prime reliance on the strike, and, in some unions, by what amounted to a breaking away of the membership from their national leaders. These leaders were now as engrossed in Labour Party politics and political work inside Parliament as the leaders of the "Old Unionism" had been in husbanding the union funds. To crown this growing disappointment in politics, industrial unionism came to the front, and a "Triple Alliance" of the three great industrial unions, the miners, railway men, and transport workers, was concluded just on the eve of the World War.

The War brought first a truce in the class struggle, both industrial and political, then Labour's entry into a coalition government. The latter did not fail to bring on and accentuate a serious labor unrest in the localities, accompanied by "unconstitutional" shop stewards' movement and by an eclipse, at least temporary, of the influence of the front bench leaders now turned cabinet members and privy councillors. Subsequently, the movement as a whole gained a fresh vital stimulation from the new and promising outlook created by the Russian Revolution and by the apparent conquest of the allied nations by the Wilsonian ideas. In 1918, the Labour Party submitted to the labor movement its first comprehensive program, a socialistic document couched in unmistakable Webbian terminology. It then proceeded to shake off the lethargy of the years immediately preceding by a reorganization which provided for local Labour Party organizations, and for the first time allowed for individual membership in addition to the indirect one as members of affiliated trade unions or of the two affiliated socialist organizations, the Independent Labour Party and the Fabian Society.

The "snap" election called by Lloyd George in December 1918 caught the Labour Party unprepared, and the victory of the "hard-faced men" shunted the labor movement onto the industrial track. After the armistice, also, the "intellectuals" reached a leading position in the movement. They sat as pro-labor members of the "public" on the Sankey Coal Commission; on the authority of the unions, they framed plans for the nationalization of the "key" industries; they conducted labor's winning publicity campaign in conjunction with the national railway strike; and they acted withal as the trusted advisers of the labor movement. However, they displayed, on the whole, a fatal underestimation of the reserve resistance power residing in capitalism. Such underestimation is an unfailing characteristic of radical intellectuals. Therefore the English intellectuals must bear at least partial responsibility for the mistakes committed, which had helped to prevent more solid labor achievements during the sunny period of the post War prosperity. Had they not helped to raise labor's hopes too high by announcing the "collapse of the capitalistic civilization", labor might then have arrived at an understanding with a capitalism which never lost its impregnable position, even at the time when labor seemed to be riding high on the prosperity wave.

With the crisis of 1920 and the ensuing depression, from which England is still to recover, came a

collapse of the high hopes from industrial action.
When the drawn-out defensive fight in 1921 in coal
mining, veritably the "Western Front" of the whole
labor movement, at last drew to an end, no one could
longer believe that capitalism was not firmly in the
saddle, and that the time had not passed for any
plans for the "nationalization" of industry. The
situation had clearly resolved itself into a struggle
for an endurable wage level and for the usual trade
union devices of job control. No change came in
the economic situation with the shortlived Mac-
Donald cabinet in 1924, while the ultimate effect on
the prospects of the Labour Party are as yet too
uncertain to warrant any judgment. Neither has the
General Strike of 1926, which was from the labor
side a strictly industrial strike in sympathy with the
hard pressed miners facing starvation wages, made
any apparent fundamental difference. From all
present indications, the whole situation is absolutely
dominated, first by the unmistakable strength of capitalism, which the General Strike has only brought
more fully into view as it has revealed the greatest
display in history of labor solidarity; and, second,
in the same degree, by the troubles of British industry in international competition. At present and as
far in the future as one can clearly discern, these
two hard facts challenge the labor movement and
set for labor its next task. This cannot be altered
by "left wing" leaders, as casual officials of the
Trades Union Congress or as spokesmen for the
ultra radical "National Minority Movement", who
proclaim revolution to be labor's task. Neither
can the intellectuals in the British Labour Party,
who would continue to rally labor to the issue

of "nationalization" of industry, do away with these two inevitable conditions. The Trades Union Congress which met in September 1927, has to all appearances brought about a liquidation of the communist "boring from within", which the British Labour Party had already accomplished two years earlier. A laboring class which, notwithstanding a shrinkage in national income, has maintained or even slightly increased its relative share, will not follow a revolutionary leadership. In the Party itself, the leadership which is emotionally wedded to intellectualist slogans, will either have to learn realism or else yield place to leaders from the trade unions, who, thanks to their more intimate contact with life, are rarely the victims of romanticism. Faced by a highly probable continuation in power of the Tories after the election of 1928, in case the anti-Tory strength should remain split, the leaders of the Labour Party will be obliged to show which of the two objectives they regard as of greater importance: gaining back for the trade unions their freedom to strike, which the Tory trades union act of 1927 took from them, or making propaganda for "nationalization" of industry.

CHAPTER V

LABOR AND CAPITALISM IN AMERICA [1]

The most distinctive characteristic of the development of the labor movement in America has not been, as in Germany, a slow but certain shedding of the philosophy originally imparted by an intellectual leadership. No intellectuals, in the true sense of the word, presided at its birth. The main feature of its development has been rather a perpetual struggle to keep the organization from going to pieces for want of inner cohesiveness. For, it has had to cope with two disruptive tendencies: First, —American labor has always been prone,—though far more in the past than now,—to identify itself in outlook, interest, and action, with the great lower middle class, the farmers, the small manufacturers and business men,—in a word, with the "producing classes" and their periodic "anti-monopoly" campaigns. Second,—and here is a tendency of a rising rather than diminishing potency,—the American employer has, in general, been able to keep his employees contented with the conditions, determined by himself, on which they individually accepted employment. Both these tendencies have seriously hindered the efforts of trade unionism towards stability and solidarity. The first tendency proved inimical because the organized wage earners would

[1] See my *History of Trade Unionism in the United States* (The Macmillan Co., 1922).

periodically be drawn into the whirlpool of politics under the banner of the "anti-monopoly" parties,— so, under the American system of party politics, invariably suffering dissension, and ultimately disintegration. The second of the tendencies mentioned has balked unionism because the employer, wielding the initiative, has been able successfully to carry his own individualistic competitive spirit into the ranks of his employees. Moreover, both factors making for disintegration go back to a common cause. For whether the labor organization has succumbed to the lure of a political reform movement aiming to shield the "small man" and the "man on the make", and has broken up in political dissension; or whether it has failed to get started because the individual laborer has accepted the incentive of a bonus wage and of a better opportunity for advancement within the framework of a non-union bargain,—the ultimate explanation, at all events, lies in the basic conditions of life in the American community—economic, political, ethnic, mental, and spiritual. Some of these are a heritage from the past, others of more recent origin, but all are closely interwoven with the present and the future of American labor.

The Basic Characteristics of the American Community

1. The Strength of the Institution of Private Property

A labor movement must, from its very nature, be an organized campaign against the rights of private property, even where it stops short of embracing a radical program seeking the elimination, gradual or abrupt, "constitutional" or violent, of the private entrepreneur. When this campaign takes the political and legislative route, it leads to the denial of the employer's right to absolute control of his productive property. It demands and secures regulatory restrictions which, under American constitutional practice, are within the province of the "police power" vested in the states and granted by specific authority to Congress; only they must, in every case, square with "public purpose", as that term is interpreted in the last analysis by the United States Supreme Court. When the same campaign follows the economic route,—the route of unionism, strikes, boycotts, and union "working rules",—the restrictions on the rights of property are usually even more thoroughgoing and far-reaching, since unions are less amenable to judicial control than are legislatures and Congress. A third form of the labor movement seeks to promote co-operative production and distribution,—neither of which is practiced appreciably in this country. This co-operative movement sets out to beat private capitalism by the methods of private business: greater efficiency and superior competitive power. To the advocates of the rights of private property, this third mode of the labor movement is the least offensive.

Because the labor movement in any form is a campaign against the absolute rights of private property, the extent to which the institution of private property is intrenched in the community in which a labor movement operates is of overwhelming importance to it. In England, the advent of industrial capitalism synchronized with an agrarian revolution which uprooted and set adrift hundreds of thousands of her peasant yeomanry to join the urban proletariat. Thus eventually the urban capitalists in the fight for their rights were denied the vital and valuable support which might have come from a land-owning peasantry. England, therefore, permitted more drastic inroads into property rights than France, where the Great Revolution created peasant proprietors on a scale far vaster even than that on which the contemporary English Enclosure movement destroyed them. The same holds for newer countries. Property rights are safer from infringement in Canada, settled by farming homesteaders, than in Australia, where, until recently, the desirable lands were owned in large holdings, by capitalistic pastoralists.

The enormous strength of private property in America, at once obvious to any observer,[1] goes back to the all-important fact that, by and large, this country was occupied and settled by laboring pioneers, creating property for themselves as they went along and holding it in small parcels. This was the way not only of agriculture but also of the mechanical trades and of the larger scale industries. Thus the harmony between the self-interest of the individual pursuing his private economic aim and the general public interest proved a real and lasting

---

[1] The utter disregard of the property rights of distillers, brewers, and others engaged in the drink traffic resulted from the intensity of the moral passion evoked—the historical heritage of puritanism. Had private property been less entrenched than it is, the property owning groups would have been more hesitant to remove even one stone of the arch.

harmony in the American colonies and states. This
Adam Smith saw in 1776, his eye on the frugal and
industrious class of masters of workshops still on
the threshold of their elevation by the industrial
revolution yet to come. Every addition to the total
of the privately held wealth was at the same time an
addition to the productive equipment in the community, which meant a fuller satisfaction of its
wants and a higher level of the general welfare.
Moreover, being held in small parcels, wealth was
generally accessible to whomever would pay the
price in industry, frugality, and ingenuity. Furthermore, this condition had not been destroyed
even with the coming in of modern "big business",
combinations, mergers, and "trusts". For, too
often does the grandeur of business on its modern
gigantic scale, the magnitude of billion dollar corporations completely hide from one's view those
other millions of small businesses. These, here and
now, may be forced to struggle hard for existence,
perhaps only to fail in the end. But failing, still
others will take their place and continue to form a
social layer firm enough to safeguard against even
a possible revolutionary explosion from below. The
earnestness with which judges will rush to stand
between legislatures and menaced property rights;
the rigor of their application of the injunction to
keep unionists and strikers from interfering with
those rights in their own way; the ease with which
a typically American middle class community may
work itself up, or be worked up, into an anti-radical
hysteria, when Soviet missionaries or syndicalist
agitators are rumored to be abroad in the land; and
the flocking to the election polls of millions to vote

for the "safe" candidate,—all are of one piece, and are to be explained by the way in which the American community originated and grew.

This social and economic conservatism, bred in the American community from the beginning, has been tested repeatedly by sections of the American labor movement,—now wittingly, now unwittingly, and invariably the test has evoked the same and identical reaction. It began in 1829, when the Workingman's Party of New York, moved by the desire to frighten employers lest they add to the recently won ten-hour day, officially endorsed the crude communistic "Equal Division" program of Thomas Skidmore.[1] A whole generation had to pass before the recollection of this brief indiscretion had faded from the public memory and ceased to plague the labor movement. Another such test of the public mind was the unplanned, but virtual anarchy of the destructive great railway strikes of 1877, from Baltimore to San Francisco. It was then that the judiciary, watching the paralysis which had seized the democratically chosen sheriffs and governors, and remembering well the Commune of Paris of 1871, resolved to insure society against a labor revolution by dint of the injunction, the outlawing of the boycott, and like measures. Nine years later, the Chicago "Anarchists", with a full-blown program of revolutionary syndicalism in all but the name itself, were made to feel the ferocious self-defense of a gigantically growing and self-

---

[1] Skidmore, a self-educated workman, published in 1829 a book entitled "The Rights of Men to Property: Being a Proposition to Make It Equal Among the Adults of the Present Generation, and to Provide for its Equal Transmission to Every Individual of Each Succeeding Generation, on Arriving at the Age of Maturity".

satisfied community against those who would import the methods of the class struggle of Russia and
of Spain. Still later, in the Pullman strike of 1894,
the labor movement saw how the courts, the Federal Executive, and the ruling forces in the country
could be counted on to act as one in crushing any
real or fancied industrial rebellion. The treatment
of the Industrial Workers of the World in the Western States, the anti-"Red" hysteria of 1919 and
1920, and the great godsend which the syndicalist
past of William Z. Foster proved to the employers
in defeating the great steel strike in 1919, which he
led,—are of too recent occurrence to necessitate
detailed discussion. The state of Kansas, a representative American farming and middle-class community, furnishes perhaps the most telling illustration of the typical American reaction to industrial
radicalism. That state, which was in 1912 a stamp-
ing ground for Roosevelt progressivism, just as it
had been the heart of the "Populism" of the nineties, showed no hesitancy, in 1919, when the coal
miners' strike had endangered the comfort of its
citizenry, at enacting a law depriving of the right
to strike, labor in public utilities and in other industries supplying food, fuel, and clothing, which the
law classed as public utilities for that purpose.

Briefly, if the century-long experience of American labor as an organized movement holds any great
lesson at all, that lesson is that under no circumstances can labor here afford to arouse the fears of
the great middle class for the safety of private
property as a basic institution. Labor needs the
support of public opinion, meaning the middle class,
both rural and urban, in order to make headway

with its program of curtailing, by legislation and by trade unionism, the abuses which attend the employer's unrestricted exercise of his property rights. But any suspicion that labor might harbor a design to do away altogether with private property, instead of merely regulating its use, immediately throws the public into an alliance with the anti-union employers. Before the Russian Revolution had intensified this fear of revolution, reform movements were probably helped by pointing out to the public that unless that and other reforms in industrial conditions were effected, a revolution might take place. But with revolution no longer a mere remote abstraction but a very lively going concern in Europe and Asia, such a threat becomes a boomerang and enthrones reaction. This is especially so because American organized labor lives in a potentially hostile environment. The American public has tolerated the labor movement, or has even aided it, as the miners were aided in their strike of 1902 against the anthracite coal combination. But a misstep can easily turn sympathy into hostility. Gompers' reiterated denunciations of communism in the disturbed years immediately following the Russian Revolution, which have been continued by his successor, seem to have been prompted at least partly [1] by the realization of the ease with which the environment of the American labor movement may be turned into a hostile environment. And this same realization that, in the American community, labor is in a minority, and is

[1] Of course the policy of the communists, and, before them, of the socialists, of trying to capture the American Federation of Labor through the tactics of "boring from within", has been the constant factor accounting for this hostility.

facing a nation of property holders, actual or potential, is at the bottom of American labor's distrust of government authority which is so puzzling
to Europeans. Experience has taught American
labor leaders that, whatever may have been the
avowed purpose when powers were extended to the
government, and whatever may have been the express assurances given to labor that such powers
would never be used against it, it is all in vain when
a crisis breaks, like a threatened strike in a vital
industry, and when the powers that be feel that
with some stretching perhaps, the law might be applied to handle the situation. It is enough to recall
that the Sherman Anti-Trust law was applied for
the first time in the Debs case arising from the
Pullman strike, and that the War-time Lever Act,
intended against food and other profiteers, was
made the basis, one year after the Armistice, of an
injunction against striking coal miners.

2. The Lack of a Class Consciousness in American Labor

The overshadowing problem of the American
labor movement has always been the problem of
staying organized. No other labor movement has
ever had to contend with the fragility so characteristic of American labor organizations. In the
main, this fragility of the organization has come
from the lack of class cohesiveness in American
labor. That American unions have appreciated the
full gravity of this problem, whether or not they
have also consciously connected it with a weak class
cohesiveness, is shown by several practices, which

they have carried to a much farther extent than unionists in other countries. It would seem as though, through these practices, they have tried to make up for the lack of a spontaneous class solidarity, upon which European unions could always reckon with certainty. These practices are ways of ruthlessly suppressing "dual" unions and "outlaw" strikes.

An "outlaw" strike is a strike by local groups, usually one or more local branches, undertaken without complying with the regular procedure prescribed in the constitution of the national union, and against the wishes of the national officers. Such strikes are invariably defeated by the national officers themselves, who, if need be, and especially if a breach of a trade agreement with the employer is also involved, will not only expel the "outlaws", but will even go to the extent of recruiting from among out-of-town members in sufficient numbers to fill the places of the strikers. In Great Britain, on the contrary, when national leaders have been thus defied by their own local branches, they have refused, to be sure, to put the strikers on the strike benefit rolls, but, on the other hand, they have never thought of visiting upon these "outlaws" anything like the reprisals employed in America. We find a similar contrast between England and America in regard to the treatment of "dual" unions. A "dual" union originates in the secession of a disaffected faction from an established union, or else it may arise as a brand new organization; in either case, it competes with the old union for membership in the same craft or industry. In America, "dual" unions are ruthlessly exterminated by the combined strength of all the unions in the American Federation of Labor. But British union leaders will view dual unionism with a complacency that seems utterly incomprehensible to American union officers. The American procedure, both in regard to outlaw strikes and dual unions, has often been decried as a bold and shameless manifestation of union "bureaucratism" and of boss-control. Much can be said in favor of this interpretation. Yet a different interpretation is equally in point. This ruthlessness, while making full allowance for the tyranny and ambition to rule by union "bosses", is at the same time a device for self-protection hit upon by labor organizations operating under conditions in which everything and everybody seem engaged in a conspiracy to undermine their solidarity within. British unions, luckily for themselves, have their internal solidarity presented "on a silver platter", as it were, by the very organization of the society in which they work. British society, with its hierarchy of classes, keeps labor together by pressure from the top. Accordingly, British workers act together in strikes, notwithstanding the rivalry between their unions. But the experience of American unionism has been that, with some few exceptions, easily explained,[1] whenever "radical" or merely impetuous local leaders defied their own union constitution with an "unauthorized" strike, or where factions have broken away to form a more "progressive" rival to the old union, the resulting fratricidal war, including mutual "scabbing", has

---

[1] The organization of the Amalgamated Clothing Workers of America in 1914, a dual union to the United Garment Workers of America, is the outstanding illustration.

always led to an all around defeat for labor, and to a total collapse of organization.

The cause of this lack of psychological cohesiveness in American labor is the absence, by and large, of a completely "settled" wage earning class. Sons of wage earners will automatically follow their fathers' occupations in the mining districts, which, because of their isolation, are little worlds in themselves. The Negroes in industry are, of course, a hereditary wage earning group. And apparently such a class has developed also in the textile centers. To be sure, the great mass of the wage earners in American industry today, unless they have come from the farm intending to return there with a part of their wages saved, will die wage earners. However, many of these do not stay in a given industry for life, but keep moving from industry to industry and from locality to locality, in search for better working conditions. Moreover, the bright son of a mechanic and factory hand, whether of native or immigrant parentage, need not despair, with the training which the public schools give him free of charge and with whatever else he may pick up, of finding his way to this or that one of the thousand and one selling "lines" which pay on the commission basis; or, if his ambition and his luck go hand in hand, of attaining to some one of the equally numerous kinds of small businesses, or, finally, of the many minor supervisory positions in the large manufacturing establishments, which are constantly on the lookout for persons in the ranks suitable for promotion. It is, therefore, a mistake to assume that, with the exhaustion of the supply of free public land, the wage earner who is above the average in ambition and ability, or at least his children, if they are equally endowed (and the children's opportunities color the parents' attitude no less than do their own), have become cooped up for good in the class of factory operatives. For today, the alternative opportunities to being a lowly factory hand are certainly more varied and entail less hardship than the old opportunity of "homesteading" in the West and "growing up with the country".

But, in a sense, the opportunity of the "West" has never ceased. In this vast country, several historical industrial stages are found existing side by side, though in demarcated areas. There is, therefore, the opportunity to migrate from older to newer and less developed sections, in which a person without much or any inherited property may still find the race for economic independence a free and open race. The difference between a section in the United States which is still underdeveloped economically and a similar one in a European country, is the difference between a navigable stream with some obstacles in its bed still waiting to be removed, and a stagnant pool without an outlet. In the former, opportunities are plentiful, multipliable by effort, and only waiting to be exploited; in the latter, the few extant opportunities are jealously monopolized by their incumbents.

If the characteristically American fluidity of economic society has preserved and created opportunities for the non-propertied individual of not much more than average ability, those with a higher ability and a gift for leadership have found their upward progression smoother still. Participation in political life in America has never been reserved to the upper classes, as until recently in England, nor to those with a higher education, as in France, but is open to all who can master the game. In the past, before the trade unions became stabilized, capable of holding both their leaders and their membership, considerable leadership material drained away from labor into politics. However, at that time industry had not yet come to appreciate the "political" talent [1] of handling men as a valuable business asset. But in the present era of "personnel management" and "industrial relations" departments, of "Welfare capitalism", and of efficiency by "inducement" and "leadership", there is room for that sort of talent, at least in the largest establishments. For the present, business men look to college trained men to fill these positions. But it is not at all precluded that what otherwise might have been union leadership talent, is being drawn into this sort of activity.

Another cause of the lack of "class-consciousness" in American labor was the free gift of the ballot which came to labor at an early date as a by-product of the Jeffersonian democratic movement. In other countries, where the labor movement started while the workingmen were still denied the franchise, there was in the last analysis no need of a theory of "surplus value" to convince them that they were a class apart and should therefore be "class conscious". There ran a line like a red

---

[1] In the bituminous coal industry, the operators began at an early date to employ ex-leaders of the miners as their "commissioners" in charge of labor relations under the agreement system with the union. These men, provided they did not practise trickery, never lost caste with the miners, any more than a member of the House of Commons does who "crosses the House".

thread between the laboring class and the other classes. Not so, where that line is only an economic one. Such a line becomes blurred by the constant process of "osmosis" between one economic class and another, by fluctuations in relative bargaining power of employer and employee with changes in the business cycle, and by other changing conditions.

Next to the abundant economic opportunities available to wage earners in this country, and to their children, immigration has been the factor most guilty of the incohesiveness of American labor. To workers employed in a given industry, a new wave of immigrants, generally of a new nationality, meant a competitive menace to be fought off and to be kept out of that industry. For, by the worker's job consciousness, the strongest animosity was felt not for the employer who had initiated or stimulated the new immigrant wave, but for the immigrants who came and took the jobs away. When immigrants of a particular nationality acquired higher standards and began rebuilding the unions which they destroyed at their coming, then a new nationality would arrive to do unto the former what these had done unto the original membership. The restriction of immigration by the quota system has at last done away with this phenomenon, which formerly used to occur and recur with an inevitable regularity.

American labor remains the most heterogeneous laboring class in existence—ethnically, linguistically, religiously, and culturally. With a working class of such a composition, to make socialism or communism the official "ism" of the movement, would mean, even if the other conditions permitted it, deliberately driving the Catholics, who are perhaps in the majority in the American Federation of Labor, out of the labor movement, since with them an irreconcilable opposition to socialism is a matter of religious principle.   Consequently the only acceptable "consciousness" for American labor as a whole is a "job consciousness", with a "limited" objective of "wage and job control"; which not at all hinders American unionism from being the most "hard hitting" unionism in any country.   Individual unions may, however, adopt whatever "consciousness" they wish.   Also the solidarity of American labor is a solidarity with a quickly diminishing potency as one passes from the craft group,— which looks upon the jobs in the craft as its common property for which it is ready to fight long and bitterly,—to the widening concentric circles of the related crafts, the industry, the American Federation of Labor, and the world labor movement.

3. The Inadequacy of the Political Instrument

The advocates of a political labor party for the United States are overlooking the fact that the political constitution of America actualizes the very "pluralist" principle which of late has become so fashionable among the younger political scientists. The American state has never been the "omnicompetent" state which these scientists abhor, because its written constitution and an ever-watchful judiciary have compelled it to treat as inviolate the autonomy of business and industry, which, though theoretically a sphere of liberty, practically are under "industrial government". The "omnicompetent" state has furthermore been prevented by a Federal system which has broken up the political sovereignty into forty-nine disjointed pieces, setting going an eternal jealousy between the largest piece, Congress, and the remaining forty-eight. Furthermore, each of the forty-nine pieces has been divided into three members, two houses of the legislature and an independent executive, all of whom must agree in order to make a law. But then it is still open to the state supreme court to annul the law, and the state cannot even appeal to the United States supreme court, although it is open to the latter to annul national laws and state laws approved by state courts. Obviously, then, American governments are inherently inadequate as instruments of economic reform. However, the American situation has at least this merit, from the point of view of labor, that it does not disguise the weakness of government, in contrast with Europe, where labor, deluded by the theoretical "omnicompetence" of the state over industry, centered on capturing that instrument, but found it wanting in actual use.

It is to this situation, more than to anything else, that the stubborn "economism" of the American Federation of Labor must be traced. For, economic action, strikes and boycotts, could never, notwithstanding court injunctions, be rendered as ineffectual as have been attempts at reform by legislation.

But not alone the inherent weakness of the state as an instrument of economic reform militates against placing reliance upon it. The prospects for success are diminished also by the now established mode of procedure for getting control of that instrument,—namely, the American political party system, so essentially different from the European. It is indeed surprising that the gild socialists should have failed to notice how exellent a type-illustration the Amerian political party is of their characteristic proposal for all industries,—a self-governing gild of all workers, high and low, with the capitalistic entrepreneur eliminated. The pertinence of this illustration in no way suffers from the fact that, in the American political industry, there are two such "gilds" competing for the contract to govern, which is awarded periodically at elections, by the voters, who are the consumers of the commodity produced by these political "gilds",—government. Each of the two political producers' gilds,—composed of "brain workers": the "bosses" or leaders; of ordinary workers: the "ward heelers"; as well as of ultra-respectable figureheads,— endeavors to guess in advance what assortment of political "goods" will please a majority of the consumers, and stocks up accordingly. Normally, there is a strong desire in each "gild" to try to hold the "patronage" of those "customers" who have extended to it preference in the past, and to cultivate their "buyers' good-will". Some of that patronage is held without an effort. Thus, with a number of "customers", the "good-will" for one or the other "producer" gild has become so absolute that it is no longer the quality of the goods that matters, but solely the label on the goods. However, so far as the other and more "choicy" patrons are concerned, the "brain workers" of each "gild" must take care not to stock up on the wrong "goods". Accordingly, when, after an election, they find that they have made a wrong guess, they not infrequently change the assortment of "goods" completely for the next election. This, however, happens much less frequently with the Republican "gild" than with its Democratic rival, because its "customers" are the "best people", the business men, to whom the rest look up as to connoisseurs in goods political. Another important wrinkle in the business of politics is that although these "gilds" are organized nationally, the managers of the local branches have practically unlimited discretion in the choice of the "goods" they wish to handle locally,—so long as their way of managing the business has a favorable effect upon the all-important national deal. It has thus come about, by an accumulation of the effects of many alignments and bargains, both old and recent, that each of the two rival "gilds" of political "producers" has developed a heterogeneous conglomerate of customers,—some of whom, by their own political prejudices, are steady and "tied" customers; whilst others, on the contrary, are "independent" customers, necessitating political managers and "bosses" with a high grade of mental agility and great shrewdness. The upshot of the whole situation is that any third concern entering into the arena, such as a "consumer"-controlled labor party set up by the labor movement, is bound to encounter the deadly competition of the expertly managed "producer"-controlled old parties. These parties have the advantage that they are capable, if need be, of a flexibility of one hundred and eighty per cent in their platforms, with extraordinary dexterity at "stealing the thunder" of the new party. As they

are out primarily to get from the voters the contract to run the government, they, like good business
men, are not rigid about consistency with their own
past professions or actions. It is to this uncanny
adaptability of the established American political
parties, meeting with the weak group consciousness
of American labor,—weakest in regard to politics
and political issues,—that the uniform failure of
American independent labor parties has been due.

To the labor movement, these realities of American politics have long been perfectly familiar. Ever
since the advent of the first labor party, the Workingmen's Party of New York in 1829, labor has
been learning through experience how slim are its
chances in competition with the old political parties.
Out of this experience there developed, as the
choice, perhaps, of the lesser of two evils, a method
of political collective bargaining between the organized labor movement and the leaders or
"bosses" of the two old parties, which consists of
trading off labor votes as payment for pledges made
by regular party politicians to carry out, if elected
to office, certain specific policies favored by labor.
Under this arrangement, organized labor is "non-
partisan", but throws its support to whichever
party comes the nearest to accepting its demands,
and "rewards its friends and punishes its enemies"
on election day. This method is, of course, most
effective when both parties are so matched that
labor holds the balance of power.

Under the system of primary elections, adopted
during the last twenty years in nearly every state,
labor has been able greatly to increase the effectiveness of its "non-partisan" political policy. Ignor-

ing now the "bosses" altogether, but making its bargains directly with individual candidates, labor is in a position to honeycomb the political parties with its own trusted men. The following hypothetical example will illustrate how labor may control an election even through a small group of loyal voters. Let us assume that in a given election district, 30,000 voters will actually cast their ballots: 14,500 Republicans (of whom 6000 are workingmen), 14,000 Democrats (of whom 8500 are workingmen), and 2000 independent labor voters. If by the candidature of an independent candidate, all the labor voters could be united, then the labor party favorite would carry by a clear majority. The unsurpassable difficulty, however, is that the majority of working men are just as staunch partisans of the old parties as the voters of the other classes are. Yet, should a labor Democrat, the choice of organized labor, run for the nomination in the Democratic primary, the 8500 Democratic labor voters who would have scorned to turn their backs upon their party to vote for an independent laborite, could be got to vote for this labor candidate, who, with the aid of the labor independents, assuming it to be an open primary, or even without their aid, would thus secure the Democratic nomination. At the regular election, then, this labor candidate would have an excellent chance to win, because he would have the 8500 labor Democrats to start with, most of the remaining 5500 non-labor Democratic voters, who would vote for him because he was the regular Democratic nominee, and the 2000 labor independents. If he got all their votes, he would win by a comfortable margin of 1000. The difference be-

tween the situations before and since the inaugura-
tion of the primary system is as follows: Under the
earlier system of a "collective bargaining" with the
political "bosses", labor, with only its 2000 loyal
voters, could have thrown the election to the less
undesirable of the two nominees of the "bosses",
but could never have dictated who should be the
nominee. Under the primary system, labor chooses
the candidate outright. Thus the "bargain" which
formerly was a two-sided "collective bargain", now
becomes a collective bargain on one side only,—
labor "bargaining" collectively, but the politicians
"bargaining" as individuals.

When a candidate so elected meets in Congress
or in the state legislature others, whether Democrats or Republicans, who like himself were nomi-
nated and elected by labor votes, and upon whom
the "yoke" of their respective party "bosses" sits
with equal lightness, the result is a non-partisan,
labor-controlled "bloc". However, in Presidential
nominations, where the convention system still rules
despite the selection of the delegates by the primary
system, the older method of "collective bargaining"
on both sides—between labor and the political
"bosses"—is still the only method.

Yet, notwithstanding the inherent limitations
of the political instrument as a tool in the hands of
labor; notwithstanding even the further difficulties
engendered by the unique American political party
system,—American labor could not afford to relinquish the political field to its enemies. Through
politics—through the non-partisan political method
—organized labor has repeatedly warded off fresh
menaces to its legal right to strike and to bargain

collectively,—notably compulsory arbitration. True, labor politics has so far failed to do away with, or even materially to mitigate, the older menace to the right to strike, the court injunction. But labor's influence, buttressed, to be sure, by the nationalistic feeling which gripped this country during and after the War, sufficed to have Congress impose a high "protective tariff" on labor power, in the legislation restricting immigration—to say nothing of the vital labor laws which have been passed by the states as well as by Congress, regarding the safety and health of wage earners and workmen's compensation, the hours of labor of women, and child labor.

The Intellectuals

Today the strongest protagonists of the idea of an American labor party are the intellectuals. The intellectuals, who, as we saw, were the prime instigators of organization in the labor movements of Germany and Russia, have been denied a similar rôle in this country. The nearest that intellectuals [1] ever came to playing a real part here was the capture by Robert Dale Owen and Frances Wright of the New York Workingmen's Party for their "state guardianship" plan for public education. This workingmen's movement of 1829, pioneer of the movement for free education at public expense, saw in that measure a means of restoring the

[1] In the earlier periods of the American labor movement, several of the outstanding "intellectuals" in close touch with it were printers who educated themselves and became editors and writers,—for instance, George Evans, Horace Greeley, Henry George, and John Swinton. In the American community, especially in the days of these men, a talented journeyman printer looked forward to just such an "intellectual" career.

original American "democracy", which, as they believed, had been sorely perverted by a usurping aristocracy. But when the intellectuals seized upon the movement, they forced upon it their own view that, to be brought up as true "republicans", children must, at an early age, be taken from their parents and placed under experts employed by the state. They apparently forgot, in their enthusiasm for a clean sweep of the irrational past, that parents, even though they might realize their inferiority to such experts, would still oppose such a flouting of their natural affections. A year later, the Workingmen's Party split apart on this issue, and finally irreconcilable dissensions undid the movement completely.

The next chapter in the history of the intellectual in the labor movement is a truly magnificent one. During the forties and early fifties, the "transcendentalism" of New England, bound up with the "efficiency" socialism of Charles Fourier, sent a group of brilliant intellectuals on a quest for an ideally and rationally organized society to be attained through a propaganda as well as through actual experimentation. Yet, splendid chapter though the quest forms in the history of American intellectual currents, it made only a slight impression on the labor movement of the time, which, owing to chronic depression, was then unstable and small, —indeed, the whole episode has left no trace in the movement of today. The only one who drank deep of the idealism of Brook Farm and at the same time stood close to the labor movement was Horace Greeley, the famous editor of the *New York Tribune*. Like the Christian Socialists in England, but not for any religious reason, he advised the organized workingmen of the forties to center on the self-governing workshop,—a Fourierite phalanstery, ultra-simplified and brought within reach of the working man.

During the seventies, we find several intellectuals as leading figures in the labor movement of the immigrants from Germany, notably F. A. Sorge, into whose keeping Marx committed the International Workingmen's Association, to keep it from falling to Bakunin and the Anarchists. At the same time, we encounter several American-born intellectuals, members of the same International but unrecognized by Marx and by the General Council in London, and whom Gompers in his autobiography makes the subject of a highly uncomplimentary description. Gompers, who had watched their thoughtless heroics in the course of the labor demonstrations held, after the panic of 1873 in New York, to demand aid for the unemployed,—heroics which ended with a riot and a number of split workingmen's heads,— never forgot what he then saw.

Henry George was the one intellectual whose influence on the labor movement, though short-lived, can be at all described in European terms. When he ran for Mayor of New York in 1886, as the candidate of the Central Labor Union, in a campaign which was watched by the whole country, he may be said to have held the labor movement of New York in the palm of his hand. But he never really understood trade unionism which to him was altogether "narrow" and a mere palliative.[1] Before long, the political movement of New York broke

[1] See below.

up in dissensions between the single-taxers and the then influential socialists, and George and the trade unions parted company for good.   The eighties, however, saw the beginning of a continuous contact between intellectuals and the labor movement, when Professor Richard T. Ely of Johns Hopkins University and his students applied themselves to a study of the labor movement.   In the eighties, also, an intellectual like the indefatigable Henry D. Lloyd began to interpret the labor movement to the reading public, in masterly "publicist" style.

At the turn of the century, we already find intellectuals interested in the workingman in considerable numbers.   They were now beginning to be manufactured in quantity by the graduate schools of the universities, by the "social settlement" houses, and by other "social service" institutions. A decade later, many of the intellectuals, ministers, writers, and others, found their way into the Socialist Party, then distinctly on the upgrade.   Also an increasing number of Americanized Jewish intellectuals in touch with the Jewish trade unions, were entering upon a general American arena from the East Side of New York.

The spectacular strike of the Lawrence, Massachusetts, textile workers in 1911, in which the leadership came from the Industrial Workers of the World, drew the interest of many of the younger intellectuals to the revolutionary labor movement. To those unfamiliar with a similar movement of the unskilled under the Knights of Labor twenty-five years earlier,—the majority of American intellectuals abhor labor history even today,—it seemed as though the long delayed revolutionary movement

of American labor had at last arrived, and that before long America would fall into line with France
and England, where syndicalism was then running
high. Measuring the American Federation of Labor
with the European yardstick, these intellectuals pronounced it reactionary, hopeless, and badly in need
of new ideas and new blood, a conviction which was
shared also by the older intellectuals, who were
neither socialists nor syndicalists but Roosevelt
Progressives. The antipathy of the intellectuals as
a whole towards the American Federation of Labor
came out definitely and decisively when a number
of them, at a representative public gathering, protested against the appointment by President Wilson
of the two labor representatives on the United
States Commission on Industrial Relations who were
recommended by the Executive Council of the American Federation of Labor, on the ground that progressive labor would thus go unrepresented on that
Commission.

With Wilson as President, the intellectuals felt
that they had at last attained a central place in
shaping the country's policy, which during former
administrations was held by the leaders of business.
This self-confidence rose especially high when the
international situation, about which the country was
ignorant, became paramount. It is enough to recall that early in 1917, when war with Germany was
imminent, the *New Republic* published an extensive
supplement with excerpts drawn from its own col-
umns for the past several years, showing how
closely the evolution of America's policy as regards
the European War paralleled the evolution of its
own policy—the country always lagging a step or

more behind in the necessarily tardy course of education.

America's entry into the War opened to many intellectuals a never-to-be-forgotten place in industry—as the "President's investigators", as members of policy-forming boards, as industrial conciliators and arbitrators, as personnel directors and advisers, and so forth; and numerous younger intellectuals filled the lower positions of the same War-time boards and institutions. Also the labor organizations now became alive to the need for the services of intellectuals who were economic and statistical experts as spokesmen before the numerous government boards with powers over labor conditions. After the Armistice, in the frequent wage arbitration cases caused by the unsettled price level, the labor movement continued to call for the services of intellectuals as experts. But the closest that the intellectuals have yet come to the labor movement, it would seem, was in the organization of the Workers' Education Bureau in 1920, subsequently taken over by the American Federation of Labor. Through the movement for workers' education, the intellectuals have attained access to the whole American labor movement, from the leaders down.

The true Marxian type of intellectual is found in the Workers' (Communist) party, and formerly was well typified by Daniel De Leon of the Socialist Labor Party. The main leaders in the Socialist Party, like the Russian Mensheviks, were revolutionists in name only, even if unbeknownst to themselves. The ethico-humanitarian type abounds in Protestant religious organizations, which frame and popularize "social reconstruction" programs, and

are doing yeoman service for social progressivism
in the midst of a country-wide reaction. The same
type is also found in the Women's Trade Union
League, and in the higher reaches of "social work".
The most "up-to-date" type is the "social efficiency" intellectual, who studies "waste" and the
"breakdown of the competitive order", and advocates the "nationalization of industry" and an approach to a "functional society".[1]

FROM "ANTI-MONOPOLY" TO A
STABLE AND JOB-CONSCIOUS TRADE UNIONISM

Historically the struggle for a program that
should express accurately labor's own point of
view, a struggle as crucial here as it was in Germany, was fought not against the supremacy of the
intellectual, which did not exist here at all, but
against the grip of the philosophy of "anti-monopoly". This philosophy, essentially the philosophy
of the "producing classes",—farmers, master workmen, and small business men,—long dominated the
labor movement and kept labor mentally tied to a
"foreign" philosophy. The causal connection between the sway of this individualistic philosophy
and the abundant economic opportunity open to the
average industrious American was noted in the first
chapter [2] as a special application of the "opportunity" theory of the psychology of economic
groups. We shall, therefore, only classify here the
several "anti-monopoly" theories current in the
labor movement from its beginning down to its

---

[1] See the classification of intellectuals given in Chapter VIII.
[2] We shall develop it further in Chapter VI.

stabilization as trade unionism, and we shall show how a stable American trade unionism came to be.

We shall begin with the land monopoly philosophies. Two "agrarian" programs, the "free homestead" program of George Henry Evans and Henry George's "single-tax", agitated the labor movement at an interval of forty years apart. They had a common diagnosis of what ailed the American body economic and in general held the same theory of therapy, only differing on the method of applying the cure. Each saw in land monopoly the source of the disappearance of the "producer's" free and abundant opportunities, and accordingly proposed to restore these by a change in the public policy towards land whereby economic individualism would again be made "safe" for the producers. But to Evans, this ideal individualistic society would be attained as soon as the government had unlocked the store of opportunity contained in its own vast land domain, by deeding inalienable homesteads limited to one hundred and sixty acres each, to all *bona fide* settlers.[1] Henry George, on the other hand, knew that the government would be obliged to meddle with land which already was held as private property. The economic crisis which hit California in the seventies, filling San Francisco with thousands of unemployed,—a crisis of whose effects he was eye-witness,—he ascribed to the fact that land speculators had been allowed to preëmpt and withhold lands in that region from use until their value had risen to a desired figure. Poverty

[1] It is noteworthy that the vastness of that domain, which to most contemporaries appeared inexhaustible, did not prevent him from specifying a "stint" of 160 acres per family.

and depression, he concluded, came when the "producer"—he did not differentiate between employer and wage earner—found the land opportunity locked away from him. The logical remedy, therefore, was to force the land speculator to reopen access to the land opportunity by putting upon him a tax equal to the economic rent of the land, whether or not the land was in actual productive use. Either program, Evans' as well as George's, contemplated that the organized producers, by going into politics, would undo the mistakes and crimes of past governments, which had permitted monopolists to rob the great majority of the people of their natural rights. The "free homestead" program gained primacy as labor's fighting program in the forties, successfully competing with producers' co-operation, Fourierism, and the other "isms", which, since the labor movement was weak and shifting, played with it almost at will. And George's single-tax, as already mentioned in connection with the intellectuals, had a meteoric career in the New York labor movement in the eighties.

The single-tax philosophy, because the socialists have fought it consistently and that on the theoretical plane,—where such clashes, since they find expression in clear-cut juxtapositions, always make an impression—has come to be regarded as the rival primarily of the socialist philosophy. When, however, the social background of American labor is taken into account, and the evolution of the American labor program, it is the philosophy of trade unionism rather than socialism that is seen to be the true opposite to the single-tax. The single-tax, starting with the premise of a natural abundance of opportunity, provides for state action to prevent monopolists from turning the abundance into scarcity by artificial means, yet rejects any interference, by the state or by the trade union, with the "producer's" relation to his opportunity, as well as with his relation to other producers. To Henry George, the trade unionists' assertion that the group must control the individual in these vital matters was extremely distasteful. He gave vent to this feeling by classing trade unionists with protectionists: "Both Trades Unionists and Protectionists have the same essential character. The Trades Unionists seek the increase of wages, the reduction of working hours, and the general improvement in the conditions of the wage earners, by organizing them into guilds or associations which shall fix the rates at which they shall sell their labor; shall deal as one body with employers in case of dispute; shall use on occasion their necessary weapon, the strike; and shall accumulate funds for such purposes and for the purpose of assisting members when on strike, or (sometimes) when out of employment. The Protectionists seek by governmental prohibitions or taxes on imports to regulate the industry and control the exchanges of each country, so, as they imagine, to diversify home industries and prevent competition of people of other countries." And although admitting that trade unions have "enabled limited bodies of working men to improve somewhat their condition and gain, as it were, breathing space", he says: "Yet it [trade unionism] takes no note of the general causes that determine the conditions of labor, and strives for the elevation of only a small part of the great body

by means that cannot help the rest. . . . To apply
the principle of trades unions to all industry, as
some dream of doing, would be to enthrall men in
a caste system. . . . Labor associations can do nothing to raise wages but by force. . . . They *must*
coerce or hold the power of coercing employers;
they *must* coerce those among their own members
disposed to straggle. . . . Those who speak of
trades unions bent on raising wages by moral
suasion alone are like those who would tell you of
tigers that live on oranges. . . . Even the most
peaceable societies (trade unions) would in their
efforts to find employment for their own members
necessarily displace others. Whereas, under the
single-tax, with the natural abundance of opportunity fully restored, "all being free to employ
themselves, the mere opportunity to labor would
cease to be a boon; and since no one could work for
another for less, all things considered, than he could
earn by working for himself, wages would necessarily rise to their full value, and the relations of
workman and employer be regulated by mutual interest and convenience".[1] While he was willing to
excuse the methods of the trade unionists on the
ground that necessity knows no law, Henry George
yet saw in trade unionism only the coercion of its
own members and of others, instead of a "scarcity
group" practicing, as the scarcity groups of by-
gone days had done, a "communism of opportunity"
and establishing "rules of occupancy and tenure of
opportunity" mandatory upon the individual.[2]

[1] Henry George, *The Labor Question, being an Abridgment of the
Condition of Labor* (pamphlet).
[2] See Chapter VI.

Henry George's philosophy never was the official philosophy of the American labor movement, except during a brief episode in the eighties, and even then mostly by the sheerest of accidents. But no other American "anti-monopoly" philosophy was so fortunate as to have for chief expounder a person with the theoretical acumen and capacity for lucid statement of Henry George. Hence it is the single-tax theory that offers the most telling comparison with trade unionism. George himself, while decidedly an "intellectual" of the highest order so far as capacity to reason on the theoretical plane went, was yet, by virtue of his personal experience and of prolonged continued contact with the life of the great American "producing class", the most representative ideologist that this class has ever had.

For an "anti-monopoly" philosophy that was truly American labor's official philosophy and which held that position over a long span of years, we must go to the "greenbackism" of the sixties and seventies. This philosophy was concerned not with the land opportunity, but with the credit opportunity. In the thirties, labor had supported Jackson in his fight against the United States Bank, and later continued to share with the West and with the master-workman class, which included the farmers, the view that the rapid accumulation of the wealth of the community in the hands of a few moneyed men was made possible by the usurious rates of interest charged by money lenders, and by denial, outright, of the credit opportunity to the honest producer, while the middleman and the speculator could command it at will. This view, that the existing banking and credit system lay at the bottom of the trouble, was given closely reasoned expression by Edward Kellogg in his book, *Labor and Other Capital,* published in 1847. Twenty years later, in 1867, Kellogg's philosophy was adopted with modifications, under the name of "greenbackism", by the National Labor Union, the national labor federation of the time.

To the money and credit reformers, the evils of contemporary society sprang from the fact that, because credit went entirely to the middleman, individual producers, or groups of producers united in co-operative workshops, were quite debarred from that all-important opportunity. Accordingly their stock remedy was to enable these producers to get abundant credit and working capital, independently of the banking "monopolist". This ideal, in the program of "greenbackism", was to be accomplished by means of the huge national debt left by the Civil War. "Greenbackism" proposed to reduce the rate of interest on the government bonds to three per cent, and to make the bonds themselves interchangeable, at the holder's option, with non-interest bearing legal tender, or "greenbacks". These greenbacks, which the bondholder received from the Treasury of the United States on depositing his bonds, he could either use in his own business, or else loan out to "producers" at a slightly higher rate than the rate on the bonds. If the market rate of interest dropped below three per cent, he could reconvert his greenbacks into bonds. Therefore, deviations from the three per cent rate, or,— to furnish the inducement for converting the bonds to begin with,—a rate slightly higher, would be no more than temporary oscillations, which would be automatically counteracted by the ebb and flow of greenbacks on the money market made possible by the feature of interchangeability. In the meantime, the individualistic ideal would have been realized— an ideal promising at once the producers' self-employment, their freedom from control either by the state or by the trade union, and a full return for their labor. Like land reform, "greenbackism" depended on political action, and produced the first national labor party in 1872. But as a quest for an individualistic economic democracy,[1] "greenback-ism" was never more than a mass wish, albeit a very disturbing one to the stability of the organization of labor. For, to trade unionism, although trade un-ionists embraced it, greenbackism proved a menace. It drew away the leaders and further tended to undermine the older movement by throwing the gates open to internal political dissensions. Fur-thermore, in essence, "greenbackism" had no place for trade unionism in its own scheme of things.

But a more constant aspiration, gripping the minds of both leaders and membership in the early American labor movement more firmly than either land reform or money and credit reform, was the equally individualistic philosophy of producers' co-operation and of the "self-governing workshop". In fact, labor embraced "greenbackism" in 1867, because, having the year before organized co-opera-tive undertakings on an ambitious scale, these soon found themselves in straits, thanks to a shortage of working capital and to inaccessibility to cheap credit. While in England the self-governing work-

[1] The Greenback-Labor Party, which polled over a million votes in 1878, was purely inflationist,

shop was the pet scheme of the "ethical" intellectuals, who introduced it to labor, in this country the idea of the co-operative workshop needed no sponsoring from the outside. To the American worker, who hankered to be rid of the capitalist "boss", a co-operative "self-bossing" seemed almost as desirable as self-employment as an independent individual—until he learned by experience how hateful co-operators may be to one another. Another attraction was the true self-governing character of this sort of undertaking and its freedom from any control outside the immediate circle of the co-operative fraternity. The strength of this natural attraction may be judged from the attitude of William H. Sylvis, the foremost leader in the sixties, who, notwithstanding that he was the efficient and systematic head of the most aggressive national trade union of the time, the Iron Molders' National Union, proclaimed that trade unionism was a mere palliative, and that labor's salvation could only come from co-operation. On the labor movement, this devotion to co-operation, which led to many experiments, had the same effect as labor's proneness at that time to rush with the other "producers" into independent politics on behalf of one or another of the above described "anti-monopoly" programs. Through either of these influences, the labor movement was long hindered from engaging in trade unionism as in anything more than a mere prosperity or "sunshine" activity. Furthermore, as the labor organizations kept constantly shifting from one of these enthusiasms to another, they remained for decades mere sieves which membership poured into only to pour out again.

Producers' co-operation was a hindrance to a stable trade unionism not only because it competed strongly for the interest, enthusiasm, and limited resources of the labor movement, which its unavoidable failures consumed in menacing proportions, but even more because the two movements were gravely incompatible. Antagonism would soon appear between the small group of co-operators and the remainder of the organized members who remained in private employment. First, the co-operative workshop, in order to get a market, would be ready from the beginning to undersell the capitalistic manufacturer, to the detriment of the labor standards in his shop. Second, in that small number of cases where the co-operative shop, by virtue of a fortunate selection of industrious and mutually congenial co-operators and of a good seller's market for its products, became a going concern, it, from these very causes, failed as a co-operative. For, when the business expanded and the working force was increased, the additions were certain to be made on the basis of hired labor. Furthermore, before long, the bulk of the stock of the association would find its way into the hands of the "smarter" co-operators. Thus, in the end, the whole labor movement had bled and toiled for the sake of the elevation to the status of capitalists of a few workingmen. Nevertheless, so well did the quest for an individualistic alternative to the wage system by the route of a "co-operative individualism" harmonize with the basic character traits of the American worker, that a crop of co-operative failures in one decade would prove futile as warning to the next, down until the middle of the eighties, when the

Knights of Labor made their experiment, the most far-reaching yet attempted. The Order of the Knights of Labor, because the lineal descendant and at the same time the most grandiose culmination of the American labor movement,—which, since its beginning in the thirties, had continued as characteristically American in outlook as the Declaration of Independence,—by their wholesale experiment and failure in the eighties permanently discredited the whole idea of producers' co-operation.[1] This failure sent the native American labor movement to school to a body of foreign-born "job" and "wage conscious" trade unionists, who had already achieved a stability for their organizations and an enduring success for their efforts, which no American labor organization—excepting a few trades in a privileged position, like the locomotive engineers, iron puddlers and rollers, and glass workers—could as yet boast. Moreover, it is more than questionable whether, if it had not been for the contribution of these foreign speaking, mostly German, groups of wage earners, the rise of a stable trade unionism might not have been delayed still further, until, at least, the turn of the century,—when the arrival of prosperity in agriculture had at last taken the ground away from under all "populistic" anti-monopoly movements.

These foreign workingmen had the advantage of being protected by their immigrant origin and upbringing from two serious dangers to the stability

[1] However, one should not overlook the parts played in the failure of the Knights of Labor by their poorly conducted strikes and by the unpsychological "one big union" principle of the organization,—both the products of the "broad" co-operative and political idealism which scorned trade unionism as opportunistic and narrow.

of their trade union organizations. Foreign to the American individualistic ideal of self-employment, they were free from the temptation to make their trade unions over into mere nurseries for co-operative shops which should fulfill that ideal. Second, their imperviousness to the call of "anti-monopoly" political movements, to which the native American labor movement usually responded so enthusiastically, kept from their organizations the risk of internal dissensions or of an infiltration of professional politicians. Moreover, it may be doubted whether even these wage earners, notwithstanding their different origin and different inherited social tradition, might have withstood any better than their native American brothers the potent sweep of the waves of "anti-monopoly" politics, had they not been fortified in advance by a philosophy of their own, which was antagonistic to the "anti-monopoly" philosophy, and which interpreted their own previous experience as a part of a European subject class with a clarity and a logic as compelling to them as was the clarity and logic of the "anti-monopoly" philosophy to the individualistic American "producer". This philosophy was the "class-conscious" philosophy of the International Workingmen's Association, which was founded by Marx in London in 1864. It was out of this class-consciousness associated with Marx, that there has grown the trade union "job and wage consciousness" of the American labor movement of today.

Before this imported socialistic class-consciousness became deep-rooted in American soil, a wage consciousness of native origin made its first appearance in the eight-hour philosophy of Ira Steward, which had its greatest vogue in the sixties. In substance, however, Stewardism was only a half-way station between the "anti-monopoly" individualism of the past and the self-confident trade unionism of the future. Stewardism shared with the "anti-monopoly" philosophy a fundamental depreciation of trade union action and a complete reliance on political action, although Steward, like George Evans of the homestead movement, twenty years earlier, did see clearly the futility of an independent labor party. He was convinced that a well-organized labor movement with a single-minded purpose to get the eight-hour day by law, could confidently use the old party politicians without being used by them instead. Second, Stewardism still saw, at the end of its shorter-hour rainbow, the old pot of gold of individualistic producers' co-operation. Where Stewardism actually anticipated the mind of modern trade unionism was in regarding as the paramount objective of the labor struggle the reform of the wage system, instead of a quick escape from it, as the "anti-monopoly" programs did. To Steward, the eight-hour day, by increasing leisure, would increase the wants of the wage earner, and by increasing his wants, lead inexorably to higher wages. "Reducing the day will increase the pay".

The socialistic class-consciousness of the immigrant labor movement was expressed in both the Lassallean and the Internationalist formulations.[1] The Internationalists were the older immigrants, not a few of them having sojourned in England on their way. Thus they were familar both with trade

[1] See the chapter on Germany.

unionism and with the pitfalls of American politics. The Lassalleans, here as in Germany, held to political action exclusively. True to their idea of the importance of trade unions as an indispensable first and long step towards an eventual struggle for socialism, the American followers of the International threw themselves into organizing trade unions in their own trades. In their own immigrant circle, especially among the Germans, they succeeded. When, however, they tried, at a national labor convention in 1876, to impress their program of class-consciousness plus trade unionism upon those remnants of the general American labor movement which had survived the depression and the preceding venture into politics, they found that that convention, as befitted a convention that carried on the established tradition, chose to succumb once more to the greater lure of "anti-monopoly" and of "greenbackism". In the following year, the Internationalists lost control even in the socialist movement, which now rushed into immediate political action. The majority of the socialists had grown impatient with a program which confined them to their trade unions until the day, which seemed remote, when these could effectually be superseded by a revolutionary political movement. Thereupon the Internationalists withdrew from all active part in the socialist movement, and devoted themselves all the more earnestly to their trade unions.

In these small but promising trade unions, the future builders of the American Federation of Labor, like Strasser and Gompers of the Cigarmakers and McGuire of the Carpenters, studied the labor question both theoretically and experimentally. They studied Marx and the other European socialists, but they were also constantly testing to see what appeals were "taking" with the working-men so that they came in as permanent members, and what appeals had only an ephemeral effect. It was in this unusual school, in which theory was mixed with direct experience, that they discovered that the union card was the only real bond that held wage earners together,—not politics, whether "greenback" or socialist. They found that a labor movement became proof against disintegration only when it was built around the job. These discoveries did not at first estrange them from socialism as a program for the future. But as time went on and they became engrossed in their "job unionism", which eschewed politics and every other quick social panacea; as they watched their organizations grow from nothing to something like the large and stable British "Amalgamated" unions, from which the International Cigar Makers' Union, reorganized by Strasser and Gompers, copied its comprehensive benefit features and centralized financial manage-ment; and as they observed with pride how their organizations, small though they still were, held together and grew steadily, in defiance of the alter-nating tides in business conditions so fatal to the labor organizations which had preceded theirs; then the original socialistic class-consciousness of these "philosophers-organizers"[1] gradually paled if not

---

[1] Gompers, in his autobiography, relates that this group, to which he himself belonged, was then known as the "Ten Philosophers." He describes their study circle in a cigar-making shop, where one of their number, usually himself, thanks to a good voice, would read aloud from Marx and others, while the others worked and listened. His loss in earnings was made up by the group.

shriveled, and in its place flourished a robust trade
unionist "job and wage consciousness".

It was indeed a new species of trade unionism
that was thus evolved. It differed from the trade
unionism that the native American labor movement
had evolved earlier, in that it grasped the idea,
supremely correct for American conditions, that the
economic front was the only front on which the labor
army could stay united. From this it followed that
when a business depression or a powerful combination of employers made the chances for advance on
that front unlikely for the time being, the correct
strategy was not, as the unions before them had
done, to shift the main strength to the political
front, because that front seemed weakly held by the
enemy. On the contrary, this unionism reasoned
that, during depression, labor's strategy should be
thoroughly to dig in on the same economic front,
awaiting the next opportunity, which was certain to
come, for advancing further; in the meantime using
every device, like benefit features, to keep the membership from dropping out. For the American labor
movement, which, during the first half century of its
existence, had been doing exactly the opposite, that
is, abandoning trade unionism for the lure and ex-
citement of "anti-monopoly" politics, this discovery
was as pivotal a discovery as that by the Rochdale
pioneers was for the world co-operative movement.
But this discovery, it should not be forgotten, could
neither have been hit upon nor later exalted into the
cardinal principle of the American labor movement,
if the class-consciousness of these "philosopher-
organizers" had not, from the beginning, rendered
them immune against being swept off their feet by

the "producer consciousness" of the individualistic
panaceas of the native American labor movement,
and thus kept them at their "study-experiment" in
their own trade unions.   In this circuitous way,
therefore, the class-conscious International of Marx
was the cause of the least class-conscious labor
movement in the world today.

In the evolution of the psychology of the American wage earner, the fruition of this "job and wage
conscious" unionism and its eventual mastery of
the whole field [1] meant a final and complete rupture
with the old "producing classes" point of view,
which saw the road to economic democracy in a
restoration to the individual, or to intimately associated groups of individuals, of access to economic
opportunity in land, marketing, and credit; this
opportunity once restored, competition alone would
suffice to preserve it all around. This philosophy,
as already noted, had issued from the typically
American premise of an existing abundance of opportunity for every industrious person,—an abundance, however, which conspiring monopolists have
artificially converted into scarcity. The predominance of the "anti-monopoly" point of view in the
American labor movement down to this time actually denoted a mental subordination of the wage
earner to the farmer, a labor movement in the grip
of a rural ideology. In contrast, the ideology of the
American Federation of Labor was both an urban

---

[1] This happened after a victory over the Knights of Labor. The
Knights, following a sudden swelling in membership in the middle
of the eighties, due to their becoming accidentally the beneficiary of
an elemental mass movement of the unskilled, threatened for a time
to engulf the trade unions, but by 1888 had fallen apart largely of
their own weight.

and a wage earner's ideology. It was based on a consciousness of limited job opportunities,—a situation which required that the individual, both in his own interest and in that of a group to which he immediately belonged, should not be permitted to occupy any job opportunity except on the condition of observing the "common rule" laid down by his union. The safest way to assure this group control over opportunity, though also a way so ideal that only a union as favored as the printers'[1] was able to actualize it entirely,—was for the union, without displacing the employer as the owner of his business and risk taker, to become the virtual owner and administrator of the jobs. Where such an outright "ownership" of the jobs was impossible, the union would seek, by collective bargaining with the employers, to establish "rights" in the jobs, both for the individual and for the whole group, by incorporating, in the trade agreement, regulations applying to overtime, to the "equal turn", to priority and seniority in employment, to apprenticeship, to the introduction and utilization of machinery, and so forth. Thus the industrial democracy envisaged by this unionism descended from Marxism was not a democracy of individualistic producers exchanging products under free competition, with the monopolist banished, but a highly integrated democracy of unionized workers and of associated employer-managers, jointly conducting an industrial government with "laws" mandatory upon the individual.

How far the unionism of the American Federation of Labor had traveled from the "anti-monopoly"

[1] See Chapter VII.

philosophy of the old American labor movement
was clearly revealed in its attitude on the "trust"
question. Early in the present century, while almost
the whole nation was insisting that the government
should break up the trusts, or at least regulate them
with most stringent legislation, many going so far
as to demand price fixing by government, the American Federation of Labor declared unequivocally
that the "trusts" were an inevitable economic development before which the law was completely
helpless, but the power of which could be controlled
by another economic power, the organized trade
union movement. Is it, therefore, a mere coin-
cidence that the German trade unions,[1] thirty years
later, facing the "trustified" Germany of today,
should equally have despaired of the poltical state as
an instrument for curbing the "trusts", and should,
like the American unionists in the late nineties, have
seen that the main road to industrial democracy
lies within the economic sphere?

Stable Unionism at Work

The American Federation of Labor entered upon
a triumphant possession of the field of organized
labor about 1890, with the virtual disappearance of
its rival, the Knights of Labor. It survived in the
struggle with the Knights because it was the product of continuous experimentation ever since the
early seventies, when Gompers' "Ten Philosophers" first developed their "theory-practice"
method of self-instruction. This experimentation
by the trade unions went on through alternating

[1] See Chapter IX.

periods of depression and prosperity,—avoiding the most serious political excitements, like the "Populist" in the early nineties; but going through with the mistaken attempt to copy the British Trades Union Congress in their first federation, the Federation of Organized Trades and Labor Unions of the United States and Canada, 1881-1886. And all the while the trade union organizations were being hammered into shape in the struggles with employers, and especially in the life and death struggle with the Knights of Labor. The resultant unionism had therefore the merit that it "fitted" both the external environment and the American workman's psychology. For otherwise, beset on all sides, without and within the labor movement, it could neither have survived, nor attained a stability thitherto unknown in American labor history. The unionism of the American Federation of Labor "fitted", first, because it recognized the virtually inalterable conservatism of the American community as regards private property and private initiative in economic life. It, too, accordingly arrayed itself on the same side, demanding only that the employers should concede the union's right to control the jobs through "recognition" embodied in the trade agreement; and in this attitude it remained unperturbed in the face of all the charges by socialist intellectuals of treason to labor or even of corruption.

This unionism "fitted", secondly, because it grasped the definite limitations of the political instrument under the American Constitution and under American conditions of political life. It therefore used the political weapon only sparingly and with great circumspection. It went into politics primarily to gain freedom from adverse interference by judicial authority in its economic struggles;—it did not wish to repeat former experiences when trade unions standing sponsor for a labor party found themselves dragged down to the ground by internecine political strife. The American Federation of Labor made itself felt politically by exercising pressure on the old parties; but it kept politics at arm's length from its own cherished trade union organization. It must be acknowledged, however, that the American movement, led by leaders risen from the ranks, could withstand the political temptation with so much greater ease than the European movements, because it saw little to choose between an autocratic capitalist management of industry and a bureaucratic one by "experts" appointed by the state.

Thirdly, the unionism of the Federation was a fit unionism to survive because it was under no delusion as to the true psychology of the workingman in general and of the American workingman in particular. It knew that producers' co-operation was a beautiful but a really harmful dream, since it only caused labor to fritter away its spiritual and material resources by shouldering itself with an impossible task of winning in the unequal competition between the capitalist-managed business undertakings, which marched like an army, and co-operatively managed ones, which were governed more by debating clubs.

This unionism was also without illusions with regard to the actual extent of labor solidarity. It knew that where wage earners were held together by the feeling that their jobs came out of a common job reservoir, as did those in the same or in closely related crafts, their fighting solidarity left nothing to be desired; provided that their unity was safe-guarded by vigilantly uprooting "dual" unions as so many noxious weeds and by enforcing a military discipline against "outlaw" actions within the union itself. The leaders of this unionism also knew, however, that they had to go slow in pressing on to greater solidarity. Where conditions made co-operation between different craft groups urgent, it was best obtained through free co-operation in "departments" of unions in the same industry,— each union reserving the right to decide for itself in every situation whether to co-operate or not. Thus, as with allied sovereign states, solidarity in action remained dependent on the sense of honor of each ally instead of on compulsion.

For that matter, the very constitution of the Federation bears testimony to the appreciation by the makers of the American Federation of Labor of the narrow natural boundaries of the solidarity of American labor. The rights granted to the Federa-tion by the international trade unions bestow no authority over strikes, but make it the most exalted tribune in the American labor world—a power, and an effective one, too—in nothing so much as in the molding of labor opinion. Yet with all that limita-tion, the Federation is practically of the greatest use to the international unions, since it protects them against the menace from "dual" unions. This it does through its power of decreeing excommun-ication, whereby city and state federations of labor are prevented, on penalty of losing their charters, from befriending such "dual" unions. It is this function of the Federation, a function largely "invisible" to the outside world, which has built up the American labor movement. So long as the Federation is succeeding in discharging this "invisible" function, its failures in carrying out its more "visible" functions,—lobbying for favorable legislation and related activities,—are overlooked within the labor movement.

It is just because the Federation has looked upon itself largely as labor's "department of the interior" that it has realized it could not afford to endanger the hard-won yet easily destroyed unity among the different crafts under the common Federation roof by disturbing the minds and unchaining strife with an authoritative *ex-cathedra* pronouncement, as the socialists would see it do, in favor of industrial unionism. No one can deny that unionism by industry has decided merits over craft unionism, or, to be precise, over amalgamated crafts unionism, which is the actual type of American unions; although all in all, this superiority may not be so overwhelming as many think. So that were the American labor movement to start anew under modern conditions of advanced technology and industrial concentration, unionism by industry would doubtless be the structural form. Such, however, is not the situation which the Federation faces. For, should the Federation—even if merely by way of recommendation,—once let go of the principle of craft unionism, it would thereby endanger the all-important "regularity" principle, upon which the internal order of the Federation depends. This would result, because, by such a pronouncement the

Federation would destroy the certainty that it would bring to bear its power of excommunication against "industrialist" secessionists from "regular" unions. On the contrary, a minority faction which favored industrial unionism might then claim the moral authority of the Federation for seceding for the purpose of joining with other unions or factions thereof in an industrial union. The result could only be a repetition of the chaos of the time of the Knights of Labor, when, in dozens of trades, "dual" labor organizations, trade unions and assemblies of the Knights, were forever engaged in war upon one another, a war from which only the employers benefited. Or, what is also likely to happen, the Federation, in response to the demand by the conservative officers and majorities of the several unions to protect them against the new "dual" unions thus arisen, would be forced to treat as "outlaws" in the labor world the very groups which, as we are supposing, had taken it at its word and proceeded to "industrialize" themselves.

The proof of the "fitness" of this unionism which came in with the American Federation of Labor lay in its stability—in the relative constancy of its membership.[1] This was due not so much to benefit features, since not many American unions copied the British model so faithfully as the cigarmakers did, as to an unrelenting campaign to control the available jobs through a multiplicity of union rules. But,

---

[1] The loss in membership from nearly four millions in 1920 to below three millions at the present time, does not contradict this statement of the situation. The growth during the War had been an "unnatural" growth, having resulted from a letting down of the bars to unionism in government-controlled (for the duration of the War) industries, notably on the railways.

behind this stability in membership, was the mental stability of the leaders, who stuck to a fighting unionism and to a program of job control. These leaders neither yielded to the temptation of taking the apparently easier path, the path of politics or of producers' co-operation; nor did they permit defeats to divert them into dangerous revolutionary paths. But neither must one overlook the stabilizing influence of the "trade agreement" of which the glass workers and the molders were the pioneers in the eighties and nineties, and which the bituminous miners made known by their spectacular victory in 1897. Even though, in the vitally important metal trades, the trade agreement system broke down, it has always remained the goal of all stable American unions, including the "socialistic" unions. The trade agreement has been supremely important as a stabilizer, since, by "pegging down", as it did, the many and increasingly numerous union rules for job control, by means of the employers' written undertaking to observe them, it simultaneously "pegged down" the membership of the union.

This "stable unionism", from the nineties to the present, has undergone many vicissitudes: alternating prosperity and depression; employers' belligerency in many industries and conciliatoriness in others; the heaping up of legal disabilities by court decisions, and the "removal" of these disabilities by legislation under friendly administrations. This unionism entered upon a new day in the emergency of the World War period, when it phenomenally expanded in thitherto barred industries,—the membership skyrocketing up to 4,000,000. Then followed an "open shop" and wage deflation campaign of equally unheard of intensity, in which most of the wartime gains were lost. Nevertheless, unionism has emerged as a permanent national force, though no more than a minority interest in the American community. As a minority interest, viewed askance by the majority, unionism has been under the necessity, if its influence and numbers were not to diminish but to grow, of exercising constant care lest by radical action on its part, the middle class public should be thrown into an alliance with the reactionaries. For this necessary caution, unionism has been attacked as passionately from the "left", as the "open shop" employers and conservative interests have, for the opposite reason, assailed it from the "right".

FROM A "DEMAND AND SUPPLY" CAPITALISM TO "WELFARE CAPITALISM"

But to say that the American labor movement has achieved in the American Federation of Labor an adaptation to American conditions and therefore a "fitness" possessed neither by the older movements with their "anti-monopoly" philosophy and essentially political methodology nor by the "left wing" movements which would revolutionize it or displace it today, is far from saying that the field belongs to the American Federation of Labor. "Fitness", in a given social environment, like "fitness to survive" in a given biological environment, is never the attribute of one single species, but different and directly competitive species are always found disputing its possession, each with a chance for success. The outcome of such a struggle in a social environment, then, is seldom completely one-sided, nor does it remain fixed for good; it is affected by temporary variations in conditions, variations which are quite consistent even with a practically constant basic social order. These variations in conditions may favor first one, then another struggling species, yet each demonstrates its essential "fitness" in that, despite the changing fortunes of war, it is never driven from the field completely.[1] The same is true of the stable unionism of the Federation and of its enemy, anti-union capitalism. Each is characterized by fitness in the same general environment: unionism, because of its discovery of a program of job solidarism least repugnant to deeply rooted American individualism; and anti-union capitalism, because that same individualism plays into its hands most directly.

But so long as anti-union capitalism depended only on force and paid a "supply and demand" wage, the danger to unionism, while often grave, was rarely critical. The manifold means by which old-fashioned capitalism sought to frustrate unionism, among which court injunctions, "yellow dog" contracts, and damage suits were not the worst, were, at least, not augmented by labor's own willingness,—unless it was immigrant labor, before it had risen to higher wants,—to align itself with the employer and against the union organizer. Thus unionism became uprooted in the steel industry only after labor had been beaten into submission; just as it has been kept out of the ever-expanding ma-

---

[1] Furthermore, in the same economic and political society, unionism will find different conditions determining survival and success in different industries with different marketing and technological situations.

chinery-producing industries by the maintenance of an army of well paid spies and strike breakers and by the same tactics of force, if less spectacularly employed, by which it is being kept out of the coal fields of West Virginia. But alongside the methods of force, there has been developing a method of inducement, in the long run by far the stronger of the two, whereby the employer had been able to "sell" his own psychology of competitive individualism to his employees. This program of "welfare capitalism" is the new labor program of American capitalism. It began thirty years ago, when the first "scientific managers" hit upon a new wage policy of bonuses and premiums, in their search for means which would lull the worker's instinctive distrust of the new methods of doing his job, which these "scientific managers" discovered through "time and motion study". They faced the problem of converting the workingman away from his belief that his opportunities are scarce to the optimistic belief that each man makes his own opportunity, that jobs cannot be "used up" by too great an output per unit of time; and that unionism is detrimental to the worker's interests as well as to his employer's. This "scientific management", in due time, broadened into a new applied science, the science of personnel management, which directs the labor policy of the triumphant "welfare capitalism" of today. In the last decade more and more employers and more and more industries have become converted to the new labor policy. One motive was to avert the demonstrated waste: of material, of the time of the supervisory personnel, and of the worker's own time resulting from a high turnover among employees. Another motive was to head off a much feared expansion of unionism, which had doubled its membership during 1917-1920. Furthermore, the rise in the wages of common labor, due to restricted immigration, has put a premium upon new ideas for getting the greatest efficiency out of each employee. Whatever the consequence to the individual workingman, the consequences to unionism have proved most serious. Unionism knew how to handle situations under the "old" capitalism. But this "new" capitalism which fights unionism with a far-sighted "preventive" method rather than with the old "remedial" one of breaking up the union by discharging agitators and imposing the "yellow dog" contract, leaves it stunned and bewildered.

The chief strength of "welfare capitalism" is that its labor policy takes, towards his problems, the worker's point of view. "Welfare capitalism" appears voluntarily to offer to the worker a "fair wage", a reasonable working day, and the security from unemployment, from injury to health, and from unjust discrimination, which unionism has always endeavored to obtain for him through its "job control". Thus the employer substitutes direct guarantees for those indirectly secured by the union's restrictive working rules. Applied all along the line, this policy of "substitution" assures the workingman the eight-hour day; more or less accurately determined wage rates safe from arbitrary cuts; profit sharing and stock distribution on favorable terms; hygienic and pleasant shop surroundings; a greater regularity of employment by means of a long distance planning of production; freedom from arbitrary discharge as a result of taking the power of hiring and firing and disciplining out of the hands of the foreman and entrusting it to special industrial relations departments; and finally, "group insurance", including life and disability insurance and an old age pension. This general policy of substitution is crowned by the "instrumental substitution" of the "company union" for historically evolved unionism, carrying out unreservedly the fundamental idea of "welfare capitalism" that the only solidarity natural in industry is the solidarity which unites all those in the same business establishment, whether employer or employed.

The wide application of the methods of "welfare capitalism", in which America leads, has coincided with a growth in industrial efficiency which is more than reminiscent of the original Industrial Revolution. The new Industrial Revolution, out of the abundance it has created, appears to have reconciled, at least for the time being, the conflicting interests of profits and wages. Moreover, with commodity prices in the last half decade at a relatively steady level, and with business conditions stable, a condition attributed by many to the policies of the Federal Reserve Board and hence promising permanence, the strongest inherent weakness in the new program of inter-class harmony has, up to the present, failed to show itself. This weakness is, of course, the complete exposure of the labor group, when limited strictly to the one establishment, to an attack upon its standards by an employer driven to that step by severe competition or by the stress of business depression.

Consequently, the latest period in American labor

history, beginning with the recovery of business
from the depression of 1921, has been wholly unique.
In the past, it was during periods of depression that
the trade union movement went through its hard
times, suffering loss of membership and strength,
since then the employer could use the upper hand
that unemployment gave him to repudiate standards
and to break up the unions; but, on the return of
prosperity, unionism invariably recuperated and expanded anew. Today, the American Federation of
Labor is failing to find prosperity favorable to
growth. This has been due, first of all, to a rapid
rise in real wages of about 26 per cent between
1913 and 1926—an unprecedented state of affairs.
Twenty years ago, when the cost of living was rising, amidst the industrial distress following upon the
financial panic of 1907, the divergence between the
agricultural cycle and the industrial cycle seemed
largely to render futile any efforts by the trade unions to obtain increased wages. Yet, on the whole,
it all redounded to the advantage of unionism.
With the barking dog of the rising cost of living
steadily at his feet, the wage earner could not afford
to be anything but profoundly wage conscious and
an attentive listener to the gospel of unionism,
especially when satisfactory business conditions dis-
pelled his fear of being thrown out of his job for
joining a union. That situation has, in the last half
dozen years, been completely reversed. Because of
the prolonged agricultural depression, retail food
prices have stayed on a low level, at about 60 per
cent above the 1913 base, while wages, after a
temporary partial deflation during 1920-1921, have,
on the whole returned to the high War-time level.

They were, in 1926, better than double the wages of 1913. Thus the spur to join a union in order to keep wages from lagging behind the cost of living, though an unfailing urge in previous prosperity periods,—has vanished in the present period.

The high American wages of today are principally the outcome of objective conditions: of the failure of the agricultural cycle to synchronize with the industrial one, and of the drastic restriction of immigration. They are not the result of deliberate policy on the part of the employers, as many of them, flattered out of their sense of reality by the compliments of investigating committees from abroad, state with a sincerity which one need not doubt. Although, once these high wages came to be, they entered into so reciprocal a connection with the use of the newer efficiency methods,—in which the initiative, of course, was the employers',—that it has become impossible to ascertain which has been cause and which effect.

The other novel and decisive factor now impeding the progress of unionism certainly has been the deliberate work of the employers. This factor is not employees' representation, since the average employee is admittedly indifferent to it. Nor is it the sale to employees of the stock of the company on advantageous terms, as that affects in a telling way only a few employees, primarily "key" employees. Nor is it even "group insurance", although its protection is extended to all employees. It is the new methods of job administration, which centralize hiring and firing in a special department, doing away largely with the exasperating tyranny of the petty boss; and which aim, by word and by deed, to convince the employees that management now is no more concerned for the regularity of the stockholders' dividends than for the regularity of the employees' jobs. It is through this new "job policy", together with the high wages, that Ameriman "welfare capitalism" is fulfilling its dearest wish: the dwindling in American labor, of a scarcity consciousness and of the feeling of solidarity that follows from such a consciousness.

Thus the American labor movement which succeeded only after many decades in replacing the individualism of the persistent "anti-monopoly" point of view with a consciousness of permanent job solidarity, now sees the employer triumphantly drawing the ranks of labor into individualistic competition for jobs and advancement,—an individualism which the "collective" principle of the company union mitigates as little as it detracts from the employer's real superiority of authority. Placed on the defensive, American unions are badly in need of an ingenious counter-move to "welfare capitalism". And the American labor movement, which thought its problem of existence and stabilization solved when it had outgrown both "anti-monopoly" and socialism, is once more troubled about the future, as it strives to regain its past "fitness", a "fitness" which availed not merely for holding its own but for growth and expansion also. Once more, therefore, as in the seventies, fundamental experimentation is the order of the day.

In a nutshell, the problem of American unionism today is, first, how to dispel the hostility of the employer, especially in the typically American industries which engage in quantity production and employ, predominantly, unskilled labor. In such industries, the employer has chiefly come to associate unionism with rules that hamper output, prevent promotion on merit, raise costs of production, and bring on strikes, in which, as in the strikes caused by inter-union jurisdictional disputes, he is often the innocent third party; rules, also which force upon industry an uneconomical wage scale. Secondly, American unionism faces the problem of winning back the public support which it has lost. The material rise in real wages and the disappearance of the more glaring abuses has robbed the labor movement of grounds for telling appeal to public sympathy. But public sympathy has been slipping from organized labor much more on account of the aggressiveness of many union groups. First came the threat of a general strike for the eight-hour day made by the railway brotherhoods in 1916,—an act which forced the passage of the Adamson law. Then the building trade unions took advantage of the post-War building boom to raise wages to a height which, to a harassed middle-class public, seemed shocking indeed. Coupled with the traditional American prejudice in favor of unrestricted private initiative, these acts of union aggression, as the public regarded them, furnished anti-union employers with an excellent opportunity to turn the public against organized labor. In the past, public sympathy for labor sprang in part from an uneasiness felt at the rise of the power of corporate wealth, for which unionism was seen as an antidote, as well as a much lesser evil in itself. In post-War America, however, the fear of big business and of "trusts" has evidently become allayed. And much the same public which, in 1912, was enraptured by Wilson's "New Freedom", went *en masse* to vote for Coolidge, to ward off the menace of La Follette who would divest the United States Supreme Court of the power to protect private property against radical legislators. Consequently, before American unionism can make any new progress, and especially before it can invade the industries from which it has been barred, it must commend itself as a constructive force. It must learn how to disarm public suspicion. It must also learn how to gain all the support possible in the camp of the industrial managerial group,—even if only to the point where they would be willing to give it a hearing and half a chance to prove itself a worth while partner in industry.

The opportunity for unionism to produce a change of attitude among the employing group is vitally affected by the shifting of power within that group itself. Ownership and management are becoming more and more divorced. The wide distribution of the stock of the giant corporations of today has created what has been aptly termed a "stock holding proletariat". When such a corporation is first formed, usually by purchase of several going business units and a consolidation of their plants and organizations, involving enormous original flotations of securities, control gets lodged in the hands of investment-bankers, who appoint the board of directors and determine the selection of the head managers. This is "banker control" of industry, which, in labor and radical circles, is held to be highly detrimental to the cause of unionism, although it is questionable whether bankers as bankers have a stronger prejudice against unionism than have other big business men, or whether they will act upon that prejudice more consistently.

But the evil of banker control as absentee control by the financier, himself divorced from actual management but dictating absolutely to management on the ground, has been greatly exaggerated. When the new corporation has proved a success, especially when it has been able to provide the capital necessary for expansion out of its earnings, or where its credit rating is so exceptional that it can sell stock directly to the public, or "over the counter", as it were, banker control is naturally at an end. Power then solidifies in the hands of professional managers, themselves with little or no stake in the business as investors, but with a momentous stake of a different order—the stake of their reputations as successful business managers. These professional managers, so long as the stockholders receive their dividends, usually enjoy an unhampered discretion in arriving at decisions, together with an assured tenure of office. They form, in other words, a business aristocracy not unlike the feudal aristocracy of old. It is very questionable whether this aristocracy of managerial executives is by nature any less intolerant of the unionist *demos,* with its "common rules" and restrictions, than is an aristocracy of absentee bankers. On the contrary, the immediacy of its contact with unionism, compared with the remoteness of the bankers', would appear to make it even more impatient with union restraints upon the employer's freedom. Yet such has been the course of American business that it is to the satisfaction of this managerial aristocracy that unionism must demonstrate its capacity to transform methods developed in a prolonged struggle to wrest job control from a greedy and exploitative capitalism, into an efficiency technique of union-management co-operation, superior even to that of the "company union". And, to add to its difficulties, unionism must perform this *volte-face* in the matter of efficiency while safeguarding the workers' ability to wage a fight against the employers if driven to it. The "new wage policy", solemnly adopted at the convention of the American Federation of Labor in 1925, promised exactly this *volte-face*. While enlarging labor's claim upon industry from a "fair" wage to a share in the proceeds of its progressive efficiency, labor pledged itself, by implication, to an unstinted co-operation towards bringing that efficiency about. In making this pledge, the Federation did no more than approve for general adoption the justly famous Baltimore and Ohio plan of union-management co-operation which, in the four years of its operation, and applying to the shop crafts on that railroad,—permitted to continue as integral parts of their respective national unions, acting through their national officers,—has proved to work far better than a company union plan. The same anxiety to pass muster before the managerial group is shown, lastly, in the renewed efforts to settle old and troublesome jurisdictional disputes in the building industry, and in the readiness displayed by several unions in that industry to join the organized employers in a constructive disposal of the apprenticeship question.

Finally, whether or not unionism will eventually, by modifying its own methods, succeed in outflank-

ing the new strategy of capitalism, there can be no
doubt as to the seriousness, for its future, of the
recent metamorphosis of the "supply and demand"
species into "welfare capitalism".

"Left Wing" Unionism

As shown above, the unionism of the American
Federation of Labor was born of a "left wing"
movement, the American branch of the International
Workingmen's Association, which gradually turned
from socialism to a wage conscious and non-socialist
unionism, eventually so hardy that it survived even
depressions,—mainly because it knew how to resist
the lure of politics. For a time this unionism and
the older socialism dwelt peacefully side by side.
Being much closer to the trade unions than to the
Knights of Labor, the socialists watched with complacency the outcome of the struggle between the
Federation and the Knights. But in the nineties
there came into existence a permanent and energetic
"left wing", directed against the Gompers leadership. For, by that time, the Federation had, by its
stubborn refusal to be seduced to socialism and a
labor party, made it plain that, despite an intellectual kinship and a common ancestry, socialism
and trade unionism had already grown poles apart.
Thus, from the nineties on, the American Federation of Labor has had to reckon with a hostile radical group, both within and without its own organization. This radical group, was, far from united,
divided between pure "industrial revolutionists"
and "political revolutionists", as also between
"dualists" and "borers from within".

The political revolutionists were the first to attack. In the middle of the nineties, the Socialist Labor Party, under Daniel De Leon, upon its failure to capture the leadership of the Federation, formed a dual federation under the name of the Socialist Trade and Labor Alliance. But an independent socialist group in the Middle West, under V. L. Berger of Milwaukee and E. V. Debs, who had espoused socialism during his recent imprisonment for contempt of court as leader in the Pullman strike, condemned "dualism" and cherished strong hopes of converting the existing trade unions by working from within. In 1900, this group combined with a faction of De Leon's party, then in revolt against the futile tactics of dualism; and the Socialist Party of North America was born. From 1901, the year of its official birth, for a period of eighteen years, the opposition to Gompersism centered in the Socialist Party. This Party, led by intellectuals as much as De Leon's party, worked through its members in the trade union organizations for the displacement of Gompers and his associates from leadership, for a declaration by the several international trade unions and by the Federation as a whole in favor of political action through "labor's class party" (meaning the Socialist Party), and for a unionism organized by industry instead of by craft. The star of the Socialist Party shone brightest during 1910-1912: its membership then exceeded 125,000; its men controlled the unions of the miners and of the machinists; and it had carried the municipal elections in Milwaukee, Schenectady, Berkeley, and elsewhere. At that time, the Socialist Party was in a fair way of becoming the Mecca of the

younger middle class progressives. But, all too
soon, this ascendancy was broken down by a sequence of circumstances arising partly within the
Party, and partly outside. In 1912, the Party
adopted an anti-sabotage resolution, and soon thereafter, in a recall election, removed William D. Hay-
wood, the leader of the Industrial Workers of the
World, from its Executive Committee, thereby creating its own opposition left wing. Coincidently,
the Party was weakened in numbers by the migra-
tion to Woodrow Wilson of many of its less radical
intellectual members, who had been brought to join
the Socialist Party only by their despair of infusing
principle into the other parties. Then came America's entry into the War, on which the Party took
a radical stand, but only a verbal one; except a few,
who braved prison. By taking this stand, the Party
literally fell between two stools. It drove away the
remainder of the younger native American intellectuals who favored the War, but failed to satisfy
the left wing, which had now become mostly composed of foreign-speaking socialists from the East
of Europe, whose revolutionary hopes were naturally raised to the skies by the Russian Revolution.
After this, the eclipse of the Socialist Party was
virtually complete. In 1919, the left wing split off,[1]
taking with it three-fourths of the membership, who
went to form two illegal Communist parties, later
to emerge from underground as the Workers' (Communist) party. These losses, which threw the Socialist Party, in membership and in political
strength, back to where it had been more than a

---

[1] Formally this secession was an expulsion of the left wing by the
National Executive Committee of the Party.

dozen years earlier, and which totally destroyed its prospects of becoming the recognized party of American labor, caused it to go still further than during its years of prosperity, in placating the trade unions, in an effort to retain a last foothold. Thus, the socialists ceased altogether to criticize the union leaders, and eagerly participated in any and every tentative political labor grouping, provided their sworn enemies, the communists, were not permitted to take part. By these means the socialists hoped to become to the future American labor party, of whose ultimate advent they still have no doubt, what the socialistic Independent Labour Party had been to the party of the British trade unions, the British Labour Party. Accordingly, the socialists joined with alacrity in the Conference for Progressive Political Action, which the railway unions organized for reasons presently to be indicated, and, in 1924, strongly supported La Follette for President. At present (1927), they are again by themselves, with the American labor party farther away than ever. They have succeeded, however, in establishing friendly relations with the leaders of the trade union movement, which they doubtless will try to utilize in the future.

The Conference for Progressive Political Action was formed in 1921 by the four railway brotherhoods outside the American Federation of Labor, the twelve railwaymen's unions inside the Federation, the socialists, and the Clothing Workers. Interpreted at the time by many as an indubitable sign of that inner urge, presumably present in every labor movement, which sooner or later drives it to reach out for a wider control of industry than a mere job control [1] by means of an independent political agency, this event clearly appears now, in retrospect, a move prompted by what then seemed to the railway unions concerned to be required by their own interests. It was a new maneuver instead of a real departure.

During the War-time period, when the United States Government administered the railways of the country, the leaders of the railwaymen's unions found themselves dealing with a management extremely friendly to their interests. While the railwaymen, especially of the better paid grades, failed to find their wages advancing as rapidly as those in other industries, the government unstintingly recognized their "union rules", amounting, in the case of the unions grouped in the Railway Employees' Department of the American Federation of Labor,—which, under private management, had failed of "recognition" except here and there, and at that grudgingly,—to a veritable revolution in their industrial status. Finding government management so responsive to their wishes, and wishing to perpetuate this desirable state of affairs, these unions, in the hearing before Congress in 1919, espoused the Plumb Plan. This was a plan for a

[1] The movement for labor banks, which began at the same time, was interpreted by the same enthusiasts as the beginning of a movement for a wide workers' control over industry by the route of power over investment and credit. In reality, the labor banks which helped unionism instead of hindering it, were the banks which were merely handy depositories for union funds, which added to the union's prestige among the membership by their mere existence, and which functioned as a species of service institution through rendering better and cheaper service to depositors than the private banks. On the other hand, the labor banking institutions which took the grand "destiny" of labor banking seriously, and followed the dangerous path of business control, turned out to be heavy liabilities to the unions which had sponsored them.

modified guild socialism, which was conceived by a brilliant and public-spirited lawyer, Glenn Plumb, independently of the European gild socialist theories; it provided for government ownership with a co-operative management by the three interests equally represented: the government, the executive personnel, and the labor unions. However, the railway unions were doomed to disappointment. Instead of adopting the Plumb Plan, Congress peremptorily returned the railways to their private owners, and, to handle the labor question, created a Railroad Labor Board with equal representation from the public, the railways, and labor. The sole power available to the Board for enforcing its awards in disputes between the management and the unions, was the moral force of public opinion. But the unions discovered before long that the Board's power over publicity virtually amounted to a coercive power over themselves, or, at any rate, sufficed to hamper them seriously in the use of whatever bargaining power they had. From liberally dispensing new union privileges and rights under the United States Railway Administration, the government, in the guise of the Railroad Labor Board, had turned to pressing for "wage deflation" and for the obliteration of valuable "shop rules". Under such conditions, the railway unions could not keep out of politics. If the government would not let them alone, they must reform the government. And since the Railroad Labor Board was the joint creation of both political parties, and since, upon Wilson's retirement, conservatism ruled both parties equally, something stronger had to be attempted than merely bargaining with the old parties at election time. Hence the Conference for Progressive Political Action.

The railway shopmen's strike of 1922, which was called forth by an award ordering a second ten per cent wage decrease inside of fifteen months, and for which the Board condemned the unions as "outlaw" organizations, greatly added to their hatred for the Board. In the Congressional election of that year, the Conference, overruling the socialists, who pressed for an immediate formation of a labor party, went into the primaries of the Democratic and Republican parties to assure the nominations of friendly candidates. It was the time honored non-partisan policy of the American Federation of Labor, but the Conference, through its several state Conferences, pursued it with greater energy and with success. In the new Congress, the "progressive bloc", headed by La Follette, had a balance of power. Yet abolition of the Board was delayed.

In 1924, the Conference endorsed La Follette for President, and the railwaymen's organizations, as well as the socialists, threw themselves with enthusiasm into the campaign. The prospects indeed seemed rosy, and expectations ran high. Therefore, great was the disappointment when the vote totalled under 5,000,000, and the electoral vote of only one state was secured. In the meantime, the Democrats in Congress, probably with the idea of punishing the labor organizations for denying support to their party,—a support upon which they had, from past experience, come to count,—chose to permit several opportunities to slip by for bringing the bill abolishing the Board to a vote. At a meeting of the

Conference for Progressive Political Action shortly after the election, the railway brotherhoods, therefore, declared their connection with the Conference at an end. Thereupon, the organization dissolved, thus ending the hope of a labor party from this source. The Railroad Labor Board was finally abolished in 1926 by a non-partisan vote on a bill which was framed jointly by the representatives of the railway companies and of the labor organizations.

Another and more explicit attempt at a labor party was sponsored during 1920-23 by the Chicago Federation of Labor. When, however, the unionist sponsors with John Fitzpatrick, President of the Chicago Federation of Labor, at the head, saw a national conference, which they had called, bodily taken out of their hands by the ever prepared communists of the Workers' party, they quickly recanted and hastened to return to the non-partisan "orthodoxy" of the American Federation of Labor. But in the Presidential campaign of 1924, the orthodoxy of the Federation itself was put to a strain by the nomination of conservative candidates by both old parties. In this difficult situation, the Federation endorsed La Follette but on a "non-partisan" basis, that is, without committing itself to him or to his group beyond that single campaign. Since then, the Federation has returned to a strict interpretation of its traditional non-partisan policy. Thus the political "left wing" has come to the end of its latest political inning, an inning in which its chances for success at first appeared to be no worse than in the nineties, when it almost captured the American Federation of Labor. At present, the only active survival of that political "left wing" is the "extreme left", the Workers' Party, which, however, is unable to make up through its virulent methods for its negligible numbers and for its failure to appreciate the basic characteristics of the social environment of the American labor movement. Its very wish to exist as a communist party is the best proof of how little it understands the nature of the problems of the American labor movement.

The industrial "left wing" movement, since the stabilization of the American labor movement in the nineties, followed three lines: a syndicalistic (the Industrial Workers of the World), a socialistic (the "New Unionism" in the needle trades), and, of late, also a communistic (the Trade Union Educational League). Syndicalism was a periodic outcropping in those industries of the West, like lumber, and, at an earlier date, metal mining, in which the pioneers' tradition of makeshift living told in a disregard of the desires of their labor personnel for the elementary amenities of civilized life, as also in an extreme irregularity of employment. Occasionally, though, syndicalism made spectacular débuts in Eastern industries, such as textiles, which pay low subsistence wages to an immigrant working force. But in neither set of circumstances did syndicalism ever grow to be more than a symptom, since "dual unionism" and a contempt for controlling the job by union "working rules" can never be compatible with numbers and stability. But the industrial movement directed by the communist William Z. Foster's "Trade Union Educational League", which rejects the dual unionism of the

syndicalists for "boring from within" the established unions, has also been completely unsuccessful
in its widely planned attempts to gain control in
the unions through raising such issues as "amalgamation". The only exception is to be found in
the clothing unions, where a revolutionary tradition
and the overwhelming prestige of the Russian Revolution have combined to raise up influential factions
in close touch with, if not under orders from, the
Communists—thereby adding another and highly interesting facet to the phenomenon of "New
Unionism".

This "New Unionism", which the intellectuals
have acclaimed as the ideal model for the other
American unions to emulate, richly deserves praise
for the consummate skill with which it has per-
formed a supremely difficult task, one which to many
students of the labor movement, both socialists and
non-socialists, long seemed like the task of Sisyphus.
It was the task of welding together into organizations with a stable membership a polyglot mass of
workers, working under the widest diversity of
conditions, from the small contractor's sweatshop
to the modern large factory, and with historically
developed national characteristics, of which a stolid
obedience to leaders is not one. In getting them
organized, the leaders have made good use of the
feeling of revolutionary solidarity which came
naturally to these workers. But revolutionary solidarity cuts both ways. While it has cemented together a body of otherwise individualistic workers,
it has also kept them peculiarly susceptible to a
point of view from which even a policy which aims
at a mark as far advanced as a "property right in

the job" under an agreement system, is considered to aim contemptibly low.

Another outstanding characteristic of the "New Unionism" is the mental nimbleness of its leaders which has fitted them to seize and employ original methods of controlling industrial situations. While at bottom these new methods accord with the very purposes which the more tradition-bound, slow-moving "old" unionists are pursuing, they have yet, through the sheer boldness and novelty of their conception, created in the minds of many a distinct contrast between the "Old" and the "New" union-ism—to the enormous advantage of the latter. An excellent example is the following: Starting from the workers' dependence on jobs, from which every kind of unionist starts, these "New Unionists" drew the practical conclusion, which "Old Union-ists" might have drawn as well, that when an em-ployer is about to go on the rocks through incom-petence,—as, for instance, through inability to ap-preciate the value of an effective cost keeping sys-tem,—it would be only good policy if the union had, in its employ, expert accountants to show such an employer the way to save his business and, at the same time, the jobs of his employees. Likewise, when the whole industry is suffering from a chronic depression, it would be good unionism to waive old established "shop customs" or even to take over from the employer a goodly portion of the task of maintaining shop discipline, if that would help re-duce production costs and stimulate a market for the commodity. Such methods, in effect a technique of "first aid" to the employer,—to enable him to stay in business, to continue risking his investment, and to continue to have jobs to give to employees,—hardly promise the "encroaching control", at the end of which the employer gets totally eliminated, of which the gild socialists talk. These new methods really stand for a "rationalization" of unionism, similar to the "rationalization" of industry—at present such a popular slogan in Europe. The credit for them must, in fairness, go in part to the advisers and economic experts from among the intellectuals who, in these unions, are working closely with the leaders.[1]

In conclusion, a proper perspective on the "New Unionism" can only be gained when due notice is taken of the difference between the character of the employer which it confronts and the type of employer in the other American industries. We saw how, in those industries, the employers' old time "will to absolute power" merged with the newer "welfare policy", created a barrier which unionism, regardless of whether it be "Old" or "New", has not yet learned how to clear away or

[1] However, it would hardly be fair to extend the same amount of credit, or perhaps any credit at all, to every union of the "New Unionism" type which has reached out towards helping solve the wider problems of its industry. For instance, in women's wear, the industry has been retrogressing from a factory organization back to a contractor shop system, coincidently with union control. Therefore the burden rests upon that union to prove that, by its claims upon the industry in wages but mostly in "rules", it has not materially contributed to the very evils which it has subsequently attempted to mitigate by its "New Industrial Program". Such union demands are more enforceable, in the very nature of things, upon the large manufacturer, who manufactures in his own shop, than upon the contractor who works for a merchant-jobber; for which reason, many a large manufacturer may have been driven to escape such burdens by metamorphosing himself into a merchant-jobber. The union's "New Industrial Program" seeks now to impose upon the merchant-jobber the responsibility for the labor standards in the shops of the contractor and sub-manufacturers whom he employs. However, there were also other contributing causes.

even to bestride. The clothing unions, on the other hand, are confronted by employers of a type who yield easily to determined pressure. This may be due to the great difficulty of inducing the individualistic Jewish employers to co-operate and offer a solid front. It may also be due to a hesitancy to expose their intraracial quarrels to a none too friendly world. Doubtless, also, many a large clothing employer became reconciled to the power of the unions as he saw them equalizing competitive costs in manufacturing and thus mitigating the cutthroat competition. Nor should one overlook the power which these unions have derived from the seasonal nature of the operations in the industry, whereby a strike during the height of the season becomes a calamity to the employer. Had it not been for this willingness of the clothing employer to have peace with or without honor; had it not been that, so far as the employer was concerned, the unions in the clothing industry were no longer fighting for their existence; then the "constructive" stage perhaps might have been delayed with them even as it was delayed with the "Old" unionism. And it may also be true that not a small share of their present "constructiveness" would have failed to emerge from behind a militancy of the same order as that shown by the "Old" unions which are still obliged to fight for their existence.

But the "New Unionism" has something else besides a "rationalized" methodology which the old-fashioned unions seem to lack at present. It has a real "will to organize" and to increase its membership to the maximum. For, to the above mentioned causes of the present standstill in American unionism, there must be added the psychology of a big majority of its leaders today—a curious blending of "defeatism" with complacency. Every union leader admits that the organization of labor must be expanded into the basic industries—steel, automobiles, farm machinery, electrical supplies, etc. But at the first encounter with the difficulties of the task,—difficulties which are admittedly enormous, made up as they are of the employers' active opposition and of the inertia on the workers' part begotten by the Coolidge prosperity and by "welfare capitalism",—or in many cases even before such an actual encounter, union officers and organizers lose their heart for the task, and rarely proceed beyond expressions of good intentions. Thereupon, —having gone through the motions of organizing in new fields, and thus eased their organizer's conscience,—the same leaders settle down to a smug survey of the well oiled machinery of their little organizations, which suggests at least a suspicion that these leaders might not entirely welcome too many new members, whose alignment in the politics of the union would at best be uncertain.

We saw how the American labor movement had acquired in the seventies, with Gompers and Strasser, the philosophy of stable trade unionism, so indispensable to its later growth, because a group of "left wingers" of that day, taught in the school of American experience, exchanged their class-consciousness for a job consciousness, and, later, in the eighties, made job conscious unionism prevail throughout the whole labor movement over the theretofore impregnable philosophy of "antimonopoly". Might it not, therefore, be that the movement in our own day, no longer facing the problem of its own stability, which is already assured, but that of expansion across the double barrier of "open shop" and "welfare capitalism", will eventually recover the indispensable "will to action" by drawing upon a modern "left wing" group, which, like its predecessor of half a century earlier, will have discovered a true path for labor's advancement in the same experimental school of American industry and society? Might it not be that men like Sidney Hillman of the Amalgamated Clothing Workers and the machinists' leaders,—the initiators of "union-management" co-operation, and classed within the Federation as of the "left", —are today in the identical stage of development towards an all-American labor leadership in which Gompers was when he was applying the economics of the First International to the problems of the Cigarmakers' Union?

PART II
A THEORY OF THE LABOR MOVEMENT

CHAPTER VI

ECONOMIC OPPORTUNITY AND GROUP PSYCHOLOGY

A theory of the labor movement should include a theory of the psychology of the laboring man. The writings of socialists, syndicalists, anarchists, communists, and "welfare" capitalists abound in embroideries on the theme of "what labor wants" or "what labor aspires to". But the safest method is to go to the organizations of labor's own making, shaped and managed by leaders arisen from labor's own ranks, and to attempt to discover "what's really on labor's mind" by using as material the "working rules", customs and practices of these organizations.[1] A study of such "rules" and customs, the products of long drawn out, evolutionary developments, will aid in distinguishing fundamental from accidental purposes. No such certainty can attach, of course, to the formulations by the "ideologists" of labor, just because these latter, being intellectuals and without the workingman's shop experience, are unable, for all their devotion, to avoid substituting their own typical attitudes and

---

[1] Unorganized workers, where they are subject to less than an iron discipline, are found to observe practices and usages identical in their purposes with the usages of organized labor. However, it goes without saying that the practices of unorganized labor are of too elusive a nature and are frequently also too unformed to serve as anything better than corroborative facts here and there.

wishes for the genuine philosophy of the laboring man.

There are, by and large, three basic economic philosophies: the manual laborers', the business men's, and the intellectuals'. Werner Sombart, in his definitions of "handicraft" and of capitalism, offers the best clue to an explanation of the essential psychologies of the "manualist" and of the business man.[1] He points out in these definitions the wide gulf between economic motives in the mediæval economy and in modern business. A secure livelihood for everyone was the aim of the gilds, but the business man has from the first been inspired by a boundless desire to amass wealth.[2] This thought, which is one of Sombart's many illuminating contributions to economic history, can be made the starting point of a more comprehensive theory of economic group psychology. It can be done by showing, first, how the psychological contrast between the two historical epochs, the gild and the capitalistic, continues in our own day, in the contrast between the psychology of trade unionism and the psychology of business, and second, how each and every type of such group psychology, past and present, can be explained through a common theory.

In an economic community, there is a separation

[1] The intellectual, in his several varieties, will be treated later.

[2] "Handicraft as a system is an economic society based on exchange between free and independent workers, who *are animated by the motive of securing a livelihood*, who follow traditional methods in their technology, and who act according to rules prescribed by a common organization." (*Der Moderne Kapitalismus*, I, 1, 188.) "Capitalism is an exchange economy, which is ruled by the profit motive as well as by an economic rationalism, and in which two distinct population groups bound by a market nexus coöperate mutually: the owners of the means of production, who are also the managers and a propertyless, wage earning group." (*Ibid.*, 319.)

between those who prefer a secure, though modest return,—that is to say, a mere livelihood,—and those who play for big stakes and are willing to assume risk in proportion. The first compose the great bulk of manual workers of every description, including mechanics, laborers, farmers, small manufacturers, and shopkeepers (since petty trade, as Sombart correctly points out, is also a manual occupation); while the latter are, of course, the entrepreneurs and the big business men. The limited or unlimited purpose is, in either case, the product of a simple survey of accessible economic opportunity and of a psychic self-appraisal. The manual worker is convinced by experience that he is living in a world of limited opportunity. He sees, to be sure, how others, for instance business men, are finding the same world a storehouse of apparently unlimited opportunity. Yet he decisively discounts that, so far as he is himself concerned. The business man, on the contrary, is an eternal optimist. To him the world is brimful of opportunities that are only waiting to be made his own.

The scarcity consciousness of the manualist is a product of two main causes, one lying in himself and the other outside. The typical manualist is aware of his lack of native capacity for availing himself of economic opportunities as they lie amidst the complex and ever shifting situations of modern business. He knows himself neither for a born taker of risks nor for the possessor of a sufficiently agile mind ever to feel at home in the midst of the uncertain game of competitive business. Added to this is his conviction that for him the world has been rendered one of scarcity by an institutional order of things, which purposely reserved the best opportunities for landlords, capitalists and other privileged groups. It may also be, of course, that the manual worker will ascribe such scarcity to natural rather than to institutional causes, say, to a shortage of land brought on by increase of population,[1] or, like mediæval merchants and master workmen, to the small number of customers and the meagre purchasing power of these. At all events, whether he thought the cause of the apparent limitations to be institutional or natural, a scarcity consciousness has always been typical of the manual worker,[2] in direct contrast to the consciousness of an abundance of opportunity, which dominates the self-confident business man.

By correlating economic types, as we do here, with an abundance or a scarcity consciousness, respectively, we are enabled to throw a bridge between our own time and earlier periods. The mediæval craftsman and gild master, notwithstanding his economic "independence", was of the same economic type as the wage earner of today. The gildsman maintained his independence solely because his rudimentary business psychology sufficed for an age when the market was limited to the locality, and the tools of production were primitively simple. Put the average wage earner back into the Thirteenth Century, and he would set up as a master; transfer a gild master into the age of modern business, and he would fall into the ranks of wage labor.

[1] See below in this chapter for the cause of the origin of the village land community.

[2] See below in this chapter for the American exception to the general rule.

While, to be sure, the economic historian was justified in refusing to see any historical continuity between gilds and trade unions, he often overlooked
their common fundamental psychology: the psychology of seeking after a livelihood in the face
of limited economic opportunity. Just as, to the
gildsman, opportunity was visibly limited to the
local market,[1] so, to the industrial wage earner, it
is limited to the number of jobs available, almost
always fewer than the number of job seekers.[2]

The economic pessimism of the manual group is
at the bottom of its characteristic manner of adjusting the relation of the individual to the whole group.
It prompts also the attitude of exclusion which
manual groups assume towards those regarded as
"outsiders". Again the manualist's psychology
can best be brought out by contrast with that of
the fully developed business man. Basically the
business man is an economic individualist, a competitor *par excellence*. If opportunity is plentiful,
if the enterprising person can create his own opportunity, what sane object can there be in collectively

[1] The mediæval period has usually been represented as the Golden
Age of the manual worker. This conception, which is dying hard, has
been begotten of the wish of many writers, socialists and reactionaries
alike, to make the picture of modern capitalism appear, by contrast
with the gild period, gloomier than the facts warrant. The economic
democracy of the early gilds, with the unimpeded advancement from
apprentice to master, has greatly encouraged this rosy view. Actually,
however, the gild age was an age of poverty, squalor, and economic
insecurity. So that the democracy of the gild age was merely the
sort of democracy under which all shared alike in the prevailing
scarcity.

[2] The average workingman considers as genuine opportunities only
jobs in his own occupation and, especially if married, only jobs which
are not too far away from home. The British unemployment insurance system gave official sanction to this view, when it held that
an insured person had not forfeited his right to an out-of-work benefit
by refusing a job outside his occupation or away from his home.

controlling the extent of the individual's appropriation of opportunity, or in drastically excluding those from other localities? Nor will this type of individual submit to group control, for he is confident of his ability to make good bargains for himself. If, on the contrary, opportunity is believed to be limited, as in the experience of the manual worker, it then becomes the duty of the group to prevent the individual from appropriating more than his rightful share, while at the same time protecting him against oppressive bargains. *The group then asserts its collective ownership over the whole amount of opportunity,* and, having determined who are entitled to claim a share in that opportunity, undertakes to parcel it out fairly, directly or indirectly, among its recognized members, permitting them to avail themselves of such opportunities, job or market, only on the basis of a "common rule". Free competition becomes a sin against one's fellows, anti-social, like a self indulgent consumption of the stores of a beleaguered city, and obviously detrimental to the individual as well. A collective disposal of opportunity, including the power to keep out undesirables, and a "common rule" in making bargains are as natural to the manual group as *"laissez-faire"* is to the business man.[1]

---

[1] "Scarcity groups" regularly endeavor to "own" as groups the limited opportunities at their disposal. Thus no issue relating to the conditions upon which they will permit an individual member to connect with an opportunity can escape becoming strongly tinged by this fundamental aspiration to "own" all the opportunities extant. It would be erroneous to try to account for an industrial struggle solely by the specific demands which are its proximate causes: wages, hours, freedom from discriminatory discharge, etc., while leaving out this group "hunger" for controlling the job opportunities to the point of "ownership". Therefore, the phenomenon of the strike is never ruled by the cold calculations of the participants, but behind each strike

In practice the same methods employed in solving the internal problem of a fair apportionment of opportunity among the "legitimate" participants are found also to answer the purpose of securing the largest possible return from the outside classes. After all, inferiority as a bargainer, when the individual acts alone, is but the other side of opportunity circumscribed.[1] When the gild or the trade union applies the "common rule" as "working rules" (or "rules for the occupancy and tenure of opportunity", as we might term them), which abolish or check competition for jobs or for patronage of customers, it creates a solid bargaining front against employer or customer, and at the same time tends to bring about a distribution of the opportunity to earn a livelihood, fair to all. Checking the race for employment opportunity tends to equalize security among the members, and simultaneously safeguards or raises the standard of life, establishes industrial liberty, protects future earning power, and increases leisure.

Does this opportunity theory explain the business man's conduct through the several stages of economic society? His individualism shows up clearest during periods of great economic expansion. When markets are becoming rapidly extended and technology revolutionized; in other words, when oppor-

there always lurks the struggle for the control of the jobs. While, for purposes of analysis, it is useful to separate the several expectancies of the worker—wages, hours, shop freedom, etc.,—these alone can never account for the real pathos displayed in industrial struggles.

[1] Labor's inferiority in bargaining follows when the employer, realizing the worker's dire needs, turns the job opportunities held by him into "silenced" opportunities, which thus do not compete for the worker. In the case of the gilds, the overlord or any other rich customer, if the gild had permitted, could have similarly traded on the bargaining inferiority of the master workman.

tunity is expanding by leaps and bounds, then his competitiveness approaches the ruthlessness of a Darwinian struggle for existence. The elder Rockefeller and Andrew Carnegie, moral men who raised competitiveness to an ethic, are indeed excellent examples. This is not to say that business men will not form "rings" even in the midst of economic revolution, nor that they cannot be taught to abate their competition in the common interest. Yet, on the whole, the "new competition" or "co-operative competition", may be said to have been given its chance only after the rush for new opportunities had already subsided of itself, due to a slackening in the opportunity-creating economic expansion.[1]

Furthermore, notwithstanding this "new competition" on the modern commodity market, there always remains a vital difference between a business men's group, with the characteristic consciousness of abundance which is normal to that economic type, co-operating to a common end, and the solidarity in action manifested by genuine "scarcity" groups. When a business men's group has been led, through fear of cutthroat competition and price wars, to resort directly or indirectly, to the rationing of market opportunity among its members, this movement has always sprung from the "head", but never spontaneously nor from the "heart", as it were, in contrast with the gilds, peasant land communities, or trade unions, which have usually taken to sharing opportunity even long before becoming

---

[1] Yet long before business men's groups learned how to stabilize their internal competition, they knew how to shut out the foreigner by a tariff wall.

formally organized. For the same reason, we never find individual business men anxious to emulate the manualist's willingness, nay, even burning zeal as shown during strikes, literally to sacrifice his own interest for the good of his group as a whole.

Thus the business men's "communism of opportunity", compared with that practiced by gilds and trade unions, appears to be a relatively feeble expression of group solidarity, in point of stability against the disruptive influence of individual self-interest; except, of course, where the combination has become a complete merger, in which case the individual has totally disappeared from the scene. And while the "new competition", which is a competition regulated by trade associations, is indeed forging to the front, it yet remains true that business men's "unions" have shown the greatest stability and longevity when one of the competing concerns of commanding position, for reasons of its own, became converted to a "live-and-let-live policy" and by its size and power, induced the other competitors to consider "playing the game" the better part of competitive valor.[1]

[1] During the stage of commercial capitalism, between the early democratic or near-democratic gild régime and modern industrial capitalism, the merchant-capitalists, who, having made their way into large scale business, rose above their manualist colleagues and took away from the latter the control of the gilds, knew how to take advantage of the traditional idea of trade monopoly to keep strictly for themselves the rich opportunities for profits in the expanding markets. Yet, while they thus kept "interlopers" and outsiders from interfering with their lucrative business, these "gild capitalists", in the chartered "national companies" for foreign trade and in the local "companies" as well, had in other respects become thoroughgoing economic individualists. As they consolidated control in their own hands, they successfully "sabotaged" all the vital old gild regulations which aimed to protect the whole producing community and to equalize opportunity among its members.

What relation has this opportunity theory of the labor group psychology to the plans of the socialists, to "workers' control", to the "abolition of wagery", and so forth?

Socialism, in its many varieties, while correctly grasping a part of the true psychology of the worker—his desire for solidarity—overlooks his unwillingness to become completely merged with his own class. Whenever and wherever full "workers' control" has been tried, by "self-governing workshops" and like organizations, history shows that sooner or later the workers have, consciously or unconsciously, opposed the creation of a solidarity exceeding a common control of opportunity and common "working rules",—that is, if the undertaking did not die at birth, or, surviving, experience a conversion, materially prosperous but spiritually degrading, into a capitalist enterprise owned by a few of the "smarter" co-operators.[1] For, the workers, it seems, will cheerfully submit to an almost military union discipline in their struggles against the employer; they will be guided by the union working rules in seeking and holding jobs; but they will mistrust and obstruct their union leaders who have become shop-bosses under whatever scheme of "workers' control". Perhaps in abstract reasoning, the wage earner might be expected to envisage the whole of the economic organization of society as the ultimate source of his job opportunity; and therefore wish for a complete "workers' control" of industry. Actually, how-

[1] See the conclusions of Sidney and Beatrice Webb after a thorough investigation of producers' co-operation in many lands—reprinted in *My Apprenticeship*, by Beatrice Webb. See also Commons and Associates, *History of Labour in the United States.*

ever, the typical wage earner, when he can express himself in and through his trade union free of domination by intellectuals, who are never too bashful to do his thinking for him, seldom dreams of shouldering the risks of management. Ordinarily he traces the origin of his opportunity not much farther back than the point where it materializes in jobs, and will grasp and support only such union policies as will enable or force the employers to offer more jobs, equally available to all fellow craftsmen, and upon improved terms.[1]

A good illustration of the true makings of the psychology of economic groups is found in Russia.

Before the Revolution, the peasants [2] owned their land in common, by village communes, which periodically divided and redivided it among the individual families, the allotments to the families being determined by their relative needs. For what the local market was to the mediæval gildsman, what jobs are to a modern labor group, this the land has been to a peasant community—a complete embodiment of its economic opportunity. The peasant

---

[1] However, in order to conserve jobs threatened by a depression and by too high production costs, workers will, if intelligently led, co-operate with the employers to enable the latter to meet a competitive price level and thus to stay in business and to continue offering employment upon attractive terms. But this still presupposes an employer willing to undertake the ultimate risks of the business.

[2] In Soviet Russia, it is the economic behavior of the peasantry rather than that of the industrial workers that offers reliable material for a study in the economic psychology of the manualist. The peasants, thanks to their strength of numbers, have escaped the regimentation at the hands of the Communist Party to which the city workers have been compelled to submit. Tomsky, the foremost leader of the Russian trade unions, frankly declared: "We do not conceal from anyone that the trade union movement has been, is, and will be directed by the Communist Party in the most centralised fashion." (Quoted in the report issued by the International Labour Office in 1927, *The Trade Union Movement in Soviet Russia*, p. 253.)

lived in a hostile world, in a world of officials and landlords, who owned the best of the land—the best of opportunity. In that world of scarcity, the peasant was a land communist; an individualist, however, in production and in distribution.[1] The in-

---

[1] Jan St. Lewinsky, generalizing from the researches of numerous Russian scholars, who have for more than thirty years investigated the forms of property found among the nomadic and settled peoples of Siberia, squarely makes scarcity of land the cause of the rise of the village land community. According to him the communal form of ownership was preceded by individual appropriation, which held so long as land continued abundant.

He describes the transition from individual to communal ownership in the following words: "The right of free occupation leads to great irregularity. Those who have great ability, more cattle, a large family, become proprietors of land, greater in extent by ten, and sometimes by one hundred times than that of the others. . . . So long as there is plenty of land this inequality injures no one. . . . [But] when all land convenient for ploughing and all meadows are occupied, when the poor, and the young who wish to form households find only inferior land or none at all, the old order of things ceases to be in the interest of all. . . . For the poor, the only means of improving their condition is to claim part of the land of the rich. . . . The probability of the poor being able to make their interests prevail becomes greater as time passes. With the increase of population, the number of those wanting land increases, and those claiming a division of the soil becomes the stronger party. . . . The fight between the opposing groups is a long one. . . . Many of the 'middle classes', fearful of losing what they already possess, join the party of the rich. . . . But, finally . . . the 'middle classes' . . . pass over to the opposition camp.

"The passage from individual to common ownership advances in accordance with the increase in the number of those who have not enough land. We can distinguish three stages in this process of evolution.

"*First Stage* There exists no equalization; the community merely restricts the right of free occupation.

"*Second Stage* The community possesses the right to transfer the property from one person to another.

"*Third Stage* The land is periodically divided."
                    The Origin of Property (London, 1913).

And St. Lewinsky concludes, basing himself on A. A. Kaufman, perhaps the greatest among authorities: "The origin of the village community has been often explained by the introduction of the collective responsibility for government taxes. The evolution of property has thus been traced back to the will of the legislator. The study of this problem in Russian Asia shows us that this factor does not play at all the important part attributed to it. . . . Only where the

tellectuals, the followers of the "Narodnik" or populist school, observing the peasant's attachment to his land commune, saw but a short step between that and socialism. Likewise, after the Revolution of 1917, when the landlords' estates went to the peasant communes, the Bolshevists repeated the same error, thinking that an easy and speedy transition could be made from communism in land to a complete communism. They discovered, however, that no consideration could lure the peasant into the producing communes which the communist state fathered. Moreover, when the landlords' power became completely broken by the defeat of the last counter-revolutionary movement, the self-same peasant started a mass flight from the land communes and an irresistible pressure for individual control of the land. The Revolution, having transported the peasants from a world of extreme scarcity into a landlordless world of broadened opportunity and of at least potentially increased returns, has thereby taken them away from a time-hallowed "communism of opportunity" to an economic individualism all along the line, akin to that of the peasants in Western Europe and of the farmers in America.

America [1] is another significant illustration of how the psychology of economic groups is shaped by economic opportunity. In this country, primarily in the non-slavery states, history has mani-

---

land has ceased to be abundant and a strong desire to introduce division existed, did the communities comply with the orders of the administration. This transition, however, took place very often without any external intervention, where the evolution was ripe for transition." *Ibid.*, 69-70. See also the chapter on Russia.

[1] See the chapter on America.

fested probably the most extensive, if not the only large-scale example of the availability to the manual worker of practically unlimited economic opportunity. This unboundedness of opportunity was the effect of easy access to the natural resources of a rich and unoccupied continent; it lay further in the simplicity of the industrial and business structure of a young community. In consequence, the great mass of American manual producers—which includes farmers, mechanics, small manufacturers, and small business men—developed a competitive psychology which greatly exceeded in intensity the competitive psychology of the very same classes in Europe, and was strongly akin to the typical business men's psychology. Surrounded on all sides by opportunity, in natural resources and in business, the thought could scarcely have occurred that opportunity needed to be rationed, or that anyone had to be kept out, or that the individual competitor needed to be controlled and restricted by his fellows, in the common interest and in the interest of his own protection from oppressive bargains. Let each individual seek his own opportunity to his heart's content, and the outcome can only be good; so ran the accepted social maxim.

Yet, the individualist millennium was far from realization, even in pioneer America. Wealth somehow showed a preference for the coffers of the few rather than for the tills of the "producers". Nevertheless the producing community was not turned away from its individualistic creed, but developed a remedial program based on a characteristic "anti-monopoly" philosophy. The trouble with America was—as the theory went—that access to opportunity was really not free: that, aided by traitorous legislators, a small number of monopolists had succeeded in locking up the legitimate opportunities of the American people. The land speculator robbed the willing producer of his chances for profitable self-employment upon the soil. The money and credit monopolist, the banker, denied to the producer a free enjoyment of credit opportunity, which was really his by right of personal integrity and by right of his toil-created physical property. Thus credit was converted into a means for exploitation, notwithstanding that it was, in the last analysis, the mere product of the producers' confidence in one another's honesty. Similarly, the mercantile monopolist and the manufacturing "trust", aided and abetted by publicly chartered banks and by other special privilege institutions—tariffs, patent rights, public utility franchises, and by a private appropriation of limited natural resources—denied to the honest producer free marketing opportunity, and forced upon him a monopoly price both as buyer and seller. The remedy was "anti-monopoly", namely, to cut away the ground from under the monopolists by destroying, through legislation, their special privileges. Once the monopolist had been forced to restore free access to opportunity, free competition could be relied upon to set up a producers' paradise.[1] It was only monopoly and the monopo-

---

[1] In Europe, too, there developed numerous "anti-monopoly" philosophies upon a similar social and psychological basis. There such philosophies, like Proudhon's in France, mirrored the aspirations of the small merchants and master workmen, who, on the one hand, had before their eyes the abundance of opportunity opened up by the commercial and industrial revolutions of the Eighteenth and Nineteenth Centuries, but, on the other hand, were chagrined to see these opportunities appropriated exclusively by merchant-capitalists, bankers

list that needed regulating—not the honest producer in his relation to economic opportunity.

That was the core of all "producer" philosophies in America—from Shay's Rebellion through Jackson, to Bryan and to La Follette. And so powerful was the grip of "anti-monopoly" philosophy upon the labor movement, that nearly three-quarters of a century had to elapse before it could shake loose and arrive at a philosophy of its own—the philosophy of trade unionism. Trade unionism, particularly the trade unionism of the American Federation of Labor, marked a clear shift in the psychology of American labor. It was a shift from an optimistic psychology, reflecting the abundance of opportunity in a partly settled continent, to the more pessimistic trade union psychology, built upon the premise that the wage earner, in a complex industrial structure, is faced by a scarcity of opportunity. The new attitude no longer called for a restoration of free competition, but for control and administration by the union of all job opportunities available to the group. This includes determination by the union of the rules under which the individual was permitted to occupy and hold his proper share of the total group opportunity. When, in the Presidential campaign of 1924, the American labor movement supported Senator La Follette, it was not a return to the former "anti-monopoly" theory, but merely an alliance cemented by the political issues

and big business men. Hence the several money and credit reform schemes including Proudhon's "Bank of the People", were designed to place the "producers" on a competitive footing with the privileged. However the European "petty bourgeoisie" rarely betrayed the same intense devotion to "anti-monopoly" programs as did the American farmers, small business men, and mechanics. Nor did these programs have there as prolonged sway as in America.

of curtailing the powers of the judiciary and of presenting a united front to reaction. The trade unionism of the American Federation of Labor, far from repeating the traditional "anti-monopoly" clamor against "big business" and for free competition, envisages unionism as the necessary counterbalance to inevitably "big business". The province of the union is, therefore, to assert labor's collective mastery over job opportunities and employment bargains, leaving the ownership of the business to the employer, and creating for its members an ever-increasing sphere of economic security and opportunity, equal to that which the craft gilds —those superb manifestations of the manual worker's aspirations and power—were able to guarantee to workingmen's communities of an earlier age.

CHAPTER VII

THE "WORKING RULES" AND PHILOSOPHY OF ORGANIC LABOR

THE GILDS

The clearest manifestation of "communism of opportunity" in the gilds is found in the "right of lot" of the early English merchant gilds. As is well known, the merchant gilds, and the craft gilds which followed them, were associations of persons enjoying a charter by public authority and endowed with an exclusive trade or craft monopoly for the locality. In the early days, when trading was on a petty scale, the merchant was primarily a transporter of goods—one who knew how to cope with the natural and other hazards of the highway. He may therefore be considered, as Sombart [1] considers him, as a "handicraftsman pursuing the trader's handicraft."

Lipson [2] defines the "right of lot" as the privilege of sharing in any purchase made by a fellow member, whether made at market or fair, or in native town. This undoubtedly amounted fully to a sharing of opportunity, since the normal scarcity of trading goods in those early days limited the trader's opportunity even more seriously than did

[1] *Ibid.*, Vol. I, Part 1, pp. 279-295.
[2] E. Lipson, *Economic History of England*, 245.

the narrow outlet available for his wares. The exercise of this right was usually, though not necessarily, conditioned on the member's being present at the making of the bargain in which he claimed a right to share. The right was laid down in either the gild charter, or in the by-laws of the borough. An excellent contemporary statement of its purpose and aim appears in a petition quoted by Lipson from the Southampton Court Leet Records.

"In times past, there hath been a very good order devised, that every burgess in this town should have a part of any bargain made with strangers for any commodity brought to the town, claiming the same in convenient time, as in the same ancient order may appear. By which device it may evidently appear to us that *the chiefest and men of greatest credit and wealth, into whose hands the best and most profitable bargains were like for the most to come, did not respect their own private gains so much as the maintenance of the state of this town,* knowing that always they were to continue in the same, but others should grow under them, and *therefore willing that the younger people should be partakers with them.*[1] Which, being so good and politic an order for the estate of this town, we desire your worship may be continued in that good sort and meaning as first it was devised."[2] Here apparently the equal sharing of opportunity was understood to concern both the established men in the gild and the younger members who were "still on the make". A Norwich custumal, also cited by Lipson, complained that "certain persons have a practice of making their purchases by two, three, or four, or more of their

[1] Italics mine.   [2] *Ibid.*, 243.

servants . . . so that they have two, three, or four
parts or more of that merchandise as against a peer
of the city''; it was therefore ordered that ''none
should henceforth make such purchases in the city
save by themselves or one of his servants only'',
so that his fellow citizens may share equally if they
wish.[1]

Scarcity of raw material was as serious a handi-
cap to the craftsman as was scarcity of trading
goods to the trader. Therefore the gild of coopers
of Kingston-upon-Hull ruled that ''noe brother of
this Societie shall buy *for himself only* any fflatt
hoopes, or any other sorte of pine hoopes, brought
to this towne, if there be above twentie of any such
sorte of hoopes. But he *shall lett every brother of
this company that shall be desirous have parte of
the same hoopes* upon paine to forfeit and pay to
the poor, one shilling''. And it was further provided that each member be *limited to* ''*half a thousand hoopes*''; should he buy more, ''the company
will seize them, so that he shall not profit un-
duely''.[2] Thus every member was held down to a
''stint'' in appropriating for himself from the common opportunity of the gild.[3]

[1] *Ibid.*
[2] Lambert—*Two Thousand Years of Gild Life*, 293.
[3] So far as merchant gilds are concerned, this right to claim a
share in the lucky purchases of one's fellows might appear to be
adequately explained as a compensation for the danger to every gild
member, when away on business in the territory of a strange borough,
to have his goods seized for debts incurred by another member. But
this can hardly serve as an explanation in the case of craft gilds,
whose members did a strictly local business. Consequently, it would
seem that the right to participate in purchases by others should be
interpreted not as a ''logical'' result of the specific consciousness of
any one particular common menace, but as a spontaneous outgrowth
of a more general ''scarcity consciousness'' prevailing in the group.
A parallel example of an undue reliance on ''logical'' connections is

A "stint" and "stint rolls" figure expressly in the minutes of the merchant gild of Dundee, Scotland: "John Jolies made one offer to this Court of eight freares (packages) of almonds, and eight freares of daittes, both at the price of ffourtie shillings. The Court accepted the offer, the members of the court who listed their names to have thair due proportione according to the last *stent roll,* and ordained Jas. Grahame to see them distributed accordinglie." [1]

Here we have a case of a joint bargain by the gild, a frequent practice, the goods thus purchased being allotted among the membership in accord with the last "stent roll".

But curiously enough, the most nicely elaborated application of the "stint" idea, coupled with a repeated employment of that term, is found in the rules of the Merchant Adventurers, which originated in the Fourteenth Century,—a national gild of wholesale merchants exporting to the Continent. The Adventurers combined the principle of collec-

presented by the theory held at one time in regard to the origin of the community in land in the Russian village. According to the theory, the communal right to allot the land among the several families was due to the governmental decree establishing a communal liability for taxes: If the community was to be held responsible for the taxes of the several families, it "logically" followed that it must also be given full power of allotting the land, since it was upon use of the land that the ability to pay taxes ultimately depended. The researches of Russian scholars in the development of the forms of land ownership in Siberia, already referred to, appear to disprove this "logical" theory conclusively. However, there is no reason to doubt a historical connection between the gildsman's right to share in purchase as applying to "production goods", both traders' and craftsmen's, and the rules aiming to assure an equality of opportunity in obtaining "consumers' goods", food and other provisions, to which apparently the term, the "right of lot", was originally applied, and which was also protected by rules against "forestalling".

[1] Warden, A. J., *Burgh Laws of Dundee*, 160.

tive control of the market opportunity, as embodied
in a rigidly enforced "stint", with another solidaristic principle common to union labor today,
namely, "seniority preference". The traders of
the Company of Adventurers, although they were
among England's first business men, retained in
their internal arrangements much of the spirit of
the early merchant gilds, when trading still closely
approximated a manual occupation. Business men
though they were, they could scarcely afford to
exchange their rigid mutual solidarity for a purely
self-seeking individualism, since they operated under unusual physical hazards and under the constant risk of sudden curtailments of business opportunity,—both of which sprang from the extremely
unstable political conditions of the time.

So they established a graduated annual stint
governing the exportation of lead, ranging from
twenty measures for members of three years' standing and below, to one hundred measures for alder-
men who had traded fourteen years or more. With
reference to the export of cloth, which was their
main business, the rule of the stint set up a gradua-
tion of from 400 pieces of cloth per year for "ffree-
men the first, second, and third year", to a maximum of one thousand pieces permitted to members
of fifteen years' standing and above. Speaking of
members of the highest standing, the rules insistently specify: "It shall not be lawfull for hym
to Shippe or Cause to bee shipped out in one yeares
space aboue the last mentioned number of one
thousand clothes . . . but he and all others of lesse
standinge, Shall Content him and themselues with
. . . the abouesaid Stint Generall . . . without

exceedinge . . . either . . . directly or indirectly, upon the penaltie of forty shillinges sterling per clothe to be forefeited and paid to the use of the ffelowshippe without favor or pardone". [1]

And the gild spirit of keeping opportunity in trust for all members speaks loudly through the following action of the General Court at London. "Upon Complaint made by the young men, that some great traders doe buy up such quantities of Clothes weekly, that the young men cannot get Cloth for their money; It was ordered that whosoever shall hereafter shipp more than *his respective Stint,* he shall pay doble imposicions and doble imprest for all that he shall soe Shipp." [2]

In the craft gilds, the customary prohibition against employing more than a limited number of journeymen and apprentices achieved the same results as the "stint" in the mercantile gilds.

Yet the gild's purpose of equalizing opportunity and raising bargaining power did not necessitate in each instance a direct allotment of opportunity, since the same could be realized with equal certainty by the indirect method of controlling competition. For, what could be more certain and more tersely to the point than the following injunction taken from the same Merchant Adventurers? "No persone shall stand watchinge at the Corners on ends of streets, or at other mens Packhouses [places of business] or at the house or place where anie Clothe merchant or draper ys lodged, nor seeinge anie such in the Street shall run or ffollow after hym with Intent

---

[1] W. E. Lingelbach, *The Merchant Adventurers of England,* "Stint of Shippinge", 67-74.
[2] *Ibid.,* 135.

to Entyce or lead hym to his packhouse, upon pain
of fyve pounds ster.''[1]

Numerous other and much better known regulations, likewise sought to equalize opportunity
within the gild, or aimed to protect it and enlarge
it, as against the world without. The refusal to
admit anyone to a share in the gild monopoly except upon the rigidly observed condition of a regular apprenticeship; the jealous watch kept lest another gild should encroach upon its own economic
jurisdiction; the frequent practice of price fixing;[2]
the prevention of inequality through direct limitation upon economic "size", as, for instance, by the
tailors of Exeter, who allowed no master more than
three servants and one apprentice "at the most"
without leave of the company,[3]—these and other
practices fall easily into one or the other of the
above-named categories. Most writers have been
disposed to view as an entirely genuine and purely
idealistic solicitude for the welfare of the consumer, the much lauded practices of suppressing
defective ware by gild authority and of imposing
money fines, and even the extreme penalty of expulsion for dishonest workmanship. Such practices, however, may be readily grasped as designed
mainly to protect the gild's collective market opportunity and its power of bargaining for a good price.

So the London hatters, in 1347, in a typical petition to the magistrates, begged that "whereas
some workmen in the said trade have made hats
that are not befitting, in deceit of the common people, from which *great scandal, shame, and loss have*

---

[1] *Ibid.*, 91.   [2] See Lipson, 301.
[3] *Ibid.*, 286.

often arisen to the good folks of the said trade,[1] they pray that no workman in the trade shall do any work by night . . . but only in clear daylight, that the aforesaid wardens may openly inspect their work."[2]

The handicraftsmen of the pre-capitalistic era lived in a world in which the producer had no rights but those he bought for money from the mighty of the land, and no economic opportunities except those he found, with the aid of his skill and primitive tools, in the limited market of his locality. In such a world, the producers, by means of a limited group control, made sure of a common disposal of economic opportunity, which meant also a pooling of bargaining power. They thus won economic security, a bargaining position equal if not superior to that of their customers, and economic independence for themselves. Coupled with these gains was an unqualified recognition of their gild organization, whereby the future was safeguarded as well. All these achievements mark off that age as an age when, notwithstanding the economic scarcity, the manual worker was pretty much the master of his destiny.[3]

---

[1] Italics mine.   [2] Lipson, 299.

[3] The "right of lot" was prevalent also in the French gilds (Martin Saint Léon, *Histoire des Corporations de Métiers*, 154. For Germany, von Below in *Das Aeltere deutsche Städtewesen und Bürgertum* (pp. 106-108), says the following: "The gilds betrayed from the very beginning an anti-capitalistic bias which was well recognized and supported by the municipal authorities. . . . The gilds sought to establish the equality of all their members, that is, of the masterworkmen, not only in law but also in fact. Nearly all gilds limited the number of journeymen and apprentices permitted to any one master—mostly to no more than two journeymen and one apprentice. In very many cases, a master was forbidden to have more than one workshop. . . . Sometimes the gilds even fixed the maximum quantity any master was permitted to produce in a given period of time, as,

Union "Working Rules"

The oldest trade union in the United States and Canada, the International Typographical Union, organized in 1851, has elaborated a code of common rules, with reference to job control,[1] altogether analogous to the rules of the gilds with reference to market control. This International Union was preceded by more than a half century's growth and persistence of local unionism, notably in Washington, Philadelphia, and New York. Such men as Henry George, Horace Greeley, and John Swinton started life as printers, and never, even after their elevation out of their trade, felt themselves to have outstripped their former colleagues of the rank and file beyond a mutual intellectual understanding. So high a level of intelligence seems to dispel any doubt as to the capacity of this group of mechanics to understand clearly what their purposes as a group are, and to devise a fitting system of control. At the same time, in common with the rest of American unions, the printers have never fallen under the spell of intellectuals not of their class. We are consequently entitled to look to the "working rules" of the printers' union, since they represent a hundred years' uninterrupted development, for safe guidance as to "what is on the worker's

for instance, in the case of the brewers. The gild ordinances frankly gave as the motive behind these restrictions the protection of the opportunity of the poorer members. The modern business man who drives smaller competitors to the wall by increasing his own output to the farthest limit possible, would have been held a criminal then."

[1] I am indebted to Mrs. Elizabeth Brandeis Raushenbush for the quotations in this chapter from the documents of the International Typographical Union and also for some of the wording relating to the Typographical Union rules.

mind''; at least as to what is on the mind of the American mechanic.

Studying the rules of the printers' union, we get a picture of a carefully worked out labor dictatorship, not, however, a dictatorship in the Russian style, but in a style all its own, since it is content to leave the employer in the unchallenged position of his property and business, and brings under a union dictatorship the employment opportunities only. This the union has accomplished by establishing and enforcing its claim that the shop rules and regulations that were fixed by ''International Law'', i.e. by the ''laws'' of the International Union, cannot be made the subject of local collective bargaining with the employers, nor be submitted to an arbitration board, but can be changed only by a national referendum of the union. Likewise, ''International Law'' can be *interpreted* only by the Executive Council of the International Union, or, as a last resort, by the Annual Convention. A failure in 1922 to renew the agreement between the union and the American Newspaper Publishers' Association illustrates this condition well. The employers had become increasingly dissatisfied over being party to an arbitration arrangement under which the more important questions were non-arbitrable. On the other hand, ''International Law'' forbade the executive officers of the Union to submit any of its ''laws'' to arbitration. Speaking of the situation thus created, International President Howard said: ''Subordinate unions desiring to incorporate arbitration clauses in new contracts are permitted to do so, provided the course of procedure agreed to properly protects their interests and

accepts *International Typographical Union Laws as
being non-arbitrable* [1]. . . . We believe our members are willing to accept a method for adjudication
of controversies which will permit them to maintain
proper standards and make satisfactory progress.
They are not, however, willing to *sacrifice what has
been won through years of effort by submitting to
unrestricted arbitration''* [2] Under these circumstances, it appears that, in the printing industry,
the industrial constitution is not a joint instrument
administered by joint or impartial agencies, but
rather a document drawn up by one party, accepted
by the other, and thereafter to a large extent administered and interpreted by the party which
enacted it. As regards a large part of the sphere
which has been called industrial relations, the employer has practically abdicated.[3] This state of
affairs goes back to a policy of practical ''job syndicalism'' [4] long pursued by the union in its dealing
with the employers.

Clearly, therefore, a union so remarkably success-

[1] Italics mine.

[2] Reports of Officers and Proceedings of the 68th Session of the
International Typographical Union, held in Atlanta, Georgia, August
13-18, 1923, page 25.

[3] This, of course, is a somewhat extreme statement which will call
for modification. In the first place, it should be noted that, while
International Law remains the supreme law, superior to any contract,
the making of local rules without negotiations with employees has
diminished greatly since the practice of signing written contracts has
begun. (Barnett and Hollander, *Studies in American Unionism*, 182.)
Also there has recently been a tendency to set up joint local boards
for the adjustment of disputes.

[4] Professor Barnett said in one of his studies of the printers, "The
unions frequently changed their scales without conferences, but the
larger unions found it advisable to consult employers before making
radical changes. . . . The practice of embodying in written documents
known as agreements the terms of employment fixed by the union and
the employers is of comparatively recent origin in the Typographical
Union." (*Ibid.*, 181.)

ful in imposing the superiority of its own "Laws" [1] upon employers, even though at the cost of frequent great struggles, should, in the manner in which it has chosen to exploit its unusual power, furnish a true exhibition of the psychology of the labor group. It is for this reason that this union's concentration, as we shall presently show, upon an absolute union control of jobs, assumes an overwhelming importance. And it is equally noteworthy that the printers, as a rule, kept rigidly aloof from any experiments in "workers' control" of industry by the route of the co-operative workshop, while, prior to the assumption of the general labor leadership by the men who made the American Federation of Labor, other labor organizations—the molders, the machinists, and blacksmiths, the Knights of St. Crispin (shoemakers), and last, but not least, the Knights of Labor—periodically displayed a most overpowering wish for such an escape out of the wage system.

"International Typographical Law" vests in the union a complete control of the jobs, which goes much beyond that achieved by other "closed shop" unions. The instrument of that control is the shop foreman, who is obliged to belong to the union. The Typographical Union has always insisted that the foreman of the shop rather than the employer himself shall do the hiring and firing, and otherwise deal with the workmen. Thus the union lays down the "law" on hiring and discharging, and the foreman, a union member, although nominally representing the employer, may be fined or expelled by the union if he does not proceed in accordance with these

[1] Wage scales, however, are subject to collective bargaining.

"Laws".[1] Where the justification for discharge is disputed, the dispute is between two members of the union, the foreman and the discharged workman; and the judicial machinery of the union decides. The worker makes his appeal to the "Chapel"—the organization of all the workers in the shop [2]—and from its decision either the foreman or the worker may appeal—to the local union. A further appeal goes to the Executive Council of the International Union. Thus the merits of the discharge are passed on by a union tribunal, and the employer has nothing to say about the matter.[3] A

[1] In 1900, President Lynch of the International Typographical Union said: "We do not expect that the foreman shall represent the union. It is understood that the foreman is engaged by the office to protect its interests and to carry out its wishes and desires. It must be remembered, however, that a union officer agrees to conduct the composition room in accordance with union rules. If he [the foreman] willingly violates a union law, or permits its violation without notifying union authority, he should be prepared to accept the consequences."
President's Letter Book (ms.), Vol. 43, p. 776.

[2] "The Chapel may also fine a foreman for infraction of Chapel rules. If he believes that he has been fined illegally, he may appeal to the local union, and thence to the International officers."
Barnett, *The Printers*, p. 297.

[3] A decision in a single case, which came up on appeal before the Executive Council, will serve as an illustration:
"McN. was an ad room employee who had served his apprenticeship in that office, and was admitted to membership at the end of four and one-half years by dispensation, upon recommendation of the foreman of the office.
"In the statement of respondent union [that is, the local union which acted as a court of first instance] it is admitted that this member had been guilty of a number of mistakes in laying out ads, with the result that he had been warned that his next offense would bring discharge. There seems to be no serious controversy as to a serious mistake in lay-out for which the member was discharged.
. . . The Executive Council is of the opinion a foreman foregoes his prerogative of discharge for incompetency where the member against whom the charge is made served his apprenticeship under said foreman. More especially so when such apprentice has been recommended by the foreman for full membership prior to expiration of full apprenticeship period." The appeal of the foreman was dismissed. (*Bulletin*

terse and accurate characterization of the Union's exclusive control of employment opportunities was given in 1923 by an arbitrator in a dispute between the associated employers and the local union at Washington, D. C., in connection with a demand by the former for the elimination from the new agreement of any reference to ''International Typographical Union Laws'':

''An analysis of the section as it now stands undoubtedly subordinates the proprietors of the printing establishments operating as closed shops to the foremen of said shops with respect to employment and discharge of journeymen. The foreman, and he alone, is to exercise discretion as to the competency, neglect of duty, and violation of office rules. In this respect, his judgment is supreme. The provision erects a standard obviously designed to withdraw from the employers all right of determination in the matters mentioned, and it leaves the employee in relation to his employer responsible for his ability and conduct to the foreman exclusively.'' The arbitrator then drafted a proviso, which the local union accepted, making the foreman subordinate to the employer. But the International Typographical Union, because this proviso took from the union its absolute mastery over jobs by virtue of its control of the foreman (and possibly because of certain others), categorically refused to underwrite the Washington agreement, on the ground that it was not in complete accord with ''International Typo-

---

of the International Typographical Union, Vol. 77, p. 72.) This case is adduced here merely to illustrate the procedure followed—not to convey an impression that the scales of union justice are not held as evenly as they should be. In a number of other cases, discharges by foremen have been upheld.

graphical Law'', which had to be protected at all hazards.

With the union ''ownership'' of the employment opportunities goes a code of ''rules of occupancy and tenure'' of such opportunities. Where there is a decrease in the amount of work, the last man to be employed is, according to the International Typographical Laws, to be discharged. And paralleling the ''rule of lot'' and the ''stint'' of the gilds, there are provisions for a compulsory sharing of the job opportunities. Where a union printer is available, none is allowed to work overtime. The six-day law of the union provides:

''Not more than 48 hours shall constitute a week's work. (In commercial offices, not more than 44 hours). No member of a subordinate union shall work more than six days in a week nor more than the number of hours constituting a day's work in any jurisdiction multiplied by six where a substitute can be obtained. Should any member work, through inability to secure a substitute, a greater number than six days in any one week, or wherever his overtime aggregates a day in hours, *he shall give to the first available substitute such accumulated day or days.*'' [1]

A penalty is provided for violation or evasion of this law. Furthermore, the law provides that, in slack times, a portion of the regular work shall be divided by limiting the regular workers to a five day week.[2] To this extent, division of work is compulsory on the individual worker.

[1] *International Typographical Union Book of Laws*, 1924, p. 87.
[2] "The subordinate unions may in time of stress enact for a period of not more than eight weeks in any one year a five-day law, by majority referendum vote of six month members." (*Ibid.*)

Voluntarily he may share his work with other printers at any time, and the employer cannot forbid it. The printer may put in a substitute at any time he desires, and the foreman cannot interfere.[1]

The union's proprietary attitude towards jobs, and its enforcement of the rules of job "occupancy and tenure" just described, are accompanied by a persistent pressure for the enlargement of the totality of the job opportunities available to the membership. Such pressure is embodied in rules which achieve this enlargement, together with strengthened control in the making of employment bargains. The "closed shop"[2] rule, that is, the rule that none but union members may find employment, is as much aimed to "conserve" the jobs as it is to make the bargaining solidarity with the employer treasonproof. Furthermore, in the printing industry especially, apprenticeship is strictly regulated, and the workers are protected in their jobs by a limitation of the number of new workers who may enter the trade. The laws of the International Typographical Union provide that no apprentice shall become a member of the union until he is twenty-one, until he has served a five-year apprenticeship (with certain exceptions), and until he has passed an examination and demonstrated his competency. It is left to the subordinate unions to fix the ratio

[1] The law reads: "Any member covering a situation that is holding a regular job on a six or seven day paper is entitled to employ in his stead, whenever so disposed, any competent member of the International Typographical Union, without consultation or approval of the foreman of said office." (*Ibid.*, p. 92.)

[2] The union control of the trade is coterminous with the extent of the closed shop, and falls short by a considerable margin of encompassing the entire trade.

of apprentices to journeymen.[1] Again, of the jurisdictional disputes with other unions, of which this
union has had considerable, many are either inspired by the job conservation or else the job
expansion motive, as the case may be, depending on
whether, in a given situation, the union in question
is in the rôle of a small nation fighting for its "right
to exist", or in that of the "imperialistic aggres-
sor". Furthermore, the Typographical Union has
to its credit the fact that, in the printing industry
par excellence, the workers have succeeded in protecting themselves from the loss of jobs on account
of the introduction of machinery. When typesetting machines began to come in, the union realized its danger, and passed an International Typographical Law which reads as follows:

"The International Typographical Union directs
in all offices within its jurisdiction, where type setting machines are used, *practical union printers
shall be employed to run them,* and also that subordinate unions shall regulate the scale of wages on
such machines"; to which a section was afterwards
added stating that "no person shall be eligible as a
learner on machines who is not a member"; and that
local unions may grant permits to apprentices during the *last six months of their apprenticeship,*
during which time they may learn to run the machines, and such apprentices shall be subject to the
rules and regulations of such local unions.[2] Thus
from the start, the union safeguarded its members
from displacement by unskilled workers as a result
of the introduction of the machine. In limiting the

[1] *General Laws, International Typographical Union,* 48-9.
[2] *Book of Laws,* 1924, International Typographical Union, p. 79.

work on machines to practical printers, and thus debarring apprentices, the union departed from its previous policy of permitting apprentices to do any work they were capable of doing. The comparative simplicity of the machines made the union afraid that employers would utilize apprentices too freely. The employers who were running "closed shops" cheerfully accepted this "International Law" as denoting a farsighted adjustment on the union's part to inevitable change, while keeping the interests of the union printers intact. According to Professor Barnett, the International Typographical Union policy in regard to machinery was instrumental in robbing the transition from hand to machine work of the hardships to the workers usually accompanying such a change.[1]

Another union rule likewise aimed at conserving employment opportunity, (which cannot, however, be placed, even by the farthest stretch of imagination, in the same class with the statesmanlike handling of the problem of the typesetting machine), is the rule which prohibits "interchanging, exchanging, borrowing, lending, or buying of matter previously used, either in the form of type or matrixes between [establishments] . . . not owned by the same individual firm or corporation" unless accompanied by the totally superfluous and wasteful operation of having "such type or matrixes reset as nearly like the original as possible, made up, read and corrected, and a proof submitted to the Chairman of the office."[2]

Thus the International Typographical Union of the United States and Canada, which, through an

[1] Barnett, *The Printers*, 197.   [2] *Ibid.*, 84-5.

early start and an excellent strategic position in the industry, has been able to work out the most far-reaching system of "job control" yet devised by any union, gives us an insight into the characteristic group psychology of the wage earner today as clearly as the gilds, vital and strong because sanctioned by religious and lay authority, reveal to us the group psychology of the mediæval master workman. Central in each instance is the vigorous claim of common "ownership" of the totality of the economic opportunity open to the membership (which is considered scarce and limited and therefore needing to be controlled), and the "common rule", that is, the commonly devised "rules of occupancy and tenure" of that opportunity obligatory upon the individual occupant. From this follows a solid bargaining front to the outside economic world, employer and customer respectively, resulting in a "fair" price or a "fair" wage, as the case may be, together with economic security and individual liberty and leisure, as well as with a reasonably protected future.

Labor's "Home-Grown" Philosophy

In the unionism of the printers' organization we have encountered a truly stable and mature type of collective behavior by labor. The printers' union qualifies as stable and mature, because it has been led by men risen from its own ranks, because it has evolved a complete "law of the job", but in a still deeper sense, because it has mastered the dilemma of serving simultaneously the individual member and the group as a whole. Such unionism is individualistic and collectivistic at the same time. It is individualistic in the sense that it aims to satisfy the individual aspirations of Tom, Dick, and Harry for a decent livelihood, for economic security, and for freedom from tyranny on the part of the boss. But such unionism is also collectivistic, since it aspires to develop in the individual a willingness to subordinate his own interests to the superior interests of the collectivity. It may be true, as Whiting Williams pointed out in his *Mainsprings of Men,* that the majority of workingmen are "on the fence", deliberately weighing the relative advantages from following the employer or the union leader, each one arriving at his own decision only after a cold-blooded calculation. However, such "Whiting Williams unionists" resemble real unionists no more than a resident of Upper Silesia would have resembled a true national of either country, had he stopped to weigh, on the memorable day of the Plebiscite, the relative material advantage from voting himself either a German or a Pole. Consequently, while it is true that a union can never become strong or stable except by attaching the individual to itself through the tangible benefits accruing to him from its administration of the job opportunities of the group as a whole, neither can it be a union in the full sense of the word unless it has educated the members to put the integrity of the collective "job-territory" above the security of their individual job tenure. Unionism is, in this respect, not unlike patriotism which may and does demand of the citizen the supreme sacrifice, when the integrity of the national territory is at stake. Just as a mere pooling by forty million Frenchmen of their individualistic self-interests will not yet produce a patriotic France, so a bare adding together of the individual job interests of five million wage earners, united in a common organization, will scarcely result in a labor movement. To have a really stable unionism and a really stable labor movement, the individual members must evince a readiness to make sacrifices on behalf of the control by their union of their collective "job-territory", without stopping to count too closely the costs involved to themselves. And like nationalism, unionism is keenly conscious of a "patria irredenta" in the non-union portion of its trade or industry.

But if unionism means an idealistic readiness on the part of the individual to offer, as the need arises, unstinted sacrifices for the group as a whole, what then of "business unionism"? May even such a unionism have an "ideology"? To many, of course, any "ideology" whatsoever in a unionism which is merely "business" and which avowedly limits its objective to a mere control of jobs, is entirely and definitely precluded. However, upon closer examination, it would seem that if, by naming the predominant type of American unionism "business unionism", it was meant to bring out that it had no "ideology", then the name was clearly a misnomer. The difficulty arises from a disposition to class as idealistic solely the professions of idealistic aims—socialism, anarchism, and the like,—but to overlook the unselfconscious idealism in the daily practice of unionism. In truth, unionism, even "business unionism", shows idealism both in aim and in method; only it does so in the thoroughly unsophisticated way of "Tom, Dick, and Harry idealism".

All unions sooner or later stress "shop rights", which, to the workingman at the bench, are identical with "liberty" itself,—since, thanks to them, he has no need to kowtow to foreman or boss, as the price of holding his job. And, after all, is not this sort of liberty the only sort which reaches the workman directly and with certainty [1] and that can never get lost *en route,* like the "broader" liberty promised by socialism? For, in practice, that other liberty may never succeed in straining through the many layers of the socialistic hierarchy down to the mere private in industry. Secondly, a union which expects its members to sacrifice for the group on a scale almost commensurate with the sacrifices which patriotism evokes, cannot be without its own respectable ideology. Frequently, therefore, the "materialism" of unionism proves only the one-sidedness of the view of the particular observer.

Yet, granting that even "business unionism" possesses ideology after a fashion, might it not be that, after all, the conception of unionism advanced here could fit only a narrow craft unionism, not a unionism with a wider conception of labor solidarity? True, the more distinct the trade identity of a given group and therefore the clearer the boundaries of its particular "job-territory", the stronger are normally the bonds which tie the members together in a spontaneous solidarity. Yet, on the other hand, the specific area of that common job-territory, or of the common opportunity which a group considers its own, is seldom fixed, but is

---

[1] Frequently workingmen are willing to resign themselves to "boss control" in their union for the sake of this liberty in the shop. In other words, they are willing to sacrifice their "political" liberty in the union so long as they may have "economic" liberty on the job.

constantly tending to widen, just as the numerical size and the composition of the group itself is constantly tending to grow. When accumulated technological changes have undermined the partitions between the several grades of labor in an industry and have thus produced a virtually undivided "job-territory" for all employed in it, the function of framing "rules of occupancy and tenure" for the job opportunities included within the now expanded job-territory will sooner or later be taken over by an *industrial* union or by an *amalgamated* union bordering upon the industrial type. And that union, when it will come to face the common enemy, will display a solidarity no less potent than the solidarity of the original craft unions, although as a job administrator the new and expanded union will endeavor to give recognition, so far as it will still remain possible, to the original particularistic job claims.

Nor need a job conscious unionism, with respect to many portentous issues, arrest the growth of its solidarity, short of the outer boundaries of the wage earning class as a whole. Many are the influences affecting union job control: the legal status of unionism, the policies of the government, a favorable public opinion, and others. Thus every union soon discovers that the integrity of its "job-territory", like the integrity of the geographic territory of a nation, is inextricably dependent on numerous wide relationships. And the very consciousness of the scarcity of opportunity, which is basic to labor's thinking, engenders in individual unions, labor's original organic cells, a wish for mutual cohesion, a common class-consciousness, and eventually a readiness to subordinate the interests of the individual cell to the aspirations of the whole labor organism. We know from history that the most craft-conscious bodies that ever existed, the mediæval gilds, left nothing to be desired so far as solidaristic action against the common overlords was concerned. There is, however, a practical limitation upon labor's solidarity, and this limitation is a very vital one, namely that, in a labor movement which has already gone beyond the emotional stage and acquired a definite *rationale* of its own, an appeal for common class action, be it through a sympathetic strike or through joint political action, will only be likely to evoke the response which is desired if the objective of the proposed common undertaking be kept so close to the core substance of union aspiration that Tom, Dick, and Harry could not fail to identify it as such.

Just as we find job conscious unionism far from devoid of idealism of a kind, so its ultimate industrial vision need not at all be limited to the job itself. In truth, such a unionism might easily acquire a lively interest in problems of management without previously undergoing mutation. It is not at all unnatural that a unionism which is intent upon job opportunities should join with management in a joint campaign to reduce the cost of operation and raise efficiency—all for the "conservation" of the current job opportunities. However, to grant so much is far from making the claim that labor might be brought to embrace "efficiency" as its primary concern instead of merely pursuing it secondarily to the primary interest in jobs. Thus it grows out of the preceding that whether one is trying to "improve" labor's "ideology", to broaden its solidarity, or to awaken its interest in "efficiency", one will indeed do well, in order to avoid wasted efforts, to steer close to the fundamental scarcity consciousness of the manual worker, which rules unionism today as it ruled the gilds of the past.

What the true purposes of unionism are (distinguished from mere verbal pronunciamentos, in which the preambles to the constitutions of some "socialistic" unions abound), and what a union does when it applies a scientific rationalism to its problems, have best been shown by the Amalgamated Clothing Workers of America. Although it is the outstanding "socialistic" union in America, it has, in practice, turned its efforts not to fighting capitalism in its industry, but to securing a thoroughgoing job control. As an organization of quite recent origin, the Clothing Workers' union lacked the advantage which the printers' union had derived from the long, evolutionary growth of a union "common law", which enforced itself almost automatically, as it were, upon the employers, through the sheer weight of trade custom. The Clothing Workers' union was therefore obliged to acquire the same control of the job through a system of *unrestricted* collective bargaining, and to secure the upbuilding of a common law, similar to that in the printing trade, through a shrewd use of the machinery for continuous arbitration, functioning under the joint agreements in that industry. The "rules of occupancy and tenure" of the employment opportunities are in the clothing industry practically identical with the printers', and, for that matter, with the rules of the railwaymen, of the miners, and of the other organized trades,—showing the same "union control of opportunity" and the same united bargaining front. But in Chicago, the Clothing Workers' union has gone a step farther, and has taken over the employment work for the whole local industry. It has installed to that end a modern employment office, originally under the management of a former chief of the Canadian system of government employment offices.

In Chicago, too, the Clothing Workers have led the way in perfecting a new method of "job preservation", rejecting both the cruder "making work" devices of the older unions and the employer's cure-all, a wage reduction. During the depression after 1920, which has not yet ended, the union has come to the employers' aid in a way altogether novel. Without itself going into business, but letting the employer remain the risk-taker and the responsible manager, this union has contrived materially to lighten his burden by considering and helping solve the problems of each concern on their merits,—up to the point of assuming responsibility for the supervision of the work. In this manner the union, through co-operating with the employer in reducing his costs and enabling him to continue in business, has saved many jobs for its members and has substantially protected the wage scale.

CHAPTER VIII

THE INTELLECTUALS' PROGRAMS FOR LABOR

In marked contrast to the actual behavior of "organic" labor groups, peasant communities, gilds and trade unions, stand the several programs for labor action mapped out by the intellectuals. This contrast is, in the last analysis, a product of two opposite ways of looking at labor. It has already been brought out how the organic groups, notwithstanding that they rigorously enforce, upon their individual members, collectively framed rules for the "occupancy and tenure of economic opportunity", yet at each turn keep in sight the concrete individual, with his very tangible individual interests and aspirations. But it has always been the main characteristic of the intellectual to think of labor as an abstract "mass" in the grip of an abstract "force". By the intellectual is meant, of course, the educated non-manualist, who has established a contact with the labor movement, either indirectly, through influence acquired over trade union bodies, or else as a leader of labor in his own right, as Lassalle was in Germany and as the leading Communists are in Russia today.

So long as the intellectual is investigating specific subjects, which have definite and calculable bearings upon the workers' welfare,—for instance, industrial accidents, unemployment, wage trends, and the like, his tendency to reduce labor in the concrete to an abstraction is restrained. But let the intellectual's thought turn from relatively prosaic matters like the above mentioned to the infinitely more soul-stirring one of "labor and the social order", and it is the rare intellectual who is able to withstand an onrush of overpowering social mysticism. Labor then ceases to be an aggregation of individuals seeking as a group to control their common economic opportunity in accord with common rules, as well as to enlarge that opportunity. Instead, labor takes on the aspect of a "mass" driven by a "force" towards a glorious "ultimate social goal". The intellectual, to be sure, is unconscious of his mysticism. On the contrary, he is generally careful to connect every move of labor towards the "new social order" which he prognosticates, with definite changes in labor conditions, with a growing wastefulness of competition, or with an equally comprehensible urge within the workingman to a greater freedom in the shop, due to an awakened self-consciousness. Yet, at bottom, the intellectual's conviction that labor must espouse the "new social order" rests neither on statistically demonstrable trends in conditions nor on labor's stirrings for the sort of liberty expressed through the control of the job, which anyone who knows workingmen will recognize and appreciate, but on a deeply rooted faith that labor is somehow the "chosen vessel" of whatever may be the power which shapes the destiny of society. The best evidence that one is here dealing with the psychological phenomenon of faith is the intellectual's persistence in that faith regardless of labor's repeated refusals to reach out for its appointed destiny and to advance materially in that direction, even when opportunity appears to beckon most promisingly.[1] When brought face to face with evidence of this sort, the typical intellectual [2] rather than admit that his original conception of labor's psychology was wrong, will take refuge in an explanation that what has occurred is merely a temporary "delay", and he will account for that delay by calling attention to the rise of a reactionary trade union bureaucracy, through whose machinations the grip of the "force" upon the labor "mass" has temporarily become weakened and its movement thus been deflected in an illegitimate direction.

While the concept of labor as a "mass" in the grip of a "force" is the common basis of all intellectualist theories of the labor movement, intellectuals fall into three distinct groupings, depending on what they take the nature of that "force" to be. The Marxian, who is a "determinist-revolutionary", pictures it as the ever growing force of material production, embodied in the tools of production and in technological methods. This "force", in seeking to break through the capitalist strait jacket which encases it and impedes its further growth, is inevitably hurling the labor "mass" against the political and legal régime established and defended by the capitalist class. Secondly, we have the "ethical" intellectual to whom the "force" that grips the labor "mass" is the force of labor's own awakened ethical perception. This "ethical" force causes labor to strive for the fullest ethical self-realization,

[1] See the chapter on Germany.
[2] Many, of course, become disillusioned and drop out.

which in turn is conditional upon labor's escape from the degradation of "wagery" into "freedom". And "freedom" is found either in the self-governing workshop of the Christian Socialist, in the "labor commune" of the Anarchist, or in the "national gild" of the Gild Socialist. Finally, there is the "efficiency" intellectual with his vision of society advancing from a state of disorganization to one of "order", meaning a progressive elimination of waste and the abolition of destitution. This type of intellectual, who is best exemplified by the Fabians, sees labor as a "mass" propelled by the force of its awakened burning interest in a planned economic order yielding a maximum technical and social efficiency.

Every one of these three types of "intellectuals" projects from his own abstract conception of "labor as a mass in the grip of a force" a mental picture of the workingman as an individual. Consequently, every one of these pictures differs widely from the real person whom employers and union leaders know. The Marxian pictures the workingman as a class-conscious proletarian who, at the dawn of a real revolutionary opportunity such as a world war or a similar upheaval, will unhesitatingly scorn all the gains in his material conditions and in his individual status which as a trade unionist he has already conquered from the employers, and will buoyantly face an uncertain future—all for the sake of the dictatorship of his class.

Unlike the Marxian, who makes a virtue of thinking in terms of the "mass", the "ethical" intellectual places the highest value upon the liberated human personality and consequently is obliged to keep the individual in the center of his vision. Yet he too falls short of a true vision, since he arrives at his individual workingman by separating him out as a molecule from the abstract labor "mass". By this process, curiously enough, the individual workingman emerges bearing a very striking spiritual resemblance to his maker, the "ethical" intellectual. To the latter, industrial freedom means the complete disappearance of all authority from above, and an opportunity for everyone to participate in the total creative planning of industry. So his "workingman", too, feels that he is still being denied his rightful chance for development of personality, if he has merely been given the opportunity, under the protection of his union, to enjoy an inalienable right to his job.

Lastly, the individual workingman of the "efficiency" intellectual, as we shall come to see, is a creature who has forever given up any claim to a vested right in any particular job, or, in common with the others in his group, to any particular "job-territory"; but is, on the contrary, totally indifferent as to who gets the job or jobs, so long as the employer observes the union standards of wages and hours. This "workingman" has presumably arrived at such a thorough oblivion of self and of his nearest group in the vital matter of securing his opportunity, because he has realized that, with such an arrangement, the employer would be free to select the fittest worker for the job and that hence the way would be opened to the highest "efficiency". Truly, the "workingman" of the "efficiency" intellectual should have no trouble in getting admitted to the Fabian Society or even perhaps into a somewhat reconstituted Taylor Society of America.

All intellectuals, whether of the "ethical", or the "efficiency", or the "deterministic-revolutionary" type, are alike desirous to make their own ideology also the ideology of labor. However, the methods which they will pursue to gain this ascendency and the lengths to which they will go, generally vary with the particular ideology each professes.

One important group of "ethical" intellectuals, the English Positivists in the third quarter of the Nineteenth Century,[1] demonstrated how intellectuals in their relationship to labor may combine a light and modest touch with a truly remarkable usefulness. These Positivists, of whom Frederic Harrison was by far the outstanding personality, notwithstanding that they labored under the urge of a potent idealism, yet were careful not to overstep that line at which even mere moral suasion, by its sheer persistence, turns into something akin to coercion. Possibly their fine self-restraint was partly owing to the fact that they rested their hope not solely upon labor but on a conversion of the whole community. Yet, in their scheme of things, an enlightened trade union movement was a powerful pledge of the ultimate realization of their ideal England, which would be liberal and humanitarian in her dealings with foreign countries and dedicated to the good life in her internal order. For that reason, they strove to win for the labor movement the status of a publicly recognized institution. It was Frederic Harrison, whose fertile brain invented the all-important stratagem whereby trade unions

[1] See the chapter on England.

could gain legal protection for their funds without exposing themselves to suits in damages brought by employers, and he thereby saved the trade unions from putting their heads into the legal noose of formal incorporation which their leaders, untrained in the law, were ready to do. Nothing, however, is more characteristic of the type of relationship between the labor movement and the Positivist intellectual group than the manner in which the bonds uniting the two were permitted to loosen and fall, once the unions had carried out their ambitious legislative program and their leaders had lost interest in outside allies. To be sure, when the trade unions had drifted away from them, the Positivists were deeply grieved, seeing in the estrangement but a sign of a growing moral flabbiness in the labor movement. Yet they permitted the connection to lapse without a protest.

Another English "ethical" intellectual group, somewhat earlier than the Positivists, were the Christian Socialists, led by Maurice and Kingsley. The Christian Socialist group were also useful to the labor movement, but only as moulders of favorable public opinion. Their contribution included no such workable and essential device as Harrison's. On the contrary, on the practical side they may be said to have done their best to put labor on the wrong track. They centered on urging an anti-capitalist panacea in the self-governing workshop, in which workmen-co-operators would own the means of production and elect their foremen and manager. To the "ethical" mind, the idea of a free association of responsible producers holds an irresistible charm. However, when labor tried it out in practice, it proved to be founded on a fallacious conception of labor psychology and on a complete misunderstanding of management problems, and, in consequence, it was a cause of material loss and of spiritual discouragement to the labor movement. Nevertheless, practical results aside, as a specimen among types of labor-intellectual interrelationships, the Christian Socialist episode may be classed with the Positivist. The Christian Socialists perhaps possessed greater fervor than the Positivists, and their program doubtless did assign to labor a more pivotal and decisive rôle. Still, they were as remote as the Positivists from the thought of trying to *control* the labor movement. Positivist [1] and Christian Socialist alike professed humanitarianism and liberty-loving philosophies; alike they abhorred every kind of coercion, physical as well as moral; and they relied equally on the moral sense of human beings to guide them to the true ideal.[2]

The anarchistic type is still another variation of the "ethical" intellectual. He may be studied at his best in the Russian "Populistic" (non-Marxian) revolutionary movement during the seventies and in the successor of that movement, the Social Revolutionary party of the Left, 1917-1919. The "Populistic" ("Narodnik") intellectual did not base his socialism, as does the Marxian, on the materialistic conception of history, but on an ethical ideal. He

[1] The Positivists hoped for the ascendency by the spiritual aristocracy over society. But industry would be free to obey it or not.

[2] A humanitarian like Lord Shaftesbury does not belong in this connection, since he distrusted trade unionism. Neither need we consider here the more democratic humanitarians like the upper and middle class organizers of the Women's Trade Union League of England and America. These intellectual women have never pretended to point to the labor movement the road which it should follow.

would be the "hero" to lead the present "masses" out of bondage to Czar and landlord, to the free land and freedom of an anarchist Russia. This type of intellectual seemed to combine an indomitable revolutionary will with an utter absence of the dogmatism that characterizes the Marxian. There are sufficient indications that had fate brought him to deal with a mass movement arisen independently of him like the British labor movement (for which, of course, neither the economic nor the political milieu existed in Russia), he would have been even more content than he actually was to rely solely on moral appeal and the contagion of the daring personal deed, and that he would have thought even less of resorting to the coercion of the spirit of labor, the favorite weapon of his Marxian adversary, through a dogmatic and presumably infallible revolutionary social science, or through the tactical means of "boring from within" the labor organizations. The "ethical" revolutionary intellectual has been, on the one hand, too individualistic to be willing to submit himself to the iron discipline of a communist party, and on the other hand, he has been too much a respecter of the liberty of others to desire to dictate to the labor movement.[1]

[1] Working-class anarchism, like French Syndicalism, has been a clever working-class stratagem to get rid of the hegemony of the intellectual. The intellectual was eliminated from the trade union movement in the name of the very revolutionary class-consciousness which he himself had helped to evoke in labor. But observe how naturally the Confédération Générale du Travail had slipped during the War into a position of opportunistic unionism. On the whole, the disappointing weakness of French unionism after 1920, exposing a deplorable instability in the movement, goes back to its constant absorption in mere matters of abstract ideology—syndicalism, reformist socialism and communism—largely the result of an earlier indoctrination, directly and indirectly, by intellectuals. Lacking a safe psychic anchorage in a body of "job control" practices, the French

But the "ethical" intellectual may be said to have entered the real broad arena of the labor struggle only with the British Labour Party. It is well known that British socialism is a blending of the ethical ideals of Robert Owen with the strategy of political mass action, which was entirely foreign to Owen. Thus, in J. Ramsay MacDonald the "ethical" intellectual is no longer the mere Christian Socialist exhorter nor the knight-errant on the model of the Russian "Populist", but the recognized leader of a great and organized movement. Our arrival at this movement furnishes a good opportunity for measuring both the goal and the strategy of the modern "ethical" intellectual type against the goal and strategy of "organic" labor.

While, at bottom, the "ethical" intellectuals and organic labor have this in common that both trace the root evil in society to the denial of "freedom" to the wage earner, there remains a broad cleavage between their respective ideologies. Unionism, perceiving the scarcity of opportunity for Tom, Dick, and Harry, proceeds, as we saw, to make that opportunity into the common patrimony of the group, to be administered in behalf of the same Tom, Dick, and Harry. The outcome is a real victory for "freedom". But freedom means two different things to

labor movement has proved an easy plaything for the gusts of wind blowing from Soviet Russia, until the frail bark has been broken on the rocks of an exceptionally entrenched capitalism. The same holds true of Italian unionism. But there is also a syndicalism which draws but little from revolutionary ideologies, but is a pure reaction to conditions. This reaction may be brought on by the ruthless exploitation by a capitalism in its first and most exploitative phase; a case in point was the great mass movement in the middle of the thirties in England. It may also be caused by a revolt against "pacifistic" leaders, who have forgotten how to lead a strike, as in England during 1910-1912 and again in 1917.

the workingman and to the intellectual. To the workingman, the freedom that matters supremely is the freedom on the job, freedom from unjust discrimination, which enables him to face his boss "man to man". Compared with this tangible sort of freedom, the "higher" freedom, the freedom to elect the managers of industry who are to supplant the present day private boss, or the freedom which the intellectual talks about, appears too remote to enter into actual calculations. So long as he may have the freedom founded on the recognition of his right to the job under conditions fixed by collective bargaining, the workingman is content to let the private employer own the capital of industry and continue taking the business risks for the sake of the profits. However, to the "ethical" intellectual, no labor movement can have an "ideology" unless it seeks to give to the workers, as the majority group in the general community or as a "producers' gild", full access to the highest reaches of industrial management and creative planning. When a labor movement fails to embrace this objective, it confesses to a second rate ethical purpose or even worse.

When the "ethical" intellectual has come to feel as a political leader of labor deeply concerned with the fortunes of the party he leads, fresh complications are bound to arise between himself and "organic" labor. The "ethical" politician may see his most carefully laid plans to win broad popular confidence for his party completely miscarry through an outburst at a critical moment, say on the eve of a general election, of a strike in one of the key industries. For it may be rather expected of unionists that they will be so materialistic as to forget the "higher" purposes of labor as soon as an opportunity heaves in sight for a wage increase or for tightening control over their jobs.[1] It is to avert such political catastrophes that the "ethical" intellectual, in the rôle of a labor party leader, will feel forced to go farther than have the other species of his type, in trying to impose his will and his views on the labor movement.[2]

A contrast to the "ethical" type is the "social efficiency" type of intellectual, who is in our times best represented by the English Fabians. Certainly this sort of an intellectual is also a humanitarian in his motives, yet it is characteristic of him that he would rather base his appeal for thorough social reconstruction on the data of the objective sciences

[1] However, when labor is still an unenfranchised class and its "struggle for citizenship" or for "equal citizenship" lies ahead of it, its political interest will at times assume a warmth which even its job interest will for the time being be unable to equal. Workingmen seek the political franchise not only for its instrumental value—to bring pressure upon the government to make labor's economic campaign less difficult—but also for the spiritual gratification that lies in having their human worth recognized as on a par with that of any other class. In that respect, the Workingmen's parties in New York and Philadelphia, the Chartist Movement in England and the Lassallean movement in Germany were all of a common psychological norm.

[2] After the fall of the first English Labour Cabinet in 1924, the trade unions appeared to act more radically than the Labour Party. This was shown in the persistent attempt by the Trades Union Congress to co-operate with the labor movement of Soviet Russia, but mainly, of course, through the General Strike of May 1926 and the protracted miners' strike of that year. However, so far as the great rank and file of British labor was concerned, this radicalism was really a manifestation of the desperate economic plight of many sections of British labor and a determination to fight to the bitter end to arrest a further lowering of standards. Even a leader like Arthur J. Cook of the miners, himself doubtless a revolutionary, in order to keep the million or more miners in line, made his battle cry "Not a penny off the wage, not a second on the time"—in reality a slogan befitting more a "business unionism" than a unionism that was clasping hands with the Red Trade Union International with headquarters in Moscow.

of economics and public administration. Instead of stressing the injustice of the existing order of things, he condemns it on the ground of its inefficiency, its general irrationality, and its waste of human energy and of material resources. Probably the Frenchman, Charles Fourier, was the first "efficiency" socialist. Unlike Robert Owen, who was mainly alive to the evils of an unjust economic distribution and to the warping of human beings by an improper social environment, Fourier spoke the language of the engineer. He would solve all the problems with a phalanstery, where industry would be "attractive", waste eliminated, and labor prosperous, despite a substantial deduction for capital and "talent". His optimism was grounded on his discovery of a psychological social science. Of course Fourier's "science" is to modern science as alchemy to chemistry. Nevertheless, his attitude was that of the scientific reformer. Like the Fabians, he set out to discover the principles underlying a proper social administration. Like the Fabians, too, he went out to permeate with his ideas all those who, regardless of the class to which they belonged, had the necessary intelligence and social idealism.

Fourier's program was non-political. He invited his followers to withdraw themselves from unscientific society and set up a miniature scientific one as an object lesson to others. By and large, he may be said to have for his modern successors our industrial engineers and personnel managers, who have reproduced both his belief in the supreme importance of industrial psychology and his contempt for politics, but rejected his socialism. But these non-political intellectuals generally have no connection with the labor movement, except for the few who "arbitrate" disputes in the clothing industry, sponsor "union-management co-operative plans", or advise labor unions on their economic policies.

Therefore the predominant type of "efficiency" intellectual associated with the labor movement is distinctly the political type. Whether his condemnation of capitalism has resulted from an inductive and detailed study of the existing waste and poverty, or whether he has reached the same conclusions more by general observations and by reflection on the inherent planlessness and "anarchy" of capitalism, his constructive program always leans heavily to governmentalism and to political action—to state-guaranteed "minima", and eventually to an organization of industry by the political community instead of by the private profit seeker. Ultimate social efficiency would come when nationalized and municipalized industries, trade unions, and consumers' co-operatives will have realized together a common unity and a common social plan under the hegemony of the state.[1]

The most serious limitation of the "efficiency" intellectual as a safe guide to the labor movement springs from his external approach to industrial problems. As a rule, he has studied industry from the standpoint of the checks put upon it by government or by trade unionism—not from the inside,

[1] The revolt by the Gild Socialists against the state-mindedness of the Fabians was a partial return to the "ethical" type. The Gild Socialists have struck the ethical note, first, in stressing the spiritual degradation of "wagery", and, second, in the encouragement which they have lent to producers' co-operation under the new form of builders' guilds. These latter, in vogue for a brief period after the War, were of a piece with the "self-governing workshops" of the Christian Socialists.

from the standpoint of the internal management of industry.[1] Even when he talks like an engineer, strictly in terms of avoidable wastes, he still shows himself the complete outsider. He placidly assumes, what a practical engineer would not do, that the reorganized economic society, from which the profit motive has been eliminated, will yet manage to retain an undiminished urge towards efficiency, which in existing society is the direct effect of the drive for profits.[2] The consequence is that, while the "efficiency" intellectual, due to an erudite scholarship, is nearly always compellingly convincing so long as he is dealing with the institutions that *regulate* industry from the outside, governmental and trade union, he fails to carry the same conviction when he turns to recommend how industry should be *operated* and managed from within.

Practical trade unionists, on the contrary, whatever may be their other limitations, rarely make such free and easy assumptions, since as "insiders" in industry, they usually know better. Occasionally they may acquiesce in the intellectual's theories, and may even carry that acquiescence to the point of demanding the "nationalization" of their industry. But at a real showdown, the union leader's inherent skepticism towards such schemes is certain

[1] A survey of the remarkable career in scholarly research which stands to the credit of Sidney and Beatrice Webb, the "efficiency" intellectuals, *par excellence*, shows, alongside of a long array of titles dealing with government administration, trade unions and co-operation (which while a management problem is yet different from the Great Industry of today) but one lone pamphlet on industrial management: *The Works Manager Today*, by Sidney Webb, written in 1917.

[2] To be sure, the entrepreneur often restricts production in order to maintain prices. But "holding the dogs in leash" does not take away from their fleetness.

to come to the surface, and will show itself through his failure to put behind these radical demands anything like the drive he puts, as a matter of course, behind demands for higher wages and for job control. The intellectual insistently recommends to labor that the seat of industrial government shall be so changed about that management shall henceforth derive its mandate no longer from the profit-seeking investors, but either from the state, in which the workers "by hand and by brain" naturally have a majority, or from the equally constituted workers' gild. To this, the thoughtful unionist clearly and directly replies, that efficient industry demands the destruction of the "bossism" by the banker over industry,[1] but not a replacement of one order of things which keeps management abjectly dependent by another order which, in effect, will do the same. The unionist knows how short his own group falls of having the requisite capacity to choose proper managers. He also shrewdly suspects that the making of paper constitutions for industries is probably an illicit occupation in a society that professes belief in evolution.

But unionists and "efficiency" intellectuals differ not alone in their theory as to what makes the wheels of industry go round. They are just as widely apart on the basic purposes of unionism. This misunderstanding of unionism by the intellectual has, surprisingly enough, been best demonstrated by the deans of the scientific students of the labor movement, Sidney and Beatrice Webb.

In their *Industrial Democracy*, the classical trea-

---

[1] It is possible that trade unionists exaggerate the menace to themselves from banker-control over industry.

tise on the practices of the labor movement, the
Webbs made the generalization, the most important
one in the book, that the trend in British unionism
has been steadily away from the device of the "restriction of numbers", towards the device of the
"common rule". They explained that they meant
by this that unionism was becoming more and more
indifferent as to who gets the job, provided there
was the assurance that the employer would observe
the union standards relating to wages, hours, and
other working conditions. In other words, a union
which has mastered the difficult problem of wage
control and knows how to prevent the employer from
"nibbling" at the standard rate (the other standards are much less of a problem to enforce), becomes willing, as a result, to relinquish the "working rules", like apprenticeship, hiring from union
lists, seniority preference, and the like, which had
previously safeguarded, on the one hand, the exclusive right of a particular labor group, say a craft, to
a particular bundle of job opportunities, and on the
other hand, the right of a particular individual to
a particular job. Under the newer unionism, which
thinks only of the "common rule", competition for
jobs, in the words of the Webbs, is becoming a free
for all competition, analogous to the one under a
meticulously conducted civil service, in which the
fitness of the candidate for the job, or for promotion
to a higher job, is the only consideration permitted
to enter. Consequently, the Webbs triumphantly
concluded, unionism is developing into a most potent
spur to industrial efficiency. First, because through
its "common rule", it is eliminating the inefficient
employer who can stay in business only through

underpaying his labor. And second, because it is now agreeing to free the employer who lives up to the common rule from any restriction whatever on his power of choosing the most efficient employee he can find. Thus, as early as thirty years ago,[1] unionism was pictured as having "caught up" with the "efficiency" intellectual, by showing a willingness to throw overboard its rules pertaining to the allotment of jobs.

Twenty years after this generalization was published,—to meet the War-time need for a greatly expanded labor personnel in industry, the unions did indeed consent to give up their rules temporarily, but only upon the pledge of the government to have them fully restored once peace was made. It was upon that occasion that Sidney Webb again displayed the characteristic aversion felt by the "efficiency" intellectuals towards union rules of the kind under discussion, as well as their deeply seated predilection for the protection of labor through legal enactment instead of by the method of collective bargaining. In his work entitled *The Restoration of Trade Union Conditions,* published in 1917, Webb spoke with positiveness of the rules having been irrevocably lost to unionism regardless of the promise of their restoration, and urgently advised the labor movement to commute that promise into a greatly broadened system of social insurance, a program of government work to take care of the unemployed, and the like. However, three years after, in the 1920 edition of the *History of Trade Unionism,* the Webbs were obliged to admit that the rules which they had given up for dead,

[1] *Industrial Democracy* was first published in 1896.

apparently without much mental anguish on their part, had come to life again. All of which goes to show that, the "efficiency" intellectual notwithstanding, unionism's deepest concern remains the right to job opportunities,—of self-conscious groups, say a craft or an amalgamation of related crafts, and of the individuals within such groups. To be sure, unionism is not hostile to the efficiency interest so dear to the heart of the "efficiency" intellectual. That this is so is shown first in the rules of eligibility for membership, which are purposely designed to keep out those who fall below a high minimum proficiency in the trade. Also, unionism has no objection if the employer, in order to attract workmen above the average, pays them above the union scale. Furthermore, no rational union will wish to become an incubus upon its own industry by handicapping it in the power to compete against other industries for the consumer's dollar. On the contrary, to improve the competitive ability of its industry, which means simultaneously its ability to furnish jobs,[1] a union will readily become a party to plans for union-management co-operation aiming to reduce costs of production by joint efforts. But, granting all this, it still remains true that unions will not permit their concern for efficiency to come between them and their interest in protecting the right to the job. So far as labor is concerned, efficiency can never be, beyond an unconditional guarantee of a good average, more than secondary consideration, coming into play only when the primary consideration has been satisfied and protected.

[1] See above for the policies of the Amalgamated Clothing Workers of America.

And this primary interest is the interest of conserving and enlarging the collective job opportunity, which the union seeks to administer with equity among all legitimate members of the group.

Although the "efficiency" intellectuals have based the program which they have submitted to labor on research and investigation, and consequently have been anything but lacking in confidence in the authoritativeness of their own recommendations, yet they have, on the whole, shown themselves entirely content to rely on the necessarily slow permeation of labor thought with their ideas. To them, after all, the "Sabbath was ordained for man", and moreover, they felt that man's decision to observe the Sabbath has to be an act of his own free choice. Such patience with the cautious pragmatism of the labor movement, or such democratic scruple, is never, however, displayed by the "determinist-revolutionary" type of intellectual, the Marxian. When an absolute confidence in one's own "science" is knitted together with an indomitable "will to revolution", and when, moreover, that science proclaims that the triumph of the proletariat over capitalism has been determined beyond recall by the objective and inexorable march of history, then patience with the trade unionists' hesitation to take the revolutionary leap in the dark ceases to be a virtue.

Labor history cannot deny to the revolutionary intellectual a truly pivotal part in the labor struggles of the past. Only in English-speaking countries did the labor movement show the capacity to arise without his leadership. On the Continent, it was from the intellectual that the philosophy and program of the budding labor movements came, just as it was the intellectual who built up the first labor organizations and directed their first campaigns. And where, as in Germany, his hegemony was long and undisputed, he managed to leave upon the labor movement an indelible imprint of idealism and of an unquestioned class solidarity, regardless of distinctions of craft and of wage levels, a solidarity which has survived, to the great advantage of the movement, even after his predominant influence had long passed. Thus few indeed will assert that without the early leadership of Lassalle and of those intellectuals upon whom fell his mantle and the mantle of Marx, German labor would have been what it is today. English labor, which lacked the intellectuals' contribution during most of its history, long retained an ingrained narrow craft consciousness; while American labor, which has never come under his influence, largely remains even today in the stage of mere craft consciousness.

Nevertheless, the basic contradiction which exists between the mentality of organic labor and that of the revolutionary intellectual must, in every instance, sooner or later become strikingly plain. The trade union leader sees the labor movement climbing a difficult road, beset with many pitfalls, towards a civilized level of existence for oneself and one's dependents. Some of these pitfalls are of the employers' making, while others are unwittingly dug by labor's devoted but impractical friends. With every stretch of the road that has been covered, labor is acquiring an ever stronger incentive to turn a deaf ear to the preachers of a complete upsetting of the established political and industrial order.

Labor leaders know that if with such a revolution there should come a disruption of production, a consequence which to practical unionists seems not at all unlikely, the hard-won labor standards would be just as much a thing of the past as the employers' profits. Furthermore, organized labor is under no illusion as to the sort of resistance that would be offered by a capitalism fighting for its very existence. But to the way of thinking of the intellectual of the "determinist-revolutionary" category, the labor movement is only an instrument of the inevitable revolution. History has irrevocably determined that the proletariat must follow the revolutionary path. The capitalists might throw labor back, but that can be only temporary. In the end, the revolutionary proletariat must win against all obstacles. If, however, organized labor hesitates and turns from the revolutionary course, the Simon-pure Marxian will admit only one conclusion: labor has fallen under a treacherous or cowardly leadership. To remove that corrupt and corrupting leadership, by whatever expedient means lie at hand, then becomes the revolutionist's first and foremost duty. If that means an inevitable factional fight within the organization, which may threaten its very existence, the risk is still worth taking. If the revolution and the ensuing dictatorship mean a more or less prolonged period of industrial disorganization fraught with fatal dangers in the case of an industrialized country depending upon exports for its food supply, the risk still remains worth taking.

This ruthless philosophy, ruthless not only towards the "bourgeoisie", but to the labor move-

ment and to the laboring people as well, was originally the product of the "will to revolution" of the
intellectual who, like the prophet of old, has heard
the voice of God and has dedicated his life to making
God's will prevail on earth—except that the "God"
of the "determinist-revolutionary" intellectual is
not a personal God but the "law" of the development
of society. But, under certain circumstances, the
non-intellectual, the manualist, may be made to worship the same God, and with the same fervor. Given
a Marxian training and a pronounced susceptibility
to the lure of Messianism, especially when unchecked by a sense of personal responsibility for
keeping one's trade union organization intact, many
a young workingman or workingwoman will display
the selfsame mentality. Moreover, in numerous
cases, that mentality may even become permanent,
showing how an early and decisive commitment to
a "foreign" philosophy, reinforced no doubt by a
suitable temperament, may block the growth of an
"organic" labor outlook. Such workingmen—
Marxians, who remain true to the faith to the last,
and some of whom, like Tom Mann of England and
W. Z. Foster in America, have attained real distinction, are generally found in "left wing" movements, like the National Minority Movement of
England, the Trade Union Educational League in
America, in "Industrial Unionist" groups, and as
leaders of the agitator type in newly and weakly
organized trades or industries. Yet even with many
of these, the revolutionary outlook has proven but
a passing phase.

Revolutionary Marxism has also proven a passing
phase with numerous intellectuals who, at bottom,

never had the revolutionary spirit, but were drawn to Marxism by the lure of its "completeness" as an intellectual system, or else were seeking to gratify a temporary youthful revolutionary mood. Some of these intellectuals turned out to have been mere "sojourning" liberals. The history of the Russian Social-Democratic movement abounds in examples of that type. Others, like Bernstein of Germany, after a long period of genuine devotion to Marxian "orthodoxy", became the "revisionist" critics of Marx, endeavoring to alter the views of the socialist movement. However, in Germany, where "revisionism" and "orthodoxy" fought their fiercest battles, it was not the "revisionist" intellectual but the trade unionist, arrived at self-confidence with the growth and success of the trade union movement, who delivered a critical blow to the leadership of the labor movement by the revolutionary intellectual. It was, as already seen, the German trade unionist who, through self-assertion, finally reduced the proud and arrogant intellectual to the modest status of a "controlled" intellectual, controlled by the trade unions.

CHAPTER IX

AN ADVANCED TRADE UNION PHILOSOPHY

German trade unions, under the influence of the sobering lessons of the recent Revolution and its aftermath, are now engaged in developing an ideology which bids fair to match, in high spiritual quality, any of the ideologies of the "ethical" intellectuals. This trade union ideology strikes a potent ethical note by rejecting the conception held by the revolutionary intellectuals, who in the past had been the absolute masters of the mind of German labor, that labor is an impersonal revolutionary mass, a conception from which there followed logically and practically the notion of a dictatorship over labor by the revolutionary party. In its place, German trade unionism is stressing the intrinsic worth of the personality of every worker, whether of the so-called "class-conscious vanguard" or merely Tom, Dick, or Harry. However, the ethical bias of this new ideology, differently from that of the ideologies of "ethical" intellectuals, has not caused it to overlook realities, whether in the make-up of the workingman or in the society in which he lives. It is thus actually building, perhaps without knowing it, upon the spontaneous, home-grown ideology which has been common to all scarcity groups throughout history. At the same time, the new ideology clearly appreciates too well how complex a mechanism modern industry is, to wish to be rid of the employer-manager for some time to come. The best exponent of this ideology is Karl Zwing, editor of the official *Gewerkschafts-Archiv,* a "Monthly for the Theory and Practice of the Organized Trade Union Movement", and the author of *The Sociology of the Trade Union Movement,*[1] published in 1925.

Zwing starts with the idea, to which he returns again and again, that political action can do little towards bringing about an "industrial democracy". He says: "It is time that the labor movement should discard its old illusion that the road to a transformed economic society lies through conquest of political power. This used to seem the only road to follow, but recent experience has proved it to be impracticable and thorny, and there is a strong probability that it will become increasingly so in the future. . . . [For] with the post-War agglomeration of economic forces, both horizontally and vertically, new centers of social and economic power have arisen, which, while capable of thoroughly disrupting the political superstructure of society, themselves are immune from disruption by political forces. By employing the political method labor might indeed stage a *revolt,* but never a *social revolution.*"[2]

"To-day politics leads but a shadowy existence, founded solely on past tradition. . . . [Therefore] labor must subject to a critical examination its tactics, which in the past it held without even questioning. If labor wishes to change the economic situa-

[1] Karl Zwing, *Soziologie der Gewerkschaftsbewegung.* Erster Teil, *Gewerkschaften und Wirtschaft.*
[2] *Ibid.,* 22.

tion, now grown so towering above the political, it must apply its organized trade union strength *directly*—not in the roundabout political way." But Zwing regretfully adds: "A way of thinking which has held sway for over a half century can only be overcome with the greatest difficulty." [1]

Political action being to Zwing at best only secondary in importance, he greatly deplores the subordination of the trade unions to the Social-Democratic Party. The trade unions, says he, were regarded as the less important pillars of the socialistic working class movement, and were ordered to limit themselves to looking after the struggles of every day only. "No one imagined that the trade unions might play a major rôle in bringing about the new society. Whatever theoretical thinking was done was from the point of view of political action." [2] So that when, in 1896, the printing employers and the printers' union concluded the first nation-wide trade agreement, which should have been acclaimed in the labor movement as a veritable turning-point in the history of German labor, the enormous significance of the event was "overlooked by all, and most of all by the laboring masses themselves, who were at the time still in the grip of the spirit engendered by the anti-socialist legislation. Consequently, what labor saw in the trade agreement idea was not the beginning of a new era and a higher form of the class struggle, but an abandonment of the class struggle idea and a spiritual surrender to the protagonists of social harmony." [3]

Zwing shows a thorough appreciation of the power of resistance in capitalism and of its undiminished

[1] *Ibid.*, 24-5.   [2] *Ibid.*, 15.   [3] *Ibid.*, 73.

vitality. He also admits freely that capitalism still has a function to perform: "The epoch which we have just lived through has demonstrated beyond the shadow of a doubt that the capitalist order does not derive its power of resistance from tradition alone, but, on the contrary, has managed to preserve plenty of good, healthy blood." [1] "The developments of recent years have made it clear that, in Germany at least, we need not expect a purely socialistic society, even as far in the future as we can now see." [2] "A real democracy in industry depends on an organic unity in industry. Therefore a life and death struggle between the two factors, labor and capital, each of which remains absolutely indispensable in the present stage of society, should be virtually ruled out from consideration. Labor fully admitted the correctness of this view when it gave up the tactics of catastrophic action. That was tantamount to an admission that the present is too deeply rooted in the past to leave the least possibility of a revolutionary change through a *coup*. Catastrophic change is least conceivable in modern economic society, since its tissues are ever assuming more and more complicated patterns. During the recent German Revolution, it was found that while the political constitution could indeed be altered in the revolutionary way, no such tactics could be effective in the economic order." [3]

This led Zwing to develop more fully his idea of the inapplicability to industry of the standard political methods expounded by the revolutionary ideologies. "It is sheer illusion to depend upon numbers or upon raw force. These methods belong to

[1] *Ibid.*, 129.   [2] *Ibid.*, 124.   [3] *Ibid.*, 129.

a time long past. But in a period like our own, which is characterized by an ever-growing refinement in industrial method and by a progressive specialization in ability and technique, victory will be with those who have a higher ability and possess a better technique. Labor must, accordingly, devote itself assiduously to its own economic education. No error could be more disastrous to labor than to fall back upon the outworn trust in mere numerical preponderance in the possession of naked physical force." [1] By "force" Zwing understands also the "force" of democratic majorities. "One frequently sees democracy identified with the principle of majority rule. But the principle of majority rule is after all nothing more than the principle of overwhelming the opposition. True democracy seeks to abolish inequalities—not to create new inequalities by means of majorities." [2] Furthermore, "democracy in industry is infinitely more complex a phenomenon than is political democracy. . . . It was for this reason that in 'autonomous industrial law' [developed under trade agreements], the majority rule principle was, from the beginning, discarded and replaced by the principle of parity or of equality between the two organized interests". [3]

With Zwing, the principle of parity (*Ebenbürtigkeit*) between labor and capital in industry ranks above everything else in importance. He does indeed envisage a future "socialization of industry". But by that he means not an expropriation of the present owners by the workingmen's state, which, as he says, only political party leaders ever wanted, [4]

---

[1] *Ibid.*, 116.   [2] *Ibid.*, 126.
[3] *Ibid.*, 127-8.   [4] *Ibid.*, 170.

but a "socialization" which will carry to the logical end the principle of the parity of classes. "Parity between capital and labor in the national economy is destined to become the guiding star for the trade unions at the present time as well as in the near future, and it truly denotes a turning-point in labor's attitude. Under the new order it will matter little who shall 'own' the means of production, but it will be of the greatest importance to establish who shall set them in motion and thus assume the real responsibility."[1] With the parity of classes fully recognized, Zwing clearly envisages a new intermediate stage between capitalism and socialism. Capitalism, in the old sense of economic individualism, has already been superseded by the capitalistic collectivism of the cartel and of the "trust". But this is merely a continuation of the old selfishness in a newer and enlarged form. It will be different in the new social stage dominated by the parity of classes. "This intermediate period during which the trade unions will play a leading rôle will see the national economy ruled neither by capitalism nor yet by socialism, but by the principle of group co-operation."[2] Next we come to a most startling admission from one who still professes to be a socialist, albeit a trade-union socialist. "When the parity of classes has been firmly established, from industry as a whole down to the elementary economic cell [the individual establishment, in which Zwing sees the greatest difficulty in the way], and when labor's ideology has triumphed over the narrow and selfishly conceived idea of property, [which is the burdensome legacy of the earliest and rudest stages of capitalism], it

[1] *Ibid.*, 124.   [2] *Ibid.*, 123.

may then well be that it will be considered an open question whether there remains any point in struggling for a change in the property-owning relations and for the elimination of the entrepreneurial class." [1] Thus socialism, in the sense in which intellectuals understand it—a mechanical change in the ownership of industry, rather than a change in its functional control, regardless of the legal forms of ownership,—gets quietly shelved as an issue for the present, and, in all probability, as an issue for the future as well.

As a corollary of the shift in emphasis from a merely mechanical change in institutions, Zwing lays new and central emphasis upon the spiritual side of the labor movement. "When a new principle sets out to overcome an older one, the decision ultimately lies not with numbers nor any other agglomeration of material elements, but with the comparative spiritual richness of the classes which are the respective carriers of these principles. . . . It will never do, especially in Germany, if the necessary spiritual qualifications exist only in a thin upper crust of the working class: to be at all effective, these qualifications must be widespread throughout the working class. He indeed worships futility who imagines that the new system could be enacted by a small spiritual aristocracy, as in Russia, through a minority dictatorship, and through indulgence in violence." [2] What Germany needs is a thorough democratization of the existing relationship, working from below upwards.

"When industry has become a feudatory to society, the worker will enjoy complete parity with his

[1] *Ibid.*   [2] *Ibid.*, 18-19.

employer, and the class struggle will be lifted to a higher and more spiritual level—in contrast with communism, which seeks to militarize the class struggle and convert it into an instrument of violence.''[1] The labor struggle, Zwing concludes, is a struggle which ''will neither be decided by the weight of numbers, nor by the weight of accumulated wealth, but by spiritual qualities''.[2] Therefore a far-sighted social policy will work untiringly for the permeation of the capitalist system of today with a higher morality. In the end, by following the route of class parity, society will achieve a complete socialization of industry and a perfect social harmony.

Significant and suggestive as Zwing's ideas are when couched in general sociological terms, he brings us even closer to the core of the matter when he turns to the concrete and specific problems of German trade unionism. His principal quarrel with trade unionism as it was during the hegemony of the Social-Democratic Party,[3] is the utter neglect of the ''shop rules'', which in British and American unionism have always ranked as of higher importance than wages. ''Aside from a few half-hearted and groping attempts to gain some control over the productive process, everything pertaining to shop management had, clear up to the War, been left in the undisturbed control of the employer class.''[4] Trade unionism, it was then thought, should concern itself only with wages, hours, and watchful scrutiny of the operations of the governmental bodies administering labor laws and social insurance. This lim-

---

[1] *Ibid.*, 54.
[2] *Ibid.*, 67.
[3] See the chapter on Germany.
[4] *Ibid.*, 80.

ited conception of the task of the trade union as pertaining to shop management revealed itself in the very term designating the trade agreement—"wage agreement" (*Tarifvertrag*). Thus German trade unionism utterly failed to put in any bid for the dozens and dozens of the job control rules achieved by American and English unions and designed to give to the membership a right to the job, freedom from overwork and arbitrary discrimination, and the protection of their bargaining power and of the trade union organization. As the sole exception to this rule, Zwing cites the same trade which in America has succeeded above all others in gaining control of the jobs—the printers of Germany. About the beginning of the present Century, he relates, the linotype began to be introduced in large numbers, but the influence of the union of the printers sufficed to make the employers agree that none but skilled journeymen should operate these machines,—precisely the same stipulation for "job preservation" exacted by the American printers' union half a decade earlier. At the time, however, this great victory went unnoticed in Germany. And Zwing adds caustically: "In the other labor circles, such matters of control on the job were then and long afterwards considered to be fully within the employer's preserve, and no one even thought of claiming the right to participate with the employers in the making of decisions."[1] For the pre-War theory was that, since the problem of the control of industry by labor was going to be decided completely and finally in the political arena, through the seizure of the power of the state, there was no call for the

[1] *Ibid.*, 80.

trade unions to engage in competition with the social-democratic party by going after such control
in a "piecemeal" way, through negotiation with the
employers.

Zwing is optimistic about immediate labor control in industry in the concrete and realistic sense of
the term, although the desire for such control dates
only from after the War, when it came coupled
with the idea of shop councils (*Rätegedanke*).
"The essence and content of the council idea is to
wring for the workers and office employees the right
to participate in decisions on all economic questions,
from production to consumption and throughout the
entire economic structure, from the individual plant
to the world trust."[1] Industrial democracy is pro-
gressing along three routes: first, through the development of an "autonomous industrial law"
(trade agreement "law"); second, through "economic parliamentarism" (representation of economic groups in economic representative institutions
linked up vitally with the state); and, third, through
the legally instituted works councils (*Betriebsräte*).
Zwing makes it plain that he is expecting the most
from the shop councils with their conceded jurisdiction over shop rules. Yet he is frank to admit
that up to the present the councils have only been
permitted to exercise the right of "joint consultation" with the employers, rather than the right of
"joint determination". Moreover, these councils
have encountered a most stubborn opposition from
the employers even in the discharge of their legally
recognized functions.

The great significance of Zwing's social philos-

[1] *Ibid.*, 69.

ophy lies in that it gives a type of labor ideology which, on the one hand, has its roots in the daily life of the working people, but, on the other, leaves nothing to be desired on the score of articulation, clarity, and theoretical consistency. Springing as it does from the "soil" of labor, it is seen to reject in nearly every particular the characteristic tenets of the intellectuals, whether of the "ethical", "efficiency", or "determinist-revolutionary"[1] description. Politics is "put in its place",[2] as compared with industrial action. The alleged decline in vigor and capacity to function of the capitalist system is shown up for the misleading fallacy that it is. Labor shall no longer strive to attain a mechanical change in property rights, but to begin forthwith a reform of capitalism by means of an all-around recognition of the union ("parity of classes"). And the question is boldly raised as to whether, when this program is carried out, it will still be necessary to eliminate the entrepreneur. Moreover, labor is no longer thought of as a "mass", nor even as history's pet revolutionary force, but as an aggregation of individuals, each of whom should be accorded full "personality" rights, thus excluding a dictatorship by the "class-conscious vanguard" and also giving an impetus to a well considered program of workers' education. But finally, and perhaps most important of all, from the standpoint of its being a new and fruitful departure

[1] The tussle of the German trade unionists was, of course, with the last named type.

[2] This, however, does not mean in the least that labor shall neglect its political opportunities, especially in view of the power of compulsory arbitration in labor disputes given to the Minister of Labor in emergency situations. It is merely a matter of determining the relative importance of the two.

for German unionism, this ideology is showing the keenest sort of an interest in the same "shop" or "working rules" which organized labor shows whenever and wherever its mind is not shaped by intellectuals from the outside, but is permitted to grow and mature along its own "organic" lines.

Is Zwing's unionism the "New Unionism"[1] we hear so much talked about? The answer is that it is neither "New" nor "Old" unionism, but just unionism. As a practical movement, it is not oriented to any specific ultimate constitution of society which is to emerge out of the labor struggle—beyond an extremely vague "socialism". On the contrary, it starts with the concrete working people and seeks to take advantage of every available opening for furthering their opportunities, which are seen to lie mainly inside the shop and industry. Lastly, it seeks to anchor its conquests securely by means of a recognized labor control.

Is Zwing's control "negative" or "positive"? Is it a control that merely binds the employer, or a control that seeks to gain greater and greater responsibility for the running of industry? Again,

---

[1] The term "New Unionism" has been given many shades of meaning. Originally and basically, however, it stood for just such a type of unionism as Germany had before the War, and from which the present day German movement has been getting away. It is essentially a unionism which expects an ultimate labor control of industry through a political labor party; although the "newer" New Unionism (since the War) also demands an "encroaching control" or a progressive invasion into the sphere of the employer's prerogative in the shop. However, this recent edition of "New Unionism" is as much stamped by the intellectual's trademark as was its predecessor, which sought salvation through politics. Its "encroaching control" seems to be solely concerned with the intellectual's purpose of pushing the employer off the board rather than with the unionist's goal of "job administration". And the celerity with which it expects the process to complete itself also betrays the intellectual's illusion that capitalism is dying.

this distinction, which is so often made, is largely an artificial one. Unionism and the striving for shop control are identical. But a unionism that thinks for itself is indifferent as to whether or not, when its campaign for control will come to be viewed in retrospect a half century or more hence, it will then appear to have been an "encroaching" control, which had whittled away the power of the employer; just as such a practical unionism will be little concerned with whether in the same retrospective view it will appear to have belonged in the category of "New" or "Old" unionism. Quite the contrary. Knowing, as it must know, as insiders and men like Zwing know, that the great and ever growing complexity of industry has ruled out the crude methods of control by majorities, whether in political campaigns or in "national gild" elections, such a unionism sees assurance for the future in a continued and broadened co-operation with the "functional group" of manager-employers.

The likelihood of that spirit of co-operation developing in unionism increases in the measure that its position in industry approaches a securely rooted "institutionalization".[1] A unionism that has become institutionalized, while seeking to continue its shop and job control, will more and more depart from the older and cruder methods of sheer restrictiveness, dictated in the past by strategic necessity and by the weakness of its confidence in its own position in industry,—and swing towards a partner-

---

[1] Unionism may reach "insitutionalization" as a result of employers' "recognition" of such long standing that to go back upon it would be tantamount to "revolution". Or, as on the Continent, it may come about by legal prescription, through legally established works' councils and legally enforceable trade agreements.

ship with the employer-manager group for the creation of a higher industrial efficiency. For unionism cannot fail to see that, after a certain point has been reached, higher labor standards can come only from a higher efficiency. Thus such latter-day phenomena as the "New Wage Policy" of the American Federation of Labor,[1] the Union-Management Cooperative Plan on the Baltimore and Ohio Railroad and other American roads, and the workers' councils in Europe, may be recognized as closely related manifestations of one and the same age-long drive by labor for an enlarged opportunity for Tom, Dick, and Harry through collective control. As circumstances change and as the plane of the industrial struggle rises, the methods of organized labor change accordingly. And as unionism takes more and more of a hand in running the productive process, it comes to depend for guidance less and less on a dogmatic anti-capitalist philosophy, but more and more on a pragmatic faith in industrial government through a co-operation of equally indispensable "functional" classes. So far as the remote future is concerned, labor is willing to leave it to be looked after in its own time by the remotely future labor movement.

But there is always the danger that in traversing this new route to industrial democracy, a route which sober reflection upon recent experience appears to have considerably robbed of its former towering and shining terminal, the labor movement might fail to preserve in undiminished strength its

[1] See above. The stress upon "co-operativeness" at present laid by the American Federation of Labor is also designed to persuade the managerial group to admit unionism into the unorganized basic industries.

original spiritual drive. It is in this connection that the intellectual might find one of the several fields for usefulness open to him in the labor movement. The intellectual can save the labor movement from succumbing to a deadening drabness, if he learns to do the following: First, how to bring out from its somber shell the kernel of the philosophy native to labor. Secondly, how to endow that philosophy with an attractiveness which only specialists in thinking in general concepts and in inventing "blessed" words for these concepts are capable of. And thirdly, he must learn how to bring this "home-grown" philosophy of labor into close correlation with broader public purpose. But to be able to perform this service today, the intellectual must always remember that he is dealing no longer with a mass which, enslaved but yesterday, might hail him as its Moses, but with a self-confident social movement which already practices and insists upon mental self-determination. The advanced model in philosophies which the intellectual has a right to expect that labor will accept, must be of a pattern that follows the main lines of the simpler model of labor's own contrivance.

INDEX

319